Deviance
TERRORISM
& WAR

The Process of Solving Unsolved Social and Political Problems

Deviance
TERRORISM
& WAR

The Process of Solving Unsolved
Social and Political Problems

John Burton

Centre for the Analysis of Conflict, Rutherford College, University of Kent

St. Martin's Press
New York

ISBN 0-312-19753-5

Library of Congress Cataloging in Publication Data

Burton, John Wear, 1915–
 Deviance terrorism & war.

 Bibliography: p.
 Includes index.
 1. Social Problems. 2. Problem solving. 3. Social
 structure. 4. Social control. 5. Authority.
 I. Title

HN18. B86 1979 309 79–16484
ISBN 0-312-19753-5

Filmset by Vantage Photosetting Company Ltd., Southampton.
Printed and bound by Richard Clay (The Chaucer Press) Ltd., Bungay,
Suffolk.

Contents

Acknowledgments

My colleagues associated with the Centre for the Analysis of Conflict have, over many years, given generously of their time to many preliminary papers and drafts written in preparation for this study. They have been destructive where this was required and, from the perspective of various disciplines, have made many positive contributions. While none would wish to be identified with the views and conclusions arrived at, all are committed in their own fields to the solution of social and political problems and regarded this exercise as part of the process of pushing at the boundaries of knowledge. In particular I wish to express my appreciation to Michael Banks (London School of Economics), Nancy Fahy (University of London), John Groom (University of Kent), Chris Hill (London School of Economics), Margot Light (University of Surrey), Richard Little (Open University), Chris Mitchell (City University), Bram Oppenheim (London School of Economics), Fran Pinter (Publisher), Tony de Reuck (University of Surrey), Dennis Sandole (University College London). Elizabeth Clarkson (University College, Swansea). Herb Kelman (Harvard University) and Ralph Pettman (Australian National University) joined our discussions during visits to London. Leone Burton, whose field of research is problem-solving, made important contributions to Chapter One, Problem-Solving, in particular. Hedda Ramsden assisted during the important final stages of exposition.

To all I owe my thanks. Acknowledgments are also due to students who have made stimulating comments and to many authors.

January 1979   *John Burton*
Centre for the Analysis of Conflict
Rutherford College, University of Kent at Canterbury

to Mark and his generation

Introduction

All countries have a range of unsolved social and political problems that can be classified by descriptive labels such as war, revolution, terrorism, hijacking, murder, assault, threat, destruction of property, etc. The range of unsolved problems is boundless because they occur at all levels within every society: in the family, in the school, at work, right through to intercommunal relations. They are also prevalent in the interstate system: first because of great power rivalries and because domestic tensions spill over beyond state boundaries and, second, because of the gap between the welfare and opportunities of the wealthier and of the poorer nations.

The behavioural scope is also boundless. It includes behaviour that appears to be 'abnormal', such as genocide or the elimination of political or tribal minorities; behaviour that is by rational people, but cannot be explained in terms other than 'mindless', such as hooliganism of many kinds; unacceptable behaviour, such as killing, but in circumstances that make the behaviour understandable as in a war or a communal conflict; illegal behaviour that is sometimes widely acceptable, such as responses to a repressive regime; legal behaviour that is antisocial, such as exploitation; behaviour that is non-rational in the sense that it is deliberate yet self-defeating, such as employing the power of the state to maintain in office authorities that are unacceptable.

However, there is a particular objective in this study that provides manageable boundaries, i.e. to determine whether there are problem-solving processes that are general in their application and which could resolve specific problems that appear to be resistant to treatment.

SOLVED AND UNSOLVED PROBLEMS

'Unsolved problems' implies that there is a category of problems that could be labelled 'solved', with a further implication that societies endeavour to solve their problems and that the category of 'unsolved' problems refers to those in which there has been no such success.

Societies deal with problems in many ways—directly through repression, indirectly through socialization, by researching into the nature of the problem, by legislation and by other means. The usual procedure is a cybernetic one rather than a problem-solving one: events are allowed to run their course and problems are dealt with as they occur. Decisions are taken and feedback leads to altered decisions, after which there is more feedback, in a continuing process until the goal is achieved. In the absence of agreed social goals and of total knowledge and foresight, the decision-making feedback process is unavoidable. That industry creates pollution is predictable, yet it is only afterwards that decisions are taken to control it. If these do not succeed in eliminating the pollution, other decisions are taken and so on. However, the processes are not as simple as this example suggests. In practice, delays and failure to respond to feedback enable the situation being tackled to alter radically in the meantime. Unemployment accompanies steps taken to curb inflation by reducing consumer demand. Individual hardship is created and measures, such as unemployment relief, are introduced. There are other social problems resulting from idleness, lack of self-respect and of social recognition, leading to deviant behaviour of many kinds. Measures are then taken to deal with these side effects. Almost inevitably the regulatory power of the state authorities has to be exercised, usually with an increasing degree of coercion. In due course it becomes overloaded with far-reaching consequences. By this process a problem may be 'dealt with' but not necessarily 'solved' and many others are created as a result of attempts to deal with the original problem.

Yet there are problems that appear to have been solved, for example, exploitation such as child labour and slavery. The institutions of child labour and slavery were not defined as problems at the time: the problem lay in the side effects, misery and violence. Controls were introduced so as to lessen these. These problems have now been solved in most countries because the institutions themselves have been eliminated. The controls exercised may have helped to eliminate the institutions by making them less profitable; but the main influences were probably altered conditions of many kinds over which authorities had little if any control, such as industrialization, capital-intensive production and the need for skills. Altering attitudes and appropriate legislation could hasten the total process only by eliminating the last vestiges of the former practices.

These are cases that can be described as structural problems: they arose out of social and political structures. There are many such structural conflicts today: in African countries where white minorities are defending their positions; in countries where religious or other minorities are struggling for recognition; in industry where demands are being made for participation and control; in particular societies and in the world society where persons experiencing relative and absolute deprivation are struggling for change. These problems are all likely to be eliminated in the long term by what some would term 'historic processes' and the violence with which they are associated is presumably part of this process.

There are other problems that are not directly related to structures which could occur in any type of society, e.g. murder of close relatives, theft by many who have no material need to steal and a variety of forms of behaviour designed to overcome boredom or to achieve recognition and status. There are also environmental problems that have social and political consequences: resource scarcity, resource inequalities and others. These types of problems cannot be solved by cybernetic processes because the motivations and environmental conditions remain. At best their character and incidence can sometimes be altered.

It would be reasonable to argue, therefore, that rarely, if ever, do policy decisions solve social and political problems. Either the course of history removes them or their nature is merely changed by the intervention of authorities.

A number of questions suggest themselves. What is the nature of the 'historical process'? To what extent can this process be assisted so as to achieve ends without unnecessary lag? To what extent can the process be controlled so that it does not include catastrophy in its repertoire, e.g. genocide as a means of dealing with a minority problem? To what extent can non-structural problems, behavioural and environmental, be solved by deliberate problem-solving techniques? To what extent can such processes overcome lag and resistance to whatever changes appear to be required in solving problems? Is there such a process as a problem-solving process that can be applied to social and political problems? Can social problems be avoided significantly more than they are at present? When they do occur for any reason outside the control of the society and its members, can there be effective problem-solving processes and adaptive policies, rather than merely controlling-processes and enforcement policies?

The answer to these questions obviously rests, first, on whether social goals can be defined consensually and, second, on the availability of knowledge of means to achieve them reliably, including knowledge of the difficulties and the problems likely to be experienced in the future. Goals and processes: these are the core concern. Is it possible to define goals that apply to all societies, goals that transcend ideologies and belief systems, on which policy decisions can be based? Are there problem-solving processes by which these goals can be attained?

THE RELEVANCE OF AUTHORITIES

All of these problems, whether they be defined as structural, behavioural or environmental, involve authorities and relationships with authorities at one level or another: responsibilities of authorities to provide leadership in solving problems, relationships with authorities, challenges to their institutions and the norms they create and support, resistance to decisions they take regarding resource distribution and to the steps taken to deal with specific situations.

In this special sense the unsolved problems of societies are finally authority problems, involving the behaviour of authorities on the one hand, and demands made upon them on the other. However, when reference is made to authorities it is not confined only to those responsible for local and central government. The authority problem that is associated with unsolved social and political problems occurs at all levels: in the family, in the school, in industry, in communal relations and in relations between states. The likelihood is that there are some features of these relationships that are common to all these levels. For instance, at each of these levels it is possible for authorities to be either coercive or to provide legitimized leadership. At all of these levels they can create frustrations and transferred aggressive responses, induce coerced or acquiescent conformity, on the one hand, or, on the other, promote flexibility, adaptability and an acceptance of change as required by those over whom they exercise authority. While there must be unique features at each of these different levels, common aspects of the authority problem may be of some significance in dealing with problems that are unsolved. Are violence and disruption, pollution and wasted resources, unemployment and boredom, communal and interstate tensions due to incompetence and weakness by authorities and absence of effective national and international enforcement procedures? Or are they an inevitable function of all social systems? Is their origin an absence of legitimized leadership? Or do they reflect avoidable low levels in flexibility of response and in problem-solving abilities and experience?

This book is in three parts. It commences the study of unsolved problems with a consideration of problem-solving as distinct from the usual processes of decision-making. The second part is devoted to a discussion of assumptions that appear to underlie conventional thought. Policies follow logically from theories and definitions of situations. Theories and definitions arise out of assumptions made about the relationship being examined. Assumptions seem, therefore, to be a logical starting point when thinking about unsolved problems. An alternative set of assumptions emerges and the third part examines these as a set to see whether they explain better the nature of social and political problems and, in particular, whether they suggest a process by which problems can be solved.

PART ONE

Problem-Solving

CHAPTER ONE

Problem-Solving

The approach to this study of unsolved problems—i.e. how they are analysed and defined—and also the conclusions of this study that dwell on processes by which specific unsolved problems may be resolved, both involve the notion of problem-solving. This is a familiar notion when it is applied to means of dealing with a situation: it is not far removed from the notion of decision-making. It is less familiar as a particular approach or technique that excludes all means of dealing with or controlling situations except those that specifically seek a resolution as distinct from a coercive settlement. It is appropriate, therefore, to consider problem-solving as an approach and as a process.

PROBLEMS AND PUZZLES

It is helpful to make a distinction between puzzles and problems. Puzzles are familiar as a form of entertainment: metal shapes that can be engaged and disengaged only by a particular order of steps; a maze to which the end can be found only by following particular paths; a quantitative 'problem' such as finding a means by which to measure a quantity of liquid by using a combination of jars. It is also a puzzle when it is necessary to find out why someone behaved as they did in a given set of circumstances, within a given pattern of behaviour. There has to be a specific explanation why someone is late home or did not send a letter. In all of these cases there are two features. First, there is a known answer: when the metal parts have been separated, when the maze has been walked through, when the late person has given the explanation, the answer is clear. The 'problem' is solved. Many mathematical 'problems' are of this kind. The solutions may not be known in advance, but it is known that there is a solution. When it is found it will satisfy the conditions of the puzzle and can be tested to ensure that this is so. (There may be more than one solution, as there may be more than one way out of a maze if it is so constructed.) Second, puzzles assume the application of known theories or a known set of techniques and these are adequate for the purpose. Third, puzzles deal with closed systems, i.e. there is no reaction to an environment that could be changing during the investigation. The late person is late in a given set of known and stable patterns of behaviour.

Much of the literature on problem-solving is, in fact, about puzzles. For example, Gagne devotes a chapter to 'problem-solving' as a means to learning and defines problem-solving 'as a process by which the learner discovers a combination of previously learned rules that he can apply to achieve a solution for a novel problem situation' (Gagne, 1973, p. 214). This is, according to our definition, puzzle-solving. The rules and conditions are given. If, in practice, it were discovered that there cannot be a solution based on the previously learned rules and the rules themselves had to be questioned and changed, this then would require the processes of problem-solving. Duncker (1943) defined a problem as arising whenever anyone has to think about reaching a goal and the problem that was studied was how to deal with an inoperable tumor. This question was in due course refined: how can radiation be focused on the tumor without affecting other parts? This is puzzle-solving. These examples are given merely to make the point that much puzzle-solving has been discussed as though it were problem-solving.

Careful, thoughtful decision-making is usually puzzle-solving, even though in popular speech it may be described as problem-solving. Pruitt's (1965) study of decision-making is titled *Problem-Solving in the Department of State* and is a description of the consultative processes that are followed. However, the discussion of the various topics under review took place in a framework which excluded many possible approaches: in each case there was a set of givens. The term 'problem-solving' was employed merely to signify that it is the role of the civil servant to make recommendations and not to

take decisions. In other words, those concerned were aware of
the dominant theories or policies within which their discussion
had to take place.

Here problem-solving is regarded as having the opposite
characteristics. First, the solution is not a final end-product. It
is itself another set of relationships that contains its own sets of
problems. The solution to a conflict problem or an authority
problem does not eliminate a party to the conflict and, therefore, creates a new set of relationships and problems. However,
this new set of problems will be the sought-for outcome and not
merely an unexpected one, as is frequently the case in cybernetic decision-making. For example, the problem of growth can be
solved deliberately to give rise to problems of leisure that have
then to be solved. A cybernetic process might achieve growth;
but a set of unanticipated problems such as inequalities and
class conflict might be the actual outcome. Second, problem-
solving frequently requires a new synthesis of knowledge or
techniques and a change in theoretical structure. Third, the
system of interactions is an open one, i.e. the parts are subject
not merely to interaction among themselves, as is the case with
a metal puzzle, but to interaction with a wider environment
over which there can be no control. While the problem is being
analysed its nature is altering and the behaviour of the parts
being analysed is altering. In the main, physical problems are
puzzles; but there can be conditions in which parts are constantly subject to change, e.g. changes in temperature, pressure,
light, etc., brought about by the environment. For this reason,
scientists endeavour to create laboratory conditions in which
variables can be held constant. In examining social and political
problems this is generally not possible. Indeed, it is the open
nature of behavioural systems that is part of the problem—a
solution to a set of relationships in a controlled situation does
not provide a solution in real life.

Because of this complexity there has always been a tendency
to 'solve' social and political problems by the more direct and
simple cybernetic processes, i.e. by making adjustments as and
when seems necessary, as the situation changes. It is also the
reason why there has been such a strong tendency to deal with
social and political problems by the direct means of coercion, i.e.

by the employment of power and influence. This is a means of preventing and ensuring conformity. It effectively transforms problems into puzzles by controlling the variables, i.e. the responses of the actor to the environment. Experience is, however, that in dealing with human behaviour such control cannot be effective permanently. The attempt to control in this way merely creates some other unanticipated and usually more difficult problems.

This distinction between puzzles and problems goes to the heart of scientific endeavour. It has been the subject of major debates between those who hold that 'normal science' is puzzle-solving within a given framework of dominant theories and those who, on the contrary, hold the view that the pursuit of science necessarily involves questioning of dominant thought systems and assumptions. The kinds of problems with which we are concerned have usually been tackled as puzzles: e.g. how can street violence or war be dealt with, given the social structure, given cultural values, given notions of law and order, given the climate of opinion, given popular thought about deviance, given the norms of psychological, sociological and legal thinking? The alternative is to question all the implied assumptions, attitudes and theories, to put forward alternative hypotheses and to examine these in the light of events. This is problem-solving. As Popper (1974, p. 52) remarked, normal science, puzzle-solving: 'is the activity of the non-revolutionary, or more precisely, the not-too-critical professional: of the science student who accepts the ruling dogma of the day; who does not wish to challenge it; and who accepts a new revolutionary theory only if almost everybody else is ready to accept it. . . . The "normal" scientist, in my view, has been taught badly'. There is a place for puzzle-solving: many situations can be dealt with within the dominant thought systems of the time. This is 'applied science'. However, unsolved problems, by definition, cannot be so dealt with. They require the approach of pure science which leads to an alternative set of assumptions and hypotheses, on which a more relevant applied science can be based. Additional tools of analysis are required. A bolder approach is required. The control of such imagination is that whatever innovative hypotheses are advanced, they must be tested and found to work.

transition
theory

PROBLEM-SOLVING BY TRIAL AND ERROR

Problem-solving is itself a problem: if we could solve the problem of problem-solving we would be well on the way to finding appropriate policies with which to deal with the problems we experience. Whether it be because power has been regarded as the effective and legitimate means of control or whether it be merely a function of the level of knowledge, the fact is that there has been little attention given to problem-solving in open systems as a conscious and disciplined procedure. An apprentice learns to use tools and to solve puzzles in his own area; but he does not learn the general rules of problem-solving and, therefore, can rarely carry over his experience into other aspects of his life. Problem-solving is not a subject taught at school or generally at universities. Consequently, the research student and the practitioner are both to a large degree engaged in activities guided primarily by preconceptions, attitudes and ideologies. They are apt not to analyse problems, but to study them in ways which relate to their own patterns of thought.

Daily experience suggests that both puzzle-solving and problem-solving tactics range from random behaviour and accidental discovery, to purposeful trial and error, to analytical approaches in which policy or action is based on an understanding of the puzzle or problem and its probable solution. This range relates in some degree to the complexity of puzzles or problems, the most difficult and least understood attract random behaviour, even frustration behaviour and remedies based on tradition, superstition and myth. The simplest open-system problems so lend themselves to action based on understanding that they seem not to warrant the term 'problem'. At most they are 'puzzles': i.e. there is either a known solution or a solution that is generally acceptable and consistent with consensual views when once it is discovered, as is the case with 'puzzles'.

While one associates random behaviour with the play of children (i.e. a type of behaviour that relates to exploration and growth and not necessarily to problem-solving), in practice much adult and professional decision-making is of this character, largely because of the complexity of the problem to hand. For example, the unpredictable consequences which unpredictable happenings, e.g. droughts or civil disturbances, have on an economic system, can make purposeful planning and action impossible or ineffective. From a practitioner's point of view, wars, race riots and criminal activities are unique events. Each is a statistic: the number of events in each category may be predicted, but no one instance can accurately be foreseen, nor can its consequences. There being no apparent patterns or regularities, except the regularity of occurrences, there can be no general explanations or controls. Randomness and repetition of already tried tactics, dominate policy. Because authorities cannot ignore a problem of public concern, random behaviour by them is sometimes politically functional, even though not designed to solve a problem.

Given a situation in which there is some understanding of the puzzle or problem, but inadequate knowledge on which to work, trial and error can be used with a precise purpose and can be orderly and conserving of energy. When someone is lost in a jungle, planned trial and error in following different paths is an appropriate strategy. Information has to be discovered. Trial and error, where success and failure are recorded, can be a useful first approach to puzzle- and problem-solving, especially where the conditions have not previously been experienced and when there are no guiding models or precedents. It can be, in this sense, an analytical device. The testing of a system to detect in which subsystem a fault lies, as is the practice of an engineer or electrician, is such a use of 'trial and error'. It is purposeful behaviour based on some understanding of the puzzle or problem. The only element of randomness may be in the order in which different tests are tried.

There are, in the real world, few occasions in which behaviour is wholly trial and error. Usually, there is a condition that invites a hunch, a predisposition to select one particular trial before another. Indeed, this is the nature of science. Events are observed, the observer has a theory and sets out to apply it or to test it. There are, therefore, two skills required in puzzle- and problem-solving: first, the skill of selecting or creating a probable hypothesis and, second, the skill of applying it. While both are necessary, the latter, no matter how well developed, is frustrated if not based on the former.

In this sense puzzle- and problem-solving ideally begin with theory making; theory is an instrument by which to solve puzzles and problems (see Frohock, 1967, p. 56). It is from theory that policy, i.e. the means by which a puzzle or a problem can be solved, is deduced.

Ideas and theories are probably a function of experience and knowledge of a wide field of science and life. Nevertheless, experience and knowledge are also the main influences that keep one within the bounds of a conventional body of assumptions, beliefs and hunches. Social and political scientists and politicians, who by dint of seniority and reputation are leaders in their field, are unlikely to solve problems with which they have wrestled over time. To experience and knowledge need to be added imagination, an ability to question conventional wisdom, a willingness to be a dissident.

The use of imagination is inherent in scientific method. In recent years its recognition has to some degree reinstated randomness. Indeed, in some quarters there has been an over-reaction to the seemingly cold logic of science, even to the promotion of anti-science. It is obvious that some problems can be solved by random behaviour. There have been accidental discoveries in science and conceivably results could be obtained quicker in some particular circumstances by these means. Accidental discovery, when it happens, is a quick and efficient method of problem-solving. However, the more laborious process of analysis is likely to be more economical in the vast majority of cases.

PROBLEM-SOLVING AS A DISCIPLINE

It is clear that different kinds of problems require different applied techniques. The case-worker who is endeavouring to solve a matrimonial problem and the policy-maker confronted by an international threat, are operating in different fields related to different academic disciplines. Are they solving their special problems by processes that are unique to each? Or is there a discipline that can be termed problem-solving that is relevant to all areas of thought and to all applied sciences?

Problem-solving, puzzle-solving and scientific analysis are closely related. It has long been argued that scientific analysis is generally applicable across academic boundaries. Various attempts have been made to detail processes. The traditional approach—which is more concerned with puzzle-solving—has been:

(i) observation and experiment	(iv) attempted validation of
(ii) inductive generalization	hypotheses
(iii) hypothesis	(v) result: knowledge.

Brecht (1967, p. 28) spells out a deductive approach in more detail:

(i) observation	(vii) deductive reasoning
(ii) description	(viii) testing
(iii) measurement	(ix) correcting
(iv) acceptance	(x) predicting
(v) inductive generalization	(xi) non-acceptance.
(vi) explanation	

This is a personal and quite formal list with limited practical significance; but the notion that there could be some agreed or accepted procedures of scientific investigation is widely held. What is needed is a less formal, applied process.

The following appear to be practical steps in problem-solving in the area of behavioural studies.

Selection of the Problem

The first step in problem-solving is the selection of the particular problem. Selection occurs because of immediate environmental pressures on the problem-solver. In an academic research environment it reflects culture, personal experience and interests or perhaps merely a desire to experiment with a new technique. In practice the problem relates to some existing theories that are found wanting: a problem is a set of circumstances not explained or of demands on a system that cannot be met within existing knowledge.

The conditions of selection, including the motivations of the problem-solver and the environment in which he operates, are important because they have a bearing on the processes that follow. Interests of many kinds are reflected in selection and carry over their influence into process. The deprived person seeking to solve problems of survival, the detective solving a crime, the police faced with deviant behaviour, all have interest motivations and options. For example, there can be solutions sought that have a personal or institutional benefit at a social cost or an immediate solution at the expense of future problems. Consequently, in assessing any attempt at problem-solving one must look beyond immediate environmental conditions to motivations in order to determine how a particular investigation came to be selected and how it is conducted. In reading and assessing any work it is relevant to ask: who wrote it, when, in what circumstances and for what reasons. The selection of a problem and initial theories are personal matters. It is the testing of theories and solutions that is of scientific interest. However, selection and circumstances can colour the rest of the problem-solving process, including testing.

This is of particular importance in the field of our present concerns. Those directly interested in the problems of our time have interests in dealing with them—personal and political. The fact that they have interests implies that they are to a large degree already committed to a particular approach: coercion of the deviant, change or preservation of social structures, alterations in educational and economic environments, etc. It is for this reason that an awareness of constraints on our own thinking is so relevant: if we seek policies that achieve a desired result, then personal theories have to be revealed and put aside, at least until the problems have been defined and analysed.

Clearly, for example, the end of violence and challenges to authority may not be desired goals, even though problems may be defined in these terms. Preservation of social and political structures may be dominant goals and violence may be tolerated as part of the cost of preserving them. In other words, the authority and violence problems may be selected for treatment. However, the interest may not be in them, but in the preservation of social and political structures. In 1975 Morocco invaded Spanish territory by a march of unarmed people. The Security Council tried to control the situation and to solve the problem. Was this to prevent war and bloodshed or to preserve sovereign integrity against a new form of invasion? There is terrorism in many countries: is interest in solving the problem of terrorism inspired by a desire to control terrorists or by a desire to alter the conditions that stimulated terrorism? There are many international and national conferences at which poverty is discus-

sed: is the interest in those experiencing poverty or, alternatively, is it in finding some means of removing a threat to existing
international and national economic and financial systems? So
with deviant behaviour of all kinds and at all levels: confusion
on motivations and mixed motives are usual.

This implies that it is necessary or at least desirable to have
some objective goal, some non-interest, non-ideological basis for
the purposes behind the selection. The only one that comes to
mind is human interest; but this requires definition if it is to
avoid personal and ideological orientations. This study adopts
the notion of 'human needs', and the motivation or reason for
selection will be seen to relate to this goal—yet to be defined.

The Process of Specification

The selection of a problem area is not simply a matter of
choosing. The selection is initially no more than an unspecific
awareness of an area of interest. The next step is to define the
focus of attention more precisely—to determine, in effect,
whether what seems to be the focus of interest is the problem
area it is thought to be. For example, suppose the area of
interest were violence. Having in mind the attention given over
the ages to problems of violence and to explanations of it such as
innate evil and human aggressiveness, violence could reasonably be designated an important interest area. However, some
forms of violence can be controlled or avoided by resource
expenditure or by agreed priorities in the allocation and organization of resources and the arrangements of relationships.
Violence is not a sufficient differentiating description of a
problem. In any event, even though it were, the researcher
would still be obliged to examine all forms of deviant behaviour
and every aspect of authority relationships, because overt violence is merely the end-result of an interaction process. If
violence were a description of an interest area, the process
leading to violence would be the problem area.

It is frequently the experience in scientific inquiry to find
that the original specification of a project is false. Tutors
supervising students encourage a project, without any certainty
that it will end up in the way in which it was intended: many
false starts are common. There is a certain scientific interest in
finding out that the specification leads to a dead end. This is

how thinking about complex subjects is extended. In the present case, the specification relates to problem-solving in connection with human needs and for this reason both of these topics are to be explored. The question being asked is whether there are goals and processes towards them that can be described and defined and by which specific problems can be solved. If there is no conclusion one way or the other this means that the specification stage has not been thought through adequately.

The Boundaries of the Area of Inquiry

The next step is to determine the operational area that relates to the specified area of interest. Assume that the area selected is conflict in the classroom or mugging in the street. Relevant to the investigation would be the educational system, the domestic environment, race relations and other specific fields.

It is at this point that there appears a clear difference between the cybernetic process of decision-making and problem-solving. The former draws the boundaries of inquiry narrowly. In the normal course of practical events, situations are categorized by reference to disciplines in academic institutions and by reference to departments in institutions of government: unemployment is for economists and departments of labour. Having been so categorized, research findings and policies are arrived at within the limits imposed by the labelling. During this century, in particular, education within academic institutions has been structured as though problems fall within fields demarcated as physical, chemical, economic, psychological, social, political or some other such 'discipline'. Policy administrators are even more departmentalized. A behavioural problem in schools is an educational one; violence in the street, theft and such crimes are matters for police authorities and courts; race problems involve boards established for the purpose; major communal conflicts are handled by the army; international tensions and conflicts fall within the jurisdiction of foreign offices and of defence departments. Each problem area has its own approach and set of remedies within the political and social order in which it occurs.

Many problems do, in practice, fall into a special category. A minor road offence is conveniently and sensibly a police matter. There are, however, few antisocial or illegal acts that can so readily be categorized: school problems are likely to be environmental rather than educational; mugging or theft could be an alienation problem; communal conflicts are usually complex in their origins and gather a momentum of their own. These and the more significant social and political problems with which societies are concerned, cannot reasonably be categorized in ways that conveniently fall within the defined scope of particular university and government departments. Whose job is it to determine whether threat and coercion are effective in deterring undesired behaviour—strategists, criminal lawyers, sociologists, psychologists? Are we to assume that if the issue is one of individual deviance it is the lawyer's or the psychologist's domain; if one of group deviance it is the concern of the political scientist and that these are separate problem areas? Who studies the legitimacy of authorities—educationalists, family guidance councils, international courts? Can we assume that the behavioural problems involved—the nature of deterrence, the nature of legitimacy—are different in each of these separate areas of responsibility?

These questions are stimulated by events in modern societies. Each deviant act can be defined narrowly by reference to the actor and to the norms of his environment. Even major communal conflict can be defined in terms of the influence of a few terrorists or the rejection of majority democratic government. However, when certain forms of deviance occur together, over a wide geographical area and in political and social systems of different kinds, some general behavioural explanations, regardless of numbers of persons involved, seem to be invited. Attempts to define and to deal with problems outside this wider context could be misleading and ineffective.

We operate in many straitjackets: cultural, linguistic, ideological and perhaps most restrictive of all, the constraints of institutionalized disciplines in both academic and policy-making fields. A problem sometimes comes to be defined according to decisions made as to who shall deal with it and such decisions are often made as administrative ones. Who shall deal with a problem is usually determined by the conventional definition of it, thus mitigating against new thinking. This separate treatment of particular categories of problems deprives researchers and administrators of the opportunity to use experience and evidence obtained in other areas. Communal conflict and interstate conflicts have much in common; but they are studied and dealt with separately. For example, in the United Kingdom the Northern Ireland conflict was deemed to be a Home Office matter before a separate department was established, while the conflict in Cyprus—a similar situation—was a Foreign Office matter. Educational problems and environmental conditions are closely linked, but these fall within the responsibility of different authorities.

There is tremendous resistance to the breaking down of boundaries of disciplines. There are obvious resistances that arise out of defence of roles both in the academic and the administrative worlds. There are intellectual objections also. The idea that conflicts between individuals and small groups could be in any way related to conflict between nations or the other way around is not generally acceptable to many scholars and administrators.

There is not even a language to bridge the gaps. Deviance is a term used to describe the non-conforming behaviour of the individual. When a nation acts against what is argued to be international law, the term is not used: aggression and intervention are more usual terms or the full description of 'contravention of international law'. Where the same terms are employed, they are given different meanings in the different contexts. Aggression by the individual is not subject to the same explanation as aggression by a large group or state. In the first case the explanation and connotation are likely to be frustration and deprivation and in the second the explanation and connotation are likely to be the opposite, assertion and superior power.

Even within separate disciplines there are further specializations and these have counterparts in public administration. There is a practice of categorizing behaviour and persons according to types: normal, abnormal; introvert, extrovert; aggressive, defensive; social, antisocial; advantaged, disadvantaged; legal, illegal; conformist, deviant. Academics who do this usually recognize that these are extreme types and that most persons and behaviour can be placed at a point along the continuum between the two extremes. The categorization is useful only as a means of drawing attention to traits in personality and behaviour. It says little about the behaviour that is described by the label. Nevertheless, in the popular view and in public policy-making, these labels are employed to describe discrete types. Justice seems to demand that this be so: justice demands that there should be no marginal cases. There are those whose behaviour is legal and those whose behaviour is illegal, normal or abnormal. Points spread along a continuum are brought together to form a group that is labelled.

This is convenient administratively for it enables a division of labour such that, for example, the abnormal or deviant can be made the responsibility of separate departments or institutions. The grouping can be altered administratively by including or excluding points along the continuum as social norms alter. The definitions or labels do not reflect any theory of behaviour and are not intended as explanation of it. They are a sufficient basis for prescription: those so grouped together, those so defined are subjected to treatment, isolation from society or punishment, as the case may be.

However, labelling is seductive. This administrative convenience has far-reaching consequences. Once categories of behaviour or persons are differentiated, there is a strong tendency to regard them as being subject to special analysis unrelated to the behaviour of all others along the continuum. Authorities are interested in why these particular persons have fallen into the behavioural groups defined as being abnormal, deviant or some other. This calls for research into the behaviour of those in these groups. This is also the academic practice. Statistically it can be determined whether those within the defined categories come from environments that are less favourable or have experienced more broken relationships on average than those who are not within these defined categories. However, such a separate analysis cannot take into account those with the same characteristics who have not been so labelled because their abnormality or deviance has not been discovered; those who would act in ways that would bring them within the definitions if need and opportunity were present; those whose behaviour could on some grounds be regarded as abnormal or deviant from many points of view that happened not to have been taken into account in the labelling process; or those so labelled who will be excluded from defined categories as social norms change. Nor does such an analysis explain the possibility that far greater numbers in a population experience the same unfavourable environments and broken relationships without behaving in ways that attract the labels to them.

Criminologists are fully aware of the problems that arise out of definitions of behaviour that are made by authoritative decision-makers in the conduct of a society. Note has been taken of the possibility that prejudice on the part of those who administer the law may result in underprivileged persons being placed in defined categories, while others who are more privileged and who have behaved in the same ways are not so labelled. The difficulties associated with interpreting motivation by observing acts are recognized: is violence in defence the same as violence that is aggressive and how can either be determined? Is theft motivated by need the same as theft by those who have adequate resources? These issues are raised in this context merely to make the point that in approaching unsolved social problems we cannot in advance prejudice the analysis by assuming different behavioural types or separating out some categories of behaviour as being distinctly different from others.

As a working hypothesis it is necessary to approach social problems on the basis that behaviour of all actors, individuals and small and large groups, is that response to the environment which seems to be the most appropriate in all the circumstances as perceived and within the limits of the knowledge available of alternative responses, such that satisfactions will be maximized. This justifies analysing all behaviour within the one analytical framework: normal and abnormal, deviant and conforming, individual and group, the haves and the have-nots, the advantaged and disadvantaged. As analysis proceeds, categories may be differentiated; but what they are must be the result of analysis and not the basis of analysis. For this reason we cannot in advance draw any disciplinary or behavioural boundaries.

Relevant Source Material

A related, but different, question to determine is what literature is relevant. Assuming the area of investigation is determined, to what degree can knowledge about behaviour at differ-

ent system levels be exploited? In the study of communal
conflict, how relevant are studies of family, race, religion, class,
majority–minority and interstate conflicts? In addition to different typologies of conflict, based on numbers involved or on
surrounding circumstances, there are different areas of explanation, psychological, physical and ideological, that raise issues
of morality, instinctive aggressiveness and structural violence.
Are some relevant and others not so?

Scholars are sharply divided on this question of relevance. Is
reference to other situations merely analogy or are there common patterns of behaviour? Some international relations
specialists claim that interstate behaviour is different in fundamental respects from behaviour at other levels of social interaction and that little reference to other levels is appropriate.
Others argue that behaviour at any one level must be analysed
in the context of knowledge of behaviour generally. The narrow
fields of industrial or interstate conflict are manageable: typically they rest on description and case studies. The wider
approach, even though it focuses on some particular type of
conflict, calls for more deductive analysis and a far greater
reliance on knowledge gained from other levels of interaction.
However, at the scientific level there should be no room for
debate: the testing of hypotheses, the application of conclusions
to policy and predictions as to the outcome of policy, should
reveal whether or not a wider or narrower demarcation of field
is valid.

Theories and their Underlying Assumptions

These are all preliminary steps, the thinking and contempla-
tion that goes into a study before the real work commences. The
next step is to examine theories and underlying assumptions. A
problem relates to the body of knowledge that is available and
has been employed in unsuccessfully trying to solve it. It follows
that a starting point is an examination of this body of knowledge.

While it is necessary both to be interdisciplinary when approaching a social problem and, also, not to prejudice analysis
by assuming in advance that behaviour is normal and conforming or abnormal and deviant, even this may be too restrictive. It
could be that we are tackling our apparently insoluble problems

within a system of thought, even if interdisciplinary and comprehensive, that excludes the possibility of solution. For example, assume that a conflictual situation were a winner-take-all one, which is how parties to a dispute frequently see their situation, then many possible cooperative outcomes would automatically be excluded from consideration. To take another example, the phenomenon of deviant behaviour could not be studied successfully within a belief system that assumed coercion as an essential control device, if in practice the origins of deviance were to have arisen out of coercion. If a belief system embraces a set of hypotheses and assumptions that prevent investigation of key elements, then solutions cannot be found. de Bono (1971) would argue that many problems can be solved only by a completely new approach, that no amount of logical refinement and accumulation of data within a given framework can avail if the original conception of the problem is false.

An altered approach comprises one or both of two aspects of thinking. There are the methods or thought processes that are followed and there are the observations and assumptions that are made in the course of this thinking about a problem. When significant changes occur in both there is bound to be what de Bono would describe as a new approach.

Take method or thought processes first. As a general rule we learn from experience. We draw general conclusions from our particular and separate observations. Sometimes we end up with a correct answer, as is evident when we can predict precisely and accurately, e.g. the rise and setting of the sun. Sometimes we end up with 'myth', such as the proposition that the best crops are planted at the rising moon. This is the empirical-inductive approach by which we observe facts, arrive at a general proposition and test this proposition against further observed facts. If the observations are backed by a theoretical explanation, which is the case with the rise and setting of the sun, then there is not total reliance on observation for validation. If, on the other hand, no explanation can be found of the observations, which is the case of the crop planting, then observations lead to propositions that have no support other than further observations. Expectation is likely to enter into the process of selection and interpretation of observations, thus leading to confirmations and not refutations. The problem of everyday life, sometimes the problem of scholarship and, frequently, the problem of policy-makers, is to know whether the general conclusions so arrived at are valid.

Thinking about social problems is especially subject to this difficulty. Social problems are thought about in a given cultural, social and political climate. Sociology, social work and industrial relations studies in particular, employ the 'case work' method. This rests heavily on observations of separate situations within a given set of assumptions and values. General statements and theories are deduced. So also in politics and in policy-making: past experiences, conventional wisdom, the values of the society, all colour the perception and definition of a situation. What is perceived, tends to confirm theories that are held. For example, statistics of arrests give some reason to believe that those administrating the law have expectations about the behaviour of certain classes and minorities in the community which influence their interpretation of behaviour, whether it is actually or potentially deviant or not (see Box, 1971, ch. 6; Pepinsky, 1976). Sometimes there is a relationship between expectations and events, the expectations in practice inducing the events: the expectation of improved business prospects promote improved business prospects and the expectation of conflict can promote conflict, thus appearing to confirm the validity of the original hypothesis.

Most historians and many social scientists follow the empirical method, even though they may be aware of the inherent danger that their observations may be influenced by the beliefs they hold and that their findings may in fact help promote the events that they predict. There seems to be no alternative if advantage is to be taken of the deep well of history and of the vast wealth of personal and social experience. Policy-makers translate their experience into ideologies and party platforms and are even more prone to observe those events that appear to confirm their view points.

It is useful to reflect a moment on the effect this descriptive or inductive method has had on thinking over the ages. Observations build on observations over the years, expectations lead to confirming observations, the observations are communicated and published, more confirmations accumulate, trends are observed, a general body of theory develops, other notions are deduced from this body of theory—and the whole process can end up with nothing more than myth, be it universally accepted myth. It is not only beliefs about the shape of the world, visits from other worlds, supernatural phenomena of many kinds that emerge by this process, but more importantly, beliefs about the handling of people, the behaviour of people, the health of people, the feeding of people, the handling of interstate strategic relations. Observations and beliefs are rarely tested in a critical manner. Within this process there is, in practice, no critical test: observations that seem to give further support are the only test and these arise out of the same subjective process by which only expected discoveries are observed.

Popper (1957) has observed: 'The question, "How did you first *find* your theory?" relates, as it were, to an entirely private matter, as opposed to the question "How did you *test* your theory?" which alone is scientifically relevant'. In his view:

> ... just because it is our aim to establish theories as well as we can, we must test them as severely as we can; that is, we must try to find fault with them, we must try to falsify them. Only if we cannot falsify them in spite of our best efforts can we say that they have stood up to severe tests. This is the reason why the discovery of instances which confirm a theory means very little if we have not tried, and failed, to discover refutations. For if we are uncritical we shall always find what we want: we shall look for, and find, confirmations, and we shall look away from and not see, whatever might be dangerous to our pet theories. In this way it is only too easy to obtain what appears to be over-whelming evidence in favour of a theory which, if ap-proached critically, would have been refuted. In order to make the method of selection work, and to ensure that only the fittest theories survive, their struggle for life must be made severe for them.

Clearly, the testing of a theory, i.e. the practical application of a conceptual notion, is in itself fertile: 'it leads to new observa-tions, and to a mutual give and take between theory and observation' (Popper, 1957, p. 135). However, despite this methodological requirement, modern behavioural sciences are heavily weighted on the side of speculative, private theories. In so far as reference is made to empirical evidence, it is more 'to find confirmations' than to test.

Whether the deductive approach is a practical one in many

circumstances is open to doubt; but it carries with it an exhorta-
tion for more precision, more honesty in selection of and collec-
tion of data, more open-mindedness and willingness to alter
approaches and explanations. Most importantly it carries with
it a powerful criticism of much of conventional thinking about
social problems which so much rests on observations made
within a particular cultural environment and value system.

Selection of events and observations tend to be controlled by
the attitudes and preconceived notions of the observer. What is
required is a declared theoretical framework in which observations can be made so that the preconceptions are explicit. Even
then the accumulation of data is not necessarily evidence: other
data could be found that is contrary. The same problem emerges
when analysis is founded on the theories that prevail. Many
writers dealing with social problems review the literature and
find contradictions, some scholars holding one view, some
another. They also find contradictions within the writings of
the one scholar. From these they draw out their own position
and the justification for it. The ideas of Aristotle, Bacon, Burke,
Hobbs, Locke, Marx, Plato, Socrates, Trotsky, Weber, and those
of Arndt, Coser, Dahrendorf, Deutsch, Durkheim, Eckstein,
Fromm, Parsons, Riesman, Verba and many others provide a
rich source for comparison and criticism. As with the reservoir
of history, they are a source from which can be drawn evidence
for support for almost any theory and for the condemnation of
any theory. Historians used recorded events, social scientists
use recorded ideas and theories. The methodological problems
are the same: in both cases there is selection of evidence. The
references to theories do not provide either validation or refutation. There are many thousand learned works that are based on
references to past and present thinking, using this thinking just
as those employing the empirical method use observed data.
The same sources are used to give quite different view points
according to the selections and interpretations made.

Past and present thinkers are invaluable as a stimulus to
thought, as are history and the observation of current events.
However, they can be no more than a stimulus. Together they
represent a description of all unsolved problems in the sense
that an unsolved problem relates to the current state of thinking about it. They, all taken together, represent the starting

point of problem-solving. The practical difficulty is that they cannot be taken together and as a whole: all events and all thinking about a particular problem is only a theoretical starting point. On the other hand, once there is selection of events or ideas the definition of the problem becomes distorted.

Some writers have attempted to overcome these difficulties by basing their thinking on islands of theory that can be culled from the thinking of others: coercion theory, value theory, socialization theory, integration theory, to name but a few. Names of writers can be associated with each and each can be explained by reference to writers and to events. In this way islands of theory serve as a synopsis of thought. The need for selection is reduced. Then it remains only to be critical of some and supportive of others within a logical framework and perhaps attempt a synthesis of the main ones, to arrive at another theory and explanation. A good example of this approach is *Revolutionary Change* by Chalmers Johnson (1966). It is one relevant to our area of interest because while his immediate concern is revolution, what he has to say about it can be applied to the wider area of social problems: he has taken a comprehensive view of past and present thinking about social relationships. There are difficulties, however. Even assuming that the selection and interpretation difficulties were overcome, perhaps the most important source of trouble remains. The contending theories frequently are developed in the same culture, within the same historical background and share the same assumptions and underlying value systems. For instance, some of the underlying assumptions of Marxism were shared by some of those against whom he was reacting. Because these assumptions are held in common they do not come to critical attention and they remain part of the new synthesis.

There are two stages in all of these approaches: refutation of past theories and the development of alternatives. The historical and comparative theory methods are both selective in the evidence used for refuting past theories and in the data used for the development of alternatives. Over the course of time there is a self-correcting process as many thinkers make their contributions by criticism and by theory building and islands of theory develop that withstand the test of time. These are adequate methods in some areas of research even though they take place within a set of cultural and value givens. This is puzzle-solving rather than problem-solving: there are answers to be found within an existing paradigm or thought system. When, however, unsolved problems are faced, the probability is that the set of givens, the axiomatic propositions and assumptions, require re-examination. The refutation of past theories and the development of alternatives, will probably need to take place in an alternative paradigm, based on a different set of assumptions.

Another approach suggests itself: to distil from thinking and from conventional wisdom the consensual and assumed assumptions, the axiomatic assumptions that are generally accepted, then to look at these in the light of events and of their internal logic in the wider perspective of an interdisciplinary and boundary free approach.

The selection for criticism of conventional assumptions is also a subjective process. There is a wide range of assumptions that are not explicitly stated and which require examination. It is not possible to isolate them all. Those that are isolated by one writer will not be the same as those that attract the attention of another. The same corrective process of continuous exploration is required. However, the process is one in which falsification is built in. If any assumption can be found not to be valid when considered as a logical deduction from others that are conventional or not valid in the light of empirical experience, then the previous approach to the problem can tentatively be regarded as being misleadingly directed. If many assumptions seem not to be valid then the whole paradigm or system of thought will tentatively be thrown into doubt. Modified assumptions and an alternative paradigm will be suggested by the criticisms made of the original ones. The original approaches will finally be falsified but the new approach is not necessarily valid. If the selection of conventional assumptions reflects the interests of the writer or if interpretations of assumptions appear to be nothing more than straw men being put up as a means of justifying another approach, the moment of truth will come when the assumptions and paradigm are assessed in relation to situations to be explained and problems to be solved. In short, the falsification processes are the same in all these three approaches; but while data gathering and comparative theory approaches will not reveal the hidden assumptions that lie behind thought within a particular framework, culture or paradigm, an examination specifically of these and their logical consistency, will at least falsify, if not offer an alternative. This is the essence of problem-solving and this is the approach adopted here.

Data

The sixth stage is one of data gathering within the new paradigm. A general definition of a situation, a general typology, needs refinement in terms of the particular problem to be tackled. For example, a behavioural relationship falling into a category of conflict needs to be spelt out in terms of systems and subsystems, parties, issues and environmental circumstances. Whether it be the Middle East situation or an industrial dispute, there will be some subsystems more directly concerned than others and in respect of these there will be several parties each pursuing their own special interests. Usually such an analysis can be made only by the parties themselves and in consultation. Other devices are necessary when this is not possible. From the point of view of the problem-solver, this is a data gathering stage, taking place within the broader definition of the problem.

In practice this stage is probably the most time-consuming in any behavioural study. Once a relationship has been defined in terms of some typology, then the details, including the history, the institutions, the personalities, the objectives and the tactics being pursued, all have to be ascertained. It can be laborious, but at the same time it can be rewarding since data gathering will constantly be casting doubt on the original conception of the problem and throwing light on theories and their hidden assumptions. For example, a communal conflict situation can be defined in accordance with some particular typology that suggests the relevant data will be found by examining the parties and their relationship. In the course of this exercise it could well be discovered that the conflict was being engineered by a third party for economic, political and security reasons.

In most situations of unsolved problems, data are not obtainable. It is possible to ask some relevant questions and to obtain some relevant statistical answers, such as numbers of political and criminal prisoners, the number of muggings that appear to have a minority relationship; but the main data are evidential and to this degree subjective. This is particularly the case in this study. While academic texts and reports are crowded with statistics, their interpretation can lead to so many different conclusions that their value is significantly reduced. Perhaps the main value of data is not to support or to refute a proposition; but merely to alert the analyst to an aspect of a problem that he may not otherwise have noted.

Paradigm Shifts

It has been stressed that assumptions and observations made when examining a problem constantly alter. A continuing part of problem-solving is to re-examine the system of thought being employed. Observations and logical deductions may be discovered that are in conflict with it. One must ask constantly whether the problem being considered can be solved within the given set of assumptions used or whether what is required is a review of basic hypotheses. One must be prepared to start again on another basis—perhaps many times.

If preconceived notions influence observations and if these are altered over time as falsifying evidence comes to light, an interesting question arises, i.e. whether the problem being observed is changing in character or whether the same problem is seen differently in different perspectives or both. It may be that a problem being examined is constantly changing as environmental conditions change, requiring constant reconsideration of the problem. It is more likely, however, that alterations in conditions are less significant than alterations in thinking about the problem.

It is no new experience to discover that widely accepted beliefs and theories can be false. Kuhn (1962) has argued that in science, i.e. in our perception and interpretation of reality, there is, at any one time, a wide professional consensus. Within this agreed set of beliefs research and experiments are carried out and policy is formulated. (Kuhn terms research within this consensual framework, 'normal science'.) However, simultaneously there are likely to be events that are unobserved, at least by most people; also observations made to which no significance is attached, merely because they do not happen to fit into preconceived ideas. For instance, continued refusal by increasing numbers of persons to accept social and legal norms should call into question the relevance of these norms and the assumption that deterrence or threat will be effective in ensuring their observation. In practice it more often leads to the idea that sanctions (that have failed) need to be increased because any other view would be contrary to conventional wisdom. Constant demands are made in most societies to increase punishment when crime rates increase. There is no conventional wisdom in which to place the idea that coercion and threat do not ensure conforming behaviour.

However, in due course, as research and policy fail to produce the desired results, disquiet is experienced: explanations are seen to be inadequate. For example, in education, in deviance studies and in industrial relations, it becomes clear that deterrence is a blunt instrument. Some other explanation of what order there is in society is sought, alternative theories emerge and different policies are advocated. This interaction between events and policies leads to an accumulation of evidence that challenges conventional wisdom to a point at which it can no longer be upheld. The prevailing pattern of belief is called into question. Dissenting social scientists put forward alternative hypotheses and definitions of situations. Western powers were blind to pre-war independence movements and expected business as usual in Asia and elsewhere in the colonial regions after the Second World War. In due course the changing political realities were forcibly drawn to the attention of governments by the people concerned. Later these had to be taken into account by scholars. To begin with, alternative descriptions and explanations of observed situations tend to be criticized by those still working within the former belief system and clashes occur between schools of thought. There is no discredited theory, no matter how out-dated, that cannot be given some empirical support. Rationalizations come easily. Independence movements were explained, quite plausibly in the political context of the Cold War, as being inspired from Moscow or Peking. Their long history, their promotion during Japanese occupation, the human and social values they reflected, were discounted in this context. In due course a new belief system, initially an uncomfortable one in which to work because it is new and requires re-thinking and re-learning, becomes familiar and a new professional consensus develops around it.

As a consequence, there appear to be occasional shifts away

from one way of thinking to another, rather than smooth and continuous changes in thought. For instance, deviant behaviour was once widely accepted as being due to demoralization or deficiency; today there is a growing acceptance of the general proposition that behaviour, deviant or not, is that response to the perceived environment which is best calculated, in the view of the actor, to achieve his objectives or values.

This represents a tremendous shift in the definition of a particular social problem. This is what Deutsch had in mind when he observed that:

> The history of many fields of science shows a characteristic pattern. There is a time in which the science goes through a philosophic stage in its development; the emphasis is on theory, on general concepts, and on the questioning of the fundamental assumptions and methods by which knowledge has been accumulated. At the end of such a philosophic stage often stands an agreement on some basic assumptions and methods—though not necessarily on all of them—and a shifting of interest to the application of these methods to the gathering of detailed facts. The philosophic stages in the development of science define the main lines of interest; in the empirical stages these interests are followed up (Deutsch, 1963, pp. 3–4).

Deutsch has used 'philosophical stage' and 'application' in ways that relate to Kuhn's 'paradigm change' and 'normal science'.

The history of thought regarding aspects of the real world is the history of perceptions of reality. The real world does not change in discontinuous jumps, neatly differentiated in epochs or centuries. The apparent discontinuity is due to the unwillingness and, perhaps, inability, to move smoothly and continuously from one image to another. An analogy is the movement of the eye across distance. The eye jumps from point to point; but what is there to be observed is continuous. The face of a person can be drawn and re-drawn progressively to the stage at which it clearly represents a different person. There is a point of time at which the observer can no longer reasonably refuse to acknowledge the change. He shifts to a new perception, a new model or image.

There has been a tendency to treat these jumps in thought, these discrete thought patterns, as inevitable and even intellectually acceptable. Important writers (see, for example, Kuhn,

1962; and Deutsch, 1963) have observed them without implying criticism of them. However, it is the acceptance, as a legitimate and logically defensible endeavour, of detailed investigation within a given belief system, detached from a wider philosophical perspective, that is a reason for our failure to solve problems. For example, the inflation in the United Kingdom of 1974–75 was attributed to a sudden and unexpected decision by oil producers to demand cartel market prices and by unions to exploit their strong bargaining power. However, what the oil producers and unions did could be put in the perspective of continuously changing relationships between those who have decision-making power and those who have been expected to act within a framework determined by more powerful states and authorities. In a similar perspective, independence and civil rights movements could be regarded as the forerunners of inflationary wage demands, in conditions in which those who have power and those who control resources are not prepared to concede an altered social and political framework. In other words, there are some longer-term trends that relate to human as distinct from institutional needs, from which it is possible to explain and predict. They are not discontinuous. All that is apparently discontinuous is the perception we have of reality as it appears to jump from one set of environmental, social and political conditions to another.

Consequently, it is the special role of social scientists, unlike that of reporters of events, to determine continuous trends, i.e. the shifts which are occurring in the real world, thereby correcting the lag in perceptions that dominates policy-making and problem-solving. This is done deductively from propositions about behaviour that can be developed and tested in the present. This implies a constant challenging of conventional thinking and theories.

The role of the social and political scientist in drawing attention to continuities is an important one politically. Changes that are perceived to be taking place at any one time seem generally to create a response of fear and frequently of attempted repression of changes. Change appears to pose a threat to some segments of society which identify their beliefs and interests with those of society itself. Change is, therefore, articulated as a threat to society. It is depicted as evidence of decay or imminent catastrophe. The 'breakdown of law and order', 'the permissive society', 'the threat to private enterprise and initiative', are typical warnings. In the longer term, after conventional wisdom is challenged by political realities, changes are seen to be acceptable, brought about by the will of the persons affected. They are not necessarily disastrous to society. Examples are the abolition of child labour, of slavery and of many ancient forms of patronage and privilege. The role of the political and social scientist is to place contemporary changes in their longer-term perspective and thus to remove some of the fear element. Society is not necessarily endangered by change; change is demanded frequently to preserve and to enhance it. If this role were enacted effectively by political scientists, many forms of behaviour that are of current concern and which are regarded as critical, undesirable and a threat to society, would be seen to be nothing more than a reflection of the demands by people for changes that are resisted by minorities who currently claim to represent the community's priorities. If the research role were enacted effectively, changes could be interpreted as part of longer-term trends and responses to demands and, therefore, as 'progressive' in the sense that society would be seen to be in transition from one phase to another. Indeed, some contemporary challenges to authority leading to widespread violence and then to structural change, could be argued to be on the credit or asset side of human affairs; we have, for example, the continuing history of independence movements. If this were so, the problems of our time could reasonably be defined as problems of accomplishing such change without violence.

To solve problems we need to experience uncertainty or disquiet at any observed event, thought or logical deduction that does not wholly and without adequate reason fit into the current mode of thought. Even so there will always be a lag between observation of realities and thought change. A switch to an alternative set of beliefs is not likely, even though a current one proves unsatisfactory intellectually and in practice, until it is clearly discerned and at least rendered credible. Credibility is not established before there is theoretical justification and testing, giving rise to acceptance and understanding.

The practical problems that concern us relate to the exercise of authority and how to harness drives to the requirements of social development: failure to maintain order while societies evolve, failure to create just societies, failure of socialization processes, failure of processes of law and order and others. The practical problems, however stated, mirror intellectual ones: failure to evolve theories of behaviour and of social organization that explain and from which would flow effective policies.

The evidence of failure both in practice and in theory is clearest, as one would expect, at the most complex levels of social interaction, international relations, including legal and strategic relations. However, the same failure is present at all other levels, in the classroom, in the streets, in business and in administration. In all these areas neither policy nor theory gives cause for satisfaction. An international lawyer, Niemeyer (1941, p. 17) declared: 'the possibilities of the existing framework of international law are utterly exhausted. There is nothing we can hope for from a further development of its basic ideas . . . with our present conceptual equipment, we are incapable of redrafting the rules of international order so as to make them fit the changed political conditions'. Thirty years later, when failure was more conspicuous, the same kind of remarks were made in respect of civil law (see quotation on p. 88).

When there are problems that have persisted over generations, when there seem to be no solutions, then the reasonable procedure is to reassess all assumptions. This is a normal process in science. By the nature of the subject matter it must be a frequent process in the behavioural sciences.

Defining the Problem

The definition of a particular social problem, as distinct from some convenient descriptive label, is possible only after analysis is complete: definition is an endproduct of analysis. It is not possible to say in advance of a solution to a problem what scope is relevant, what disciplines, what literature, what experience, what data. Take, for example, a terrorist act such as the holding of hostages. Within a narrow conception it can be defined immediately as an illegal act. This, however, is merely a label. It is not an analytical description or a definition from which some insights into terrorism can be obtained with a view to its handling or prevention. There might be political motivations, alienation aspects and others: it would be misleading to draw boundaries in advance of a full analysis.

We are concerned with unsolved social problems. Defining

the problem of unsolved problems is no less an endproduct of the analysis. At the outset no separate categories are differentiated with a view to their exclusion or inclusion. We are concerned with the total problem area of unsolved social problems, at all levels, cutting across all disciplines. What we seek is a definition that is itself a perspective, even a social theory, within which they can be tackled.

The definition of a situation, including the interpretation given to observable acts, determines what steps should be taken in dealing with it. Consequently, definition is the basis of policy formation. It is this which most engenders academic and political argument. Mostly, definition reflects personal philosophies and interests; because policy flows from definition, policies reflect them also. Returning again to the example of a political establishment confronted by a minority, the situation could be defined as a law and order issue or, alternatively, as a problem of change. If law and order, the policy would be police and military repression of dissidents. If a problem of change it would be consultations with them. In such cases there is a strong probability that ideologies and interests will determine interpretations of behaviour and definitions of situations. To a greater or lesser degree all behaviour is observed on the basis of expectations of it and the preconceived notions that affect observation.

The distinction between action and behaviour is important in this context. Action is observable. Behaviour is the motivation, the reason for the action. It cannot be observed. Observing behaviour is interpretation of action and, as such, may not coincide with the actual motivations leading to the action. It is necessary to differentiate motivation, observed behaviour and interpretations of observed behaviour. The apparent deviant, the apparent conformist, members of minorities engaged in violence, members of majorities calling for law and order, nations confronting or supporting the international system presumably are all behaving in ways calculated to maximize their interests. Their acts, however, could be interpreted by those who observe them as aggressive, hostile, irrational behaviour. The defence measures of other countries are seen to be aggressive, those of one's own as defensive. The acts of minorities opposing a system are interpreted by establishments as undemocratic, lawless and violent, while defensive acts to defend establishments are similarly interpreted by minorities. Thus 'double-standards' emerge in political and social life. The same acts can be interpreted sympathetically in one case and critically assessed in another. Violence is justified in one set of circumstances, but not in another. Behavioural science is concerned with reducing the gap between behaviour and interpretations of behaviour.

It is clear, then, that we should explore means by which definitions of situations in social and political life can be more valid. The definition must be that of the actors, not that of the observer, otherwise the gap between observed action and intended behaviour will persist. Interchanges between parties involved in conflictual relations, in industry, in school, in the family, deliberately constructed to focus on the ascertaining of motivations, are probably a necessary part of the process of definition of a behavioural problem. Once there is an agreed definition, there is more likely to be an agreed solution. Indeed, definition and solution cannot readily be separated.

A definition of a situation is always subject to change as additional acts are observed and altered interpretations occur. However, there are inhibitions to such change. The research worker tends to acquire a vested interest in his hypotheses. In political and social life alteration of definition and, therefore, of policy, is frequently interpreted as a sign of failure or lack of determination. Policies that fail thus tend to lead to more of the same medicine rather than to a search for alternatives. This applies to all levels of social interaction, from the family to the interstate system.

An important policy consideration is raised here. It cannot be assumed that those dealing with a problem necessarily wish to solve it. It might seem expedient not to solve the problem or to argue that a holding position is the sought-after 'solution'. What appear to be difficulties in defining and solving a problem may well be an absence of any desire to define it or to solve it. For example, it could be convenient not to define certain delinquency, truancy or other social problems because the definition would point to the desirability of policies and structural changes that were not acceptable to society or to decision-makers. There may be no acceptable solution to an immediate problem, even though technically a solution may be possible.

Problems at the international level and many domestic problems seem unresolvable except by structural changes which themselves would be unacceptable. Indeed, this could be regarded as the typical case in political and social life, at the heart of conflict between opposing ideological parties. Thus there appears to be something remote and idealistic about much sociological and political theory. Theory seems to be of little relevance to the practitioner.

Some legal scholars, having examined means of settling disputes, came to the conclusion that they were adequate. The difficulty was that parties were not prepared to use them. The problem was, therefore, one of willingness and not of procedures (see David Davies Memorial Institute, 1966). The absence of willingness to use existing procedures should have been included within the definition of the problem, so that the causes of the unwillingness could be examined and alternative processes explored. A definition of a problem must include all attitudes and interests of all actors, not just those that happen to be shared by the analyst.

The tendency to exclude variables from the definition of a problem and thus to make studies of problems remote, arises in large degree out of the fragmentation of knowledge and interests into separate disciplines. Problem-solving appears too complex unless it can be conducted within the boundaries of a particular discipline or department of government. Yet part solutions are rarely helpful and are frequently self-defeating. It is at this point that policy-makers are in greatest difficulty: how to define a problem realistically, yet within a political context.

Testing and Prescription

While a problem may be regarded as 'solved' it still has to be proved or tested before it can be regarded as solved to the satisfaction of others. The 'solution' to a complex behavioural phenomenon or event has to be readily testable. It has to be tested in full view of others, i.e. it needs to be a test process that others can work through. Furthermore, the test needs to be capable of proving false the original hypotheses.

Tests cannot be made of a bold theory, especially in complex behavioural relationships. Aggressiveness of man has been an untested theory cropping up in most behavioural thinking. To be tested the theory has to be broken down into testable propositions that can be deduced from the theory. That man is aggressive in certain specified conditions is a testable proposition.

Perhaps in complex behavioural relationships there is no test of a hypothesis that meets these requirements, except perhaps prediction. Prediction is not in itself proof; but it does allow for disproof. Prediction is a game all people indulge in, especially political analysts; but it has not become a scientific game. Being wise after the event, rationalizing some general observations, horoscoping, are popular games. Prediction precisely formulated, recorded and objectively assessed, is not common among political analysts. If general and significant behavioural propositions are valid, e.g. propositions about deterrence, identification, participation, legitimacy, role behaviour, aggressiveness, structural violence, learning methods and law enforcement, then it should be possible to predict the consequences of policies in particular situations.

Like prediction, prescription follows logically from explanation. Prescription can be regarded as a form of testing. If the explanation is valid, the prescription will alter the situation as required.

Prescription presents special problems in behavioural sciences. In behavioural sciences prescriptions are likely to cut across ideological and belief systems of all kinds. Prescriptions relating to treatment of deviants could be clear cut; but they may run counter to views held by society generally and be unacceptable as policy. In other words, the analysis of a problem and the consequent prescription, could turn out to be one that is made from a particular point of view or within the framework of a particular set of beliefs. If prescription finally cuts across belief systems, then the problem was not defined sufficiently broadly initially. The ideologies and views that exist in the wider environment are part of the problem. It is not until the analysis is made, until prescription is decided and is tested, that the relevant responses in the wider environment can be determined. A great many political analyses of contemporary situations fail at this point: they conclude with what 'ought' to be policies and what 'could' be accomplished if only authorities or parties concerned had the will and were prepared to effect the necessary changes. A problem is not solved if unrealizable conditions have to be included in the solution.

Process

Finally, this observation leads to a consideration of process. Some 'solutions' prove not to be relevant. Others may appear to be irrelevant unless processes by which they can be made to be effective can be demonstrated. In the behavioural field this is an important and greatly neglected aspect of problem-solving. It relates, in particular, to the dynamics and processes of change and adjustment and to the means by which these can be accelerated. There will be few 'solutions' to problems of behavioural relationships that do not directly or indirectly relate to altered perceptions and attitudes, altered belief systems, considerations of options previously not considered, altered structures and roles. No 'solution' is complete, no test is adequate, unless accompanied by exploration of processes by which the solution can be rendered acceptable. The instructions for application must accompany the packet.

This is a neglected field because the history of civilizations so far has been a history of interplay between authorities and subjects, culminating in the law and order structures with which we are familiar. Decisions made, i.e. 'solutions' arrived at, have been enforced. They have, therefore, had the appearance of real solutions and have been commonly regarded as such. There has been no need to resolve problems. It has been sufficient to settle them.

The traditional approach to social sciences is for the observer or analyst to stand at a point outside the situation or events under study. The situation is perceived by the observer in terms of his normative standards, his interpretations of behaviour, his knowledge of various pieces of history, sociology, politics and other aspects of the total situation. However, it is the common patterns of the behaviour of the actors which are the subject of study, not the common patterns of their overt behaviour as perceived by different observers. The only reality that is relevant is that of the actors, not the reality of the observer.

For example, only those involved in a conflict can judge which variables are relevant, which patterns of behaviour are applicable. The conflict to be resolved is that which is perceived by the actors. Their interpretations of behaviour and events are part of the reality. Clearly they are likely to alter their perceptions and interpretations with increased knowledge. If the processes of resolution include increased information, by reason of increased communication between the actors or injections of information by a third party, then the 'reality' will alter.

We are led, therefore, to seek processes in which observations of patterns of behaviour are made from within the situation, by the actors themselves. These same conditions are those in which knowledge about patterns of behaviour can be fed back to actors, allowing them to select what is perceived to be relevant and giving them the opportunity to alter their selection as new information seems to require.

These conditions suggest themselves. The actors need to be placed in conditions which enable them to check on their perceptions of each other and the social order they are confronting, to assess the costs of pursuit of their goals in terms of loss of other values and to explore alternatives that are available once this reperception and reassessment have taken place. The third party is an observer in a scientific role. He makes no assessment, suggestions or interventions except to communicate what may be relevant patterns of behaviour drawn from other situations. He is wholly supportive of all actors. His knowledge of the situation is confined to the perceptions of the actors, conflict being a perceived relationship, even though it usually has structural components.

In short, the contribution of social science to problem-solving is to detail a process for the analysis by the actors of their situation and to provide specific information, the relevance of which is to be determined by the actors. The answer to the question, what is the solution to a particular behavioural problem and what should be done, is: there is a process to be followed, including the making available of all those pieces of knowledge which the actors find relevant and significant. The particular and detailed outcome of this process is unknown in advance even to the parties. It is likely to be very different from their expectations because of likely changes in preferences and cost assessments. But it is an outcome which emerges as a result of knowledge of the motivations of all actors, the costs of pursuit of goals and whatever relevant knowledge about organizational behaviour that exists.

The study of processes in organizational behaviour is only just commencing. Decision-making processes have been an important theme since the fifties, but even as yet tested processes have been applied only in some larger businesses and institutions. It is processes that social sciences have to offer—not ready-made solutions. The processes offered include, as a main ingredient, an analysis, hypothesis, a probable 'solution', an input of pieces of theory, much of which has the support of tests at one behavioural level or another. The actual solution is for the parties to determine. Their decisions are the final test of the scholars' analysis and tentative 'solution'.

A characteristic feature of contemporary times would seem to be that traditional 'solutions' are not in practice solutions of problems and not accepted as such. In this sense problems of violence, deviant behaviour and the others must be defined tentatively at the outset of analysis in a way which includes the three components: belief systems of the subjects concerned, the ideological orientations of the societies concerned and processes by which solutions may be applied. Problem-solving to date stops at the selection of a theory. Prescription and the processes by which it can be applied are essential parts of the exercise. Process is discussed further in Chapter Ten.

PART TWO

Assumptions

Introduction

The starting point could be a statistical analysis of behaviour associated with unsolved problems, the form it takes, the circumstances which seem to contribute to it, age groups, and all other possible 'facts' about it. Indeed, this is the usual starting point and attempts have been made on the basis of such data to arrive at explanations and prescriptions. However, this is an approach that suffers from some self-fulfilling prophesies. The observer is gathering data within a conventional definition of deviance or some other problem area, on the basis of a set of assumptions about society and authority that ensure that what he observes and analyses falls within these conventional notions. A more fundamental re-thinking of a problem seems to be required whenever policies are seen to fail to achieve objectives. An alternative to asking 'what are the facts?' is to ask 'what are the assumptions on which "facts" are selected and interpreted?' This is an approach which states the problem in terms of those assumptions and policies which in practice have proved to be inadequate as an explanation of it and as a basis of policy in dealing with it. It is what we think now, the conventional wisdom, that gives us the starting point. This includes prevailing value-systems, definitions of problem behaviour, conceptions of morality, notions of law and order and ideas about the role of authority.

Questioning of generally accepted belief systems can be disturbing. Conventional notions of deviant behaviour, for example, are in accord with values attached to discipline, social responsibility, respect for authority, law and order and earned social status. Deviance, in conventional terms, is the negation of these. Why then call into question these values when searching for the reasons for the erosion of authority and for deviance? A definition and explanation of deviance and a remedy for it that requires changes in these conventional values and beliefs would seem to be a movement towards surrender to deviance. This is a valid argument. If, for example, it were to be shown that unsolved problems, nationally and internationally, were

41

due to income inequalities, to the working of the free enterprise system, to the existence of centralized authorities, to conventions allowing freedom of protest, to trade union organization, to a free press and, in addition, if these conditions were nevertheless held to be essential for the desired way of life and for peace and security, then it would be valid to argue that the problems that persist would be the price that has to be paid. This situation would present conditions that had perpetually to be contained, not problems that required solutions. It would be logical to argue that existing structures, institutions and values had to be maintained and that problems of deviance should be examined within this framework, without questioning the framework.

However, both attributing deviance to existing structures or institutions and asserting that existing institutions should be maintained without change, are extreme positions. The probability is that there are many types of deviant behaviour with many causes. No less, there are undoubtedly some institutions and social norms that need adjustment. Deviance is behaviour that does not conform with certain norms: it cannot be defined or conceptualized outside a framework of norms. Social norms change and, therefore, behaviour that is classified, for example, as deviant or conforming, must be reclassified from time to time. A re-examination of social norms is continuous in all societies. In the interests of law and order it is expedient to ask questions about the nature of authority, of its erosion, of inequalities and of all structures and institutions that could be relevant to deviant behaviour and to other challenges to authority. All assumption and theories out of which arise beliefs and policies must be open to question. The position could be confirmed that much non-conforming behaviour, while to some degree being a response to existing institutions, is a burden societies have to bear, that challenges to authorities have sometimes to be met by some means other than accommodation to demands for change, that conventional values and beliefs are soundly-based. However, this cannot be assumed to be the case without first examining them.

The assumptions that appear to be implicit and significant in conventional thought and policies are discussed in the following five chapters: those concerned with the social system (Chapter Two), institutional values and human needs (Chapter Three), control mechanisms (Chapter Four), the settlement of disputes (Chapter Five), legitimacy (Chapter Six) and role defence (Chapter Seven).

Clearly a wide literature is relevant to this Part and to the third Part which deals with an alternative paradigm— virtually the whole of philosophical and behavioural studies of the last four of five decades. While references are made in the text, these merely provide examples. There is not, for obvious reasons, the usual attempt to review the relevant literature. Yet the reader has a right to expect an historical context, some evidence of continuity of thought, especially when conventional wisdom is being criticised and an alternative paradigm suggested.

There are three strands of thought that are especially relevant. First the philosophical. A paradigm shift from institutional to human values seems to have begun consciously at about the time Christian Bay wrote the classic *The Structure of Freedom* in 1958. No reference is made to this in the text for it pervades the whole: no publication serves better as an historical foundation for the arguments in this and the next Part.

There is a second body of literature that is taken for read in these next two Parts. Stemming from the challenge that Bay and others have made to traditional 'scientific observation' and to the exclusion of seeming value judgments, is a wide and growing literature on ethnicity, recognition, control and other human needs. It is a literature that is largely anthropological and sociological. Typical is the work of Epstein *Ethos and Identity* (1978) and the great many references that are given in his appendix. The combination of the philosophical and the scientific provides the basis for an inter-disciplinary theoretical-prescriptive study such as this.

There is a third strand that is also taken as read. When a paradigm shift, involving as it does a new language and unfamiliar conceptual notions, is well under way, there are attempts at greater precision and at operational definitions. 'Needs' and 'values' present great difficulties in this respect. A paper by Singer, 'Individual Values, National Interests, and Political Development in the International System' (1970) is a major contribution in this respect and, along with the thinking of Bay and the scientific findings of political and social science, provides a foundation for Parts Two and Three.

CHAPTER TWO

The Social System

SOCIETIES AS INTEGRATED SOCIAL SYSTEMS

An underlying assumption in conventional thought is that a society is a coherent system or, alternatively, that the goal of a society is to establish and to preserve itself as a coherent social system. 'Cohere' is the term used by Dahrendorf (1959, p. 157): '... the most puzzling problem of social philosophy: how is it that human societies cohere?' Cohere (according to the *Concise Oxford Dictionary*) means remain united, well knit, stuck together. It is implied that there are some attractions among the parts that bind them together, even though they may have had to be socialized into this attraction in the first place. Coherence implies a lasting unity or integration, not just an association of units that are otherwise hostile and held together only while pressures are applied to keep them together. A contrary view is that the appearance of coherence is misleading: that societies are not coherent societal systems and that attempts to establish them and to preserve them as such lead to reactions that are, in the view of those making these attempts, dissident and deviant.

There are far-reaching implications in these opposing viewpoints and for this reason they should be examined. For example, consider the widespread existence of we–they relations in industry and in many segments of society where management and leadership are clearly necessary. The approach that assumes the existence of integrated social systems, as a fact or as an ideal, would suggest agreed principles that enabled those in the we–they system to cooperate. It is, nevertheless, just as reasonable to assume that the structure is unacceptable to one side, that no principles of social cooperation overcome the conflictual structural problems, that in practice the two oppos-

44

ing societies each have their own set of values and principles on which to confront the other. In the latter view the question to be asked would not be what principles, what enforced contract make possible an integrated society, but what are the conditions and principles that enable different and opposing societies to function harmoniously; alternatively, what are the structural changes that are required to eliminate we–they relationships in the social system. Re-phrasing we could ask, can the 'we' occupants of roles be placed by the 'they' occupants into legitimized roles and by what processes; alternatively can the we–they relationship be removed? Similarly, take a case of communal conflict such as in Northern Ireland or the caste relationships that exist in India. In these cases it would be absurd to refer to coherent societies. Part of the argument that follows is that there probably are shared *needs* in all societies: they are shared because they are universal. However, such *values* that are described as shared by coherent social system theorists, in practice are values that frequently are inimical to the pursuit of these needs. There enforced observation may be a cause of behaviour that is labelled as deviant or problem behaviour. In short, the assumption that societies are integrated social systems and should be preserved as such, if not wholly valid, may be both a source of many unsolved social and political problems and also a reason why they are not solved. We should examine, therefore, theories that assume the existence of integrated social systems.

SOCIAL SYSTEM THEORIES

The arguments about what makes societies cohere have generally centred on the relative significance of coercion and of shared values as controlling influences. Coercion theory is associated with Hobbes who held that a society is a form of social order imposed by some on others by threat and coercion. It is based on the empirical observation that societies are significantly, even basically conflictual. The variety of desires, ideas and interests in any society is recognized. In addition it is noted that 'the fundamental inequality of social structure, and the lasting determinant of social conflict, is the inequality of power

and authority which inevitably accompanies social organization' (Dahrendorf, 1959, p. 64). It follows that '... it is not
voluntary cooperation or general consensus but enforced con-
straint that makes social organizations cohere' (Dahrendorf,
1959, p. 165).

Such a view is confronted by many who would argue that to
the extent societies rely on coercion they are likely not to cohere.

> There is a wealth of evidence and principle that repressive
> policies defeat their purposes. The public order is most
> effectively maintained—it can *only* be maintained—when
> means are provided within it for men to work towards the
> attainment of their aspirations. This is not an ethical
> judgment, or rather not just an ethical judgment. It ap-
> proaches the status of a scientific law of social organization
> (Gurr, 1970, p. X).

Nevertheless, coercion theory attracts wide support. It is at the
heart of traditional thinking about authority relationships. Out
of it arises the rights and obligations approach to law (discussed
further on p. 85) and the we–they attitudes that prevail in
industry and in most large organizations. The theory seeks to
explain the assumption that societies are an entity, that there is
a social system, despite the empirical evidence, on which the
theory is also based, that societies are conflictual. It is a theory
that assumes coherence yet explains it by a theory that argues
that there is none except to the extent that there is coercion. Yet
there is no theoretical evidence that coercion can succeed in
promoting coherence.

As is always the case, when one embarks on a theory that has
a false premise, one is led into many false notions that are
logically deduced. Dahrendorf, with most lawyers, is led to
argue that authority relationships are always relationships
between 'super- and sub-ordination' and employs the terms
'domination' and 'subjection' alongside the term authority.
Such an approach virtually eliminates problem-solving. Situations are dealt with within a power-coercive framework on the
basis of those norms that are being upheld within this
framework.

With value theory there are associated Weber, Durkheim and
Parsons who have argued that societies are maintained by the
existence of certain shared values that are sufficiently powerful

in their influence to ensure the acceptance even of limited inequalities and social injustices. Value theory, like coercion theory, assumes the existence of an integrated social system and then sets out to explain it. The explanation appears to confront much empirical evidence of greatly differing values within the one society, dissident groups prepared to disrupt and to use violence, religious and other minorities that oppose authorities and social norms. As is the case with coercion theory, there is no evidence given of the existence of the phenomenon to be explained, i.e. the existence of an integrated society.

The assumption of social integration—or coherence—is reflected in earliest notions of fairness, justice and law. The theory of the social contract, as found in Locke, Rousseau and Kant, assumes that those who engage in social cooperation choose together the principles on which social behaviour will rest. This may be a valid assumption when applied to small, face-to-face relationships; but it is not a logical extension to assume that all persons living in a complex industrial nation-state belong to the one social system in which the principles of social cooperation have been agreed. There could be many such social systems—even in infinite number having in mind the multiple role behaviour of each inhabitant—in the one state. The controlling authority is likely to be drawn predominantly from one or some only. The 'social contract' is probably a mythical notion; but the notion has been and is employed to legitimize the existence of social norms and their enforcement.

Coercion and value theories appear to reflect opposing views as to the nature of controls that give rise to social organization. However, the differences are ones of emphasis only: neither wholly excludes an element of the other. It is not difficult to arrive at a synthesis between the two, as Chalmers Johnson (1966, p. 35) has done, on the grounds that value theory needs to be supplemented with a consideration of non-normative conflict and, therefore, some element of coercive control. All have in common the view or assumption that societies are coherent or integrated social systems. All are concerned with an explanation of this coherence or integration and all are concerned with discovering means by which societies can be preserved as coherent or integrated social systems.

There are social scientists who accept the existence of social systems, yet obviously are aware of disintegrative tendencies despite coercion, socialization and some shared values. Hence an interest in functional conflict Coser (1956), following Simmel, gives many examples of the ways, such as external threat, by which conflict can be used to promote internal cohesion of social and political groups. In an extensive reader on conflict resolution (Smith, 1971), a number of articles are included that deal with the integrative functions of social conflict, including the functions of racial conflict (e.g. giving a sense of identity within the racial community).

Popular conventional wisdom is in accord with the value or goal of integration and political policies are invariably directed towards it. The United Kingdom government regarded its role in the conflict in Northern Ireland as an endeavour to hold together the society, the Nigerian authorities resisted cesession, in Cyprus the national and international goal was initially an integrated society. On a subsystem level, the general assumption is that racial and language minority groups should be integrated into the majority community and share its values and institutions.

The notion of integration as a social goal has some far-reaching intellectual consequences that themselves create problem areas. Coercion theory and the related notion of conflict as 'functional', have led to intellectual and policy positions that are divisive and intellectually and emotionally disturbing. It is in this framework that violence comes to be justified: if conflict is functional, then it can be argued that violence employed in conflict can be functional. The argument has to apply with equal force to all parties, so conflict and violence have to be assumed to be functional also for those defending their positions.

Another example shows how the assumption of a social system as an entity leads those who think about social issues into positions that promote even more serious problems, intellectual and practical. Chalmers Johnson adopts the notion of social system, implying an integrated system or, to use his phrase, a 'value-coordinated social system'. From this assumption he is led to make a distinction between rebellion and revolution. Rebellion is a condition in which there is revolt within the value-coordinated social system. It is not widespread and does not effectively challenge it. Rebellion is, therefore, not legitimized. Revolution, on the other hand, has a legitimized status: it is the withdrawal of a mandate. It is a challenge to the values being coordinated. 'True revolution is neither lunacy nor crime. It is the acceptance of violence in order to cause the system to change when all else has failed, and the very idea of revolution is contingent upon this perception of societal failure' (Johnson, 1966, p. 12). He quotes with approval Ortega y Gasset:

> Man has always had recourse to violence; sometimes this recourse was a mere crime and does not interest us here. But at other times violence was the means resorted to by him who had previously exhausted all others in defense of the rights and justice which he thought he possessed. It may be regrettable that human nature tends on occasion to this form of violence but it is undeniable that it implies the greatest tribute to reason and justice (Johnson, 1966, p. 12).

Unsolved social problems are thus defined away. 'Mere crime' and 'rebellion' are to be repressed. They have nothing to do with the need for structural changes, which can be brought about only by revolution. The same argument could be used in relation to football 'hooligans' who have been deprived of education, jobs and a stimulating social environment; in relation to violent minorities suffering discrimination; and in relation to all other dissatisfied groups that believe that they have tried all possible means to achieve just ends. 'Purposive political violence' either justifies all protest or none.

Historically and currently the value attached to an integrated society and the assertion that societies are in fact integrated by shared values and by coercion, seems to be due to normative influences. The desire for an integrated society is probably a leadership desire that stems from leadership needs and national security. However, a thought system that includes this assumption excludes important orientations that may be relevant to the solution of many social and political problems. In the wider context of modern world society, there may be good reasons for not promoting national entities that are integrated by socialization or coercion. Even in the narrower context of national society, there may be good reasons for not attaching a value to the integration of different social systems. On the contrary, unsolved social problems at all levels, from the small group to the world system, may well stem from thought systems and policies that assume integrated social systems as a fact or as a goal. Such thought systems and the entities created by coercion, could promote conditions that in due course disrupt societies generally.

At the empirical level there are good grounds for questioning the assumption of integrated social systems. The fact that authorities throughout modern history have had to struggle with problems of social integration—unlike more 'primitive' and smaller social systems—itself would suggest that large populations, often diverse in language, ethnic origins, ideologies and beliefs, do not form integrated systems even with a high level of coercion. This should call into question integration as a social goal, while not denying necessarily that it is an elite or leadership goal. It should certainly call into question the assumption that an integrated society can be created by socialization of values and by coercion, without at the same time creating social problems of the type that fall within the category of unsolved social problems.

TRANSACTIONAL THEORIES

Social and political scientists who are working on specific problems appear to adopt a neutral position on the question whether societies are coherent wholes. They appear to be little interested in the coercion-value debate. They are focusing on interdependence and transactions, the structures that promote functional cooperation and the behavioural requirements that need to be catered for within structures if they are to be functional. They are concerned with process, for it is through processes of interaction that the required structures and transactional patterns emerge.

Let us dwell on this because there is here a criticism of Marxism and traditional thought that appears to be missed by many social scientists—and by some activists and terrorists whose motivations are sometimes laudable but whose activities are unacceptable and in any event self-defeating. Drucker (1950) and Mayo (1949) are typical of those working at the coalface in endeavouring to explain industrial society by supposing that any discordent element is due to psychological disturbances: provided management and organizations are efficient, making use of skills and thereby providing recognition and role, the personal sense of security and the absence of discord are high. Note that this formulation can be made to apply to socialist as much as to free-enterprise systems. Blake *et al.* (1964) are concerned with intergroup conflict in industry and they have concentrated on process, how to resolve conflict by processes of conflict resolution. They do not need to start from any assumption about integration or disintegration, coercion or values. Through process structural conflicts are revealed and dealt with. There is a recognition here that membership of a group, especially a functional group, is not the same as identification with a group. Dahrendorf (1959, p. 115) in commenting on such approaches argues: 'The trend of sociological analysis founded on metatheoretical assumptions that deny the possibility of analysing social conflict as a structural phenomenon intrinsically rejects, of course, the very idea of a theory to replace Marx's. Thus, for Drucker and Mayo there is no point in any theory of conflict, since systematic antagonisms have no place in their image of society'. This is a serious misinterpretation. Such social analysts do not deny the existence of 'structural violence' through which results the damage to or lack of development of the individual. They do not deny structural conflict. What they deny is that it can be resolved only by coercion. They further deny that structural conflict is zero-sum or win–lose in its nature. For coercion theorists it is necessarily zero-sum. 'With respect to authority, however, a clear line can at least in theory be drawn between those who participate in its exercise in given associations and those who are subject to the authoritative commands of others' (Dahrendorf, 1959, p. 170). Such a view rests on a narrow definition of authority and excludes possibilities of legitimized authority that derives its legitimacy from those over whom it is exercised—a type of authority that we shall later describe as differentiated role enactment (see p. 131). Furthermore, it is a misinterpretation to argue that those who do not adopt the structural conflict approach have no theory of conflict. On the contrary, process is a theory of conflict. It is a theory that argues that conflict may be

positive sum, provided that the processes are such that parties
to the conflict are in a position to analyse their values, goals and
costs and to seek to solve problems experienced in relationships
by finding outcomes that are positive sum. Process is a means by
which structures may be altered so as to overcome problems of
structural conflict. As Dahrendorf makes clear, this is a departure from Marxism: the latter is more concerned with confrontation and power outcomes than with problem-solving processes.

The apparent cohesion of societies is due to functional transactions that are taking place and to alterations in structures
that take place as a result of transactions. However, it is only a
superficial appearance of coherence. Different social groups,
with different values, resistant to coercion from any authorities
that are not legitimized by them, operate in every society and
across functional groupings. Neither coercion nor shared values
explains what transpires; functional transactions do not require a basis in either. In this view, neither more coercion nor
more socialization towards shared values is the appropriate
remedy for social problems. The remedy is a greater attention to
processes whereby transactions are facilitated, whereby problems arising are dealt with within the different value systems
of the parties concerned and by means that enable alterations in
relationships and in the structures in which they take place.

The probability is that there are never integrated societies. In
the perspective of coercion theory a society is not a voluntary
association. It is one that is imposed on members by enforced
constraints. In the perspective of value theory a society is
largely a voluntary association of individuals that have shared
common values. Neither notion describes societies as they, in
practice, exist. Nor does the compromise notion of a 'value-
coordinated social system'. All imply social interactions within
a geographical area, controlled by an authority, which is the
notion of a nation or a state. Societies, meaning nations and
states, comprise numbers of individuals and groups of individuals holding a wide range of values, resistant frequently to any
socialization processes and coercion designed to impose social
values. The only integrated societies that do exist comprise
face-to-face associations and groups of persons who have some
shared interests and values along with many that are not so

shared. These shared values may be incompatible with what are described as the shared values of society. Such societies may or may not have any connection with national boundaries. This is not what is in the minds of those who have been analysing integrated social systems. They are reflecting conventional ideas about nations and nation-states. They are interested in the forces that do or can organize nation-states into integrated societies. They are reflecting thinking that could have been regarded as relevant in times in which populations were organized around elites, largely separate from other such societies, each concerned with its own preservation from external attack and from internal revolution. The notion of integrated social systems is not one that can readily be applied to a modern industrial society comprising very many different interest groups, cultural groups, ideological groups, class groups and others that have their own values and attitudes to society. As Moore (1970, p. 131) has observed: 'The conception of an "integrated" social system, which informs much of the writing in contemporary sociology—often implicitly—is a model useful for many purposes, but is clearly contrary to fact'. We could go further: it is a conception that may lead to objectives and policies that create serious and damaging social and political problems.

In practice, any grouping, be it the nation, the state or the world society, comprises an infinite number of societies and an unlimited cross membership of societies. Integration is a meaningless notion when applied to a population living within a particular geographical area, except in so far as interests can be identified that are shared by all. This would be an unusual circumstance. The nearest approximation would be survival in times of foreign threat and even then there would not be a full consensus. Integration is a sociological concept: the boundaries of societies that are relevant are social, not geographical, boundaries. The attempt to impose integration, in a given territory, either by coercion or by socialization processes that are designed to promote shared values, is likely to be counterproductive. Part of the counter-productivity may be dissident behaviour and deviance in one form or another.

The reasons why this is so will become clearer in Chapter Three in a discussion of values, both institutional and human.

Here, it is sufficient to point out that the conventional notion of and value attached to integration of a society as an entity characterized by shared values and conforming behaviour within a consensual set of norms, is one that does not accord either with reality or with the nature of needs and aspirations of the actors concerned. We will see that stemming from this notion many others emerge, notions of law and order, social norms, deterrence and others. They are all notions that pre-suppose certain social goals, which appear not to be the goals of the members of the social group concerned. We cannot assume the existence of shared values, either as a result of coercion or as a result of socialization process, nor can we assume that social integration is a consensual goal.

The relevant questions to pose when considering unsolved social problems are not whether shared values, coercion or both create an integrated society and how to promote an integrated society; but under what conditions and by what processes can there be a harmonious and cooperative society despite the absence both of shared values and of coercion.

CHAPTER THREE

Institutional Values and Human Needs

The assumptions have been examined that societies are coherent or integrated social systems, or that if they are not it is the purpose of leadership to achieve integration: the assumption that social values do or ought to take precedence over individual values.

Legal scholars and philosophers have asserted the primacy of social values ever since relations between citizens and the state were first considered. The justification for this view is that the interests of most citizens, over the long term, are best catered for by the preservation of social institutions and structures (including the institutions providing for change) even though in the short term, and in some particular cases, there may be some curb on individual freedom and development. On the face of it there can be no objection to this mode of thought. It is widespread: most regimes and authorities tend to take this view, as do usually those over whom they exercise their authority.

However, there is another assumption implied in the notion of an integrated social system that seems to destroy the validity of this mode of thought. It is that integrated social systems are possible as the result of shared values and some element of coercion: individual values can be subordinated to social values. This is an important assumption for coercion theory and for any value theory that admits the existence of non-normative behaviour which must be controlled. Both attribute deviance to imperfect socialization or to a failure of the system to impart and to enforce its values, to 'role strain' resulting from a conflict between social and individual values and to ambiguities and inconsistencies in the social value system. Johnson (1966, p. 33) comments: 'These are extremely important sources of potential conflict, violence, and even revolt; and they are sufficient in themselves to warrant institutions of authority to enforce social behaviour'. The assumption is that enforcement is not merely desirable, but also possible.

Both of these assumptions, that individual values need, in the general interest, to be subordinated to social values and can be so subordinated, require examination. Neither may be valid, thus revealing possible sources of unsolved problems, for attempts to coerce that are unnecessary (in the sense that an integrated social system is unnecessary) or impossible are likely to stimulate hostile responses including deviant behaviour. Furthermore, even though both assumptions were justified by experience, even though the need for coercion were present and coercion were effective, it could be that the process of coercion, while achieving immediate compliance, is itself in the longer term a source of deviance and revolt. Asserting the need for coercion and its practical effectiveness without taking into account its consequences, may be merely defining social problems out of existence. Consequently there is a reformulation of this assumption that requires examination, that individual values can be subordinated to social values without the side-effects of destructive consequences for society and individual abnormalities in behaviour that threaten the system itself. A contrary proposition would be that, if an attempt is made to subordinate individual values to social values, then, because it is not possible to enforce social values that are inconsistent with individual values, there will be responses that are damaging both to the individual and, through him, to the social system.

Two questions come to mind. First, are there human values held by all people in all societies by reason of their being individuals living within social organizations, that may be important and perhaps essential to individual social interactions, but which may be incompatible with some of the values of a society? For example, there may be a universal value attached to participation in decision-making, to a sense of control over one's own destiny, either generally or in relation to a particular environment. If social and political structures and values attached to them have their origins in the relative influence of competing interest groups, i.e. if roles and their occupants are the outcome of relative power positions, there is a strong presumption that these same structures and roles may impede growth and the full expression of personality of the majority by depriving them of this participatory experience. It is generally assumed that this is the case; but it also held that such a sacrifice is part of the price the individual in society is expected to pay to be a member of a society and to benefit from the security and services it offers. However, a second question relates to this last observation. Assuming there are such human values, can they be frustrated by a socialization process or by some other means, without endangering, not just individual development, but the stability of the society which the socialisation process seeks to establish? For example, can an ideal form of organization, with justice and equality built in, so overcome a desire for a sense of control as to guarantee social stability? May it not be that no process of socialization, no coercion, can suppress or sublimate certain universal human values that are not provided for within the value system of a society?

These are clearly fundamental questions; but they are capable of being answered both within a theoretical and an empirical framework. Indeed they have been answered in contemporary thought, at least to a degree that casts grave doubt on the assumption that individual values can be subordinated to institutional values and, therefore, doubt on the proposition that social systems can be made to cohere by coercion and by socialization into shared values.

THE DISTINCTION BETWEEN VALUES AND NEEDS

At the heart of the problem of social and individual values is the notion of values itself. If by values is meant only those superficial attitudes and behavioural patterns that are acquired because they are found to be useful in living within a particular society or civilization, i.e. cultural values, then it is axiomatic that respect for institutions and the norms of society will take precedence over any merely idiosyncratic individual values. However, individual values may not be limited to those that are successfully internalized through the socialization process. There may be values which are held by individuals as individuals—human values. Some societies may not be conducive to their pursuit because of their size, their particular system or for some other reason. Further, there may be values required by society that are not and cannot be internalized, because they are incompatible with these human values.

The likelihood is that there are, in addition to cultural values, more basic and fundamental human drives, common to all humans and shared generally by developed organisms. There are systemic properties common to all living organisms, ranging from dependence on oxygen to repair and adaptive capabilities. These and basic physical requirements common to all members of the human species are acknowledged. We are presently concerned with individual needs that have a societal significance, i.e. those needs without which there cannot be on-going social relationships and harmonious organizations. It is a reasonable hypothesis that there are systemic needs of the individual that are operational at the level of social organization. They are the needs of individuals interacting within a social group and of social groups interacting within larger societies: they are relevant to all levels of behavioural relationships.

Classical and conventional thinking does not draw a distinction between (cultural) values and (universal) needs. On the contrary, they are all seen to be in a continuum. The more obvious needs of survival have been regarded as basic needs, e.g. shelter, food, sex and reproduction, the satisfaction of which leads to other needs such as participation and recognition. In this view it is reasonable to draw a line at some arbitrarily determined welfare standard, according to stages of development of society and the nature of political control, other needs being a luxury or non-essential increment that can be earned by, or that happens to be the lot of, some individuals and some nations. If, however, it were found that there are certain human needs that are universal in the sense that they are a systemic requirement of the individual and that no society can be harmonious or survive indefinitely unless they are satisfied, then the argument about freedom and organization takes on another complexion. For freedom we would need to read certain requirements of the individual which, if not met by society, makes the individual a malfunctioning unit, finally destroying the total system. If there are needs that must be satisfied before there is individual development and socialization, then the relegation of these to the category of values, some of which are mere luxuries to be experienced only after others are satisfied, would be a sufficient explanation of dissidence and of deviant behaviour.

There is a problem of language in this discussion about values and needs which must be dealt with before proceeding further. There is no generally accepted word that signifies human needs in the sense used here. We are familiar with 'values' or 'needs' signifying the basic requirements of the individual, such as food, shelter and others; but there is no agreed term that covers the basic needs of the individual as a social unit and which are, therefore, basic to social organization. Needs, values, wants, are all used in different senses by different writers, sometimes interchangeably. Whatever use is given implies a notion, a theory. Davies (1963) equates wants and needs, whereas Burns (1977) makes a clear distinction between the two. For Burns wants relate to those goods and services that one lacks; needs imply a more socialized phenomenon: needs are the more widely sanctioned wants. In this view it will obviously be the role of leadership to transform wants into needs.

'Needs' are being used here in quite a different sense to describe those conditions or opportunities that are essential to the individual if he is to be a functioning and cooperative member of society, conditions that are essential to his development and which, through him, are essential to the organization and survival of society. Again, this use of the term implies a theory: the efficient and harmonious functioning of society (as distinct from its integration) is not explained by coercion or by shared values, but by the development and functioning of its component parts, individuals and groups. These requirements are not 'wants' or 'values'; they are needs that are more fundamental than either. It would be useful to have some agreed vocabulary that would make thinking clearer and enable better communication, but in practice we have to use words in common speech and to give them a precise meaning in the particular context in which they are used. Spelling out the theory implied in the special use of the terms is one way in which this can be done: new theories, new insights, new perspectives lead to an enriched language and more precise employment of words. However, the reader cannot always divorce himself from the meaning he is accustomed to attach to these words. In this case he is probably saying to himself that these needs cannot be satisfied in every case until societies have developed further, until more pressing wants have been met. Such a response would lead to the point of the argument being lost. What we are referring to in this context are needs that are always present: individual needs that are as basic to harmonious social relationship as food and shelter are to the individual. They do not depend on stages of development. The argument is that without the satisfaction of these needs the individual will find the norms of the society in which he behaves—primitive, traditional or industrial—to be inappropriate because these norms cannot be used by him to secure his needs. He will invent his own norms and be labelled deviant, or disrupt himself as a person, rather than forego these needs.

The assertion of systemic needs, i.e. needs that are universal within the human species, is not inconsistent with the existence of cultural values. The relationship between needs and cultural values is that the latter include not only the local manifestations of needs, but also, like social norms, the tools used to pursue needs. In one culture property is a means to recognition, in another the giving of property, in one aggressive behaviour satisfies a need and in another cooperative behaviour is the tool to satisfy the same need. In the same culture the deviant seeks recognition in one way, the business man in another. As Maslow (1954, p. 67) reports: 'There is now sufficient anthropological evidence to indicate that the fundamental or ultimate desires of all human beings do not differ nearly as much as do their conscious everyday desires.... In one society, one obtains self-esteem by being a good hunter; in another by being a great medicine man or a bold warrior or a very unemotional person, and so on'.

However, not all cultural values are manifestations of universal human needs. Some are clearly acquired and relate to interests. For example, there is evidence that some cultural norms and behavioural patterns relate to class, occupation and ideologies. They exist across national and ethnic groups. There is a student, a professional, a deviant and a working class culture and associated values that cut across geographical boundaries.

One way of determining needs is to postulate that the expression of values in cultures over time reflects human needs and that attention can therefore, be focused on cultural values (de Reuck and de Reuck, 1974, p. 429). The argument is that members of societies, each rational and in competition and cooperative with each other, evolve and inherit a set of values that, by a process like a fine market mechanism, maximize satisfactions. Individual choices and hierarchies of preference create the cultural values. As in a market mechanism, some values are sacrificed as a means of securing others. In the main, these are 'shared' values. Nevertheless, even this approach does not necessarily assume that cultural values so arrived at reflect a consensus, since people occupying different locations and situations within the society have correspondingly different interests and performances, forming subcultures. Because of power relationships within the society and consequent market 'imperfections', the recognized social values tend to express the values associated with higher status and elite role occupations. There is no reason to believe that cultural values so arrived at, even over long periods of time, reflect human needs. On the contrary, the probability is that past societies and civilizations failed to develop precisely because the 'shared' or cultural values were skewed in favour of particular elites and powerful authorities, were not adaptive to altering conditions and demands and were destructive of the whole society.

Kelman (1977) has argued that universal values are reflected in 'all major ethical systems and acknowledged in as many national constitutions. They are even formalized in international agreements, such as the Universal Declaration of Human Rights. . . . The existing consensus can at least serve as a starting point for continuing transnational exploration and specification of criteria that would have universal validity'. However, even these international declarations reflect a special value system, that of authorities and, furthermore, authorities in only some cultures and political systems. They are not necessarily a reflection of any universally held values, as we shall see on p. 168 when the difference between human rights and human needs is discussed.

Whether or not there are such attributes as universal needs and behavioural patterns that are universal as a consequence, it has long been assumed that this is the case, even though there has been little attempt to be specific as to what they are. Take, for example, general works such as that of Gurr (1970), and the reader edited by Davies (1971). The authors are prepared to generalize universally, about the consequences of deprivation, the coercive balance between values and constraints, the relationship between frustration and aggression and many other aspects of human relationships. In other areas the same general assumption of universal patterns of behaviour and means of control are in evidence, as for example in the reader edited by Thomas and Bennis (1972).

HUMAN NEEDS AS A NAVIGATION POINT

Before turning to define and to be specific about human needs, there is one other proposition to examine. Traditional scientific thought has argued that there can be no objectivity about human goals and, therefore, no objectivity about policies. There can be a purely scientific approach only to description —conditions of life as they exist, degrees of relative poverty, altering levels of crime, the incidence of war and such matters. This is a description of 'reality'. In this view there cannot be any scientific determination of goals: it cannot be argued scientifically that wealth is more important than freedom or stability more important than progress. Hence we are led to 'scientific value relativism'. There are hypotheses that a goal of societies (and of political science) is, for example, the greatest happiness for the greatest number. In short, it has been argued that there are no scientific navigation points, no references by which value priorities can be determined, no guides to policy that are outside and above ideology, class or cultural prejudice. Western political science and governments have been content to rest on a vague consensus, that defies precise interpretation in any practical situation:

> that government should be based on respect for the dignity of man and on freedom of conscience; that there should be

independent judges, equality before the law, no slaves, no torture, no cruel punishment; that the principles of habeas corpus should give every arrested person the right to be heard by a judge who could, if detention was not warranted under the law, free him with or without bail; and that science, art, and press must be uncensored. (Brecht, 1967, p. 6)

In this conventional view, human needs and social values are asserted as part of religion, ideology and class or cultural philosophy. Different assertions lead to different structures and policies. Changes in governments lead to changes in policies. Different value orientations lead to quite opposite conclusions in academic discussions. Left–right, hard–soft debates dominate discussion about the handling of situations. As a result problems are not approached as such with a view to a solution.

We are asserting that if there were to be discovered a definite set of human needs on the basis of which societies could be harmonious, major methodological problems in behavioural sciences and in policy-making would be avoided. If there were agreement as to human needs then there would be a logical starting point of behavioural analysis, for there would be a scientific basis for determining goals. Institutional forms and social values could be assessed in relation to known needs and the efficacy of public policies and processes could be judged by reference to them. There would then be a shared value system; we would know what was and was not adaptive behaviour by authorities for it would be assessed by reference to human needs; we would have some means of judging the relevance of social norms and conventions; we would have valuable knowledge about what causes frustrations and, therefore, about some conflict situations; and we could examine particular problem areas—industry, education, kinship, law and order—and be quite precise about policy orientations that would reliably achieve these known and agreed needs. We could analyse the human condition, how people and social organizations behave and will behave, on the basis of what is, not what ought to be, what will inexorably evolve, not what is thought to be desirable.

Normative and culturally-oriented lists of human needs imply that social and political structures and cultures evolve

over time, guided by and reflecting human needs. This rein-
forces the idea that what evolves is 'natural', even ordained,
justifying the classical emphasis on the preservation of institutions and structures that have evolved over time. An
empirically-based list of human needs, on the other hand, could
reveal marked discrepancies between evolved structures and
human needs. For example, there could be a differentiation of
power or some elite leadership influences, that over time
created structures that frustrated the fulfilment of human
needs, even though satisfying in the shorter term the special
interests of elites. There could be non-adaptive behaviour from
the point of view of the society generally, while there appeared
to be satisfaction of norms and interests as articulated by elites.

This is not to say, however, that a list of culturally or ideologi-
cally based human needs would not overlap an empirically
based one. On the contrary, religion and ideology are vehicles by
which experience and conventional wisdom are transmitted.
The connecting link in the history of thought between ideological viewpoints and empirically determined ones are the observations and insights of observers, especially in conditions of
change that stimulate observation and constant revision of
ideas.

A social system is made up of units that are themselves
entities. Each of these units enacts many roles in the complex
society of which it is a member. The quality of social interaction,
the adaptive and problem-solving potential of the total society,
bears a direct relationship to the quality of behavioural response of the units that comprise it. Personalities are the
guardians of the accumulation of knowledge and experience in
societies and of the process of change (Parsons, 1956, presents a
similar view). The satisfaction of human needs and desires is,
consequently, of systemic interest. The patterns of response of
units within a system are the basis of observed systemic properties. For this reason it can be deduced that systems and subsystems will have behavioural properties in common. Recognition, control and security are human needs in the sense that
individuals require them; but no less do small and large groups.
In these cases the display of these needs are described as
'independence struggles', 'nationalism' and 'freedom'. In this
sense human needs are the navigation or reference points, not

only for psychologists, but no less for sociologists, and students of politics and international politics.

The selection of a particular unit of analysis has a significant effect on interpretations of data. The psychologist, taking the individual as the unit, defines a situation in one way—e.g., some form of maladjustment—the sociologist, taking the group as a unit, defines the same situation in another—e.g., some structural condition leading to deviant behaviour. Thus, the definition of a problem becomes confused. If 'system' is adopted as the unit of analysis, a different perspective occurs for it is a notion of interaction that is general. In a system 'authority' is not the relevant or all-important centre of attention as it is when relationships in some particular social structure are being analysed. There are some systems, e.g. the international system, in which it is difficult to find the locus of authority or even to determine whether an authority exists (see Barkun (1968, p. 28ff) for further discussion). It could be that in social analysis that focuses on individual or group behaviour the existence of authorities is assumed and given a locus, even though they do not exercise influence. What is relevant are the patterns of behaviour and frequently these will show regularities despite different authorities and different cultures. It is the existence of human needs and interests or the denial of them, that is the basis of these regularities in patterns of behaviour. Take, for example, the problem of identity. Worldwide there are tribal, religious and language difficulties, in addition to class and cultural clashes. The strong tendency to identify with ethnic and other such groups, even with football teams, is self-evident. The need to identify is experienced by everyone when threatened or insecure. It is a phenomenon that can probably be explained in terms of security and recognition. So with legitimization, role behaviour and other forms of relationships, including deviant behaviour.

If we could postulate and find empirical evidence of fundamental or universal needs and desires, rather than changing cultural values, we would have a firm basis on which to judge whether knowledge and policy were being applied to human development—or merely to some speculative notion of it. In a discussion of the authority problem this is clearly important. It is authorities that articulate values and create institutional frameworks. Their legitimized status can be assessed only by reference to the degree that they promote adaptive behaviour. Adaptive behaviour can be defined only by reference to human needs and desires—whatever they prove to be. In the meantime, in the absence of any certain knowledge of human motivations and drives, we can operate deductively. This could be the better methodological course in any event. We arrive at a list of needs which is the best we can do at the moment, then we seek to test it by asking whether on such a basis, we can arrive at definitions of problems and at policies that more reliably achieve their stated purposes. Can we give more meaning to conceptual notions about which as yet there is little agreement or clarity, can we predict social developments? Modifications of the notion of human needs and desires will undoubtedly be required as we proceed: but methodologically we will have taken an important step in moving from induction to deduction, from analysis and classification to testing by falsifying.

This position is now widely recognized. Indeed, it will be difficult to be credible in the future without taking into account the influence of needs, which Sites (1973, p. 9) argues 'is many times stronger than the influence of the social forces which play upon man'. Those concerned with law and order will still continue to argue on the basis of social norms and their enforcement and many politicians will find it expedient also to adopt this approach; but sociological and political analysis is without any sure foundations without this conceptual notion of needs. This is not the occasion on which to review contemporary writings and to demonstrate the prevalence of a needs approach. Sites (1973, p. 7) has already done this, concluding: 'The point we wish to make here is that basic needs do exist and that they are more universal, and thus less specifically cultural, than some behavioural scientists would have us believe'. In elaboration he points out:

> In using the need concept we must ever be conscious that we are operating at an abstract conceptual level and that in the last analysis the actual basis of the need is tied up with certain psychophysiological processes which are in interaction with the environment and which are not at this point in our scientific development directly observable. The fact that these processes are not directly observable, however,

should not prevent us from working with the need concept if it allows us better to understand and to explain human activity. (The atom was conceptualized long before it was 'observed'.) That is, if we observe certain kinds of activity (or lack of activity) in behaviour which we need to account for, and can do so with the use of certain concepts which do not do violence to other things we know and which are consistent with other data which cause us to think in the same direction, there is no reason why we should not do so. We can always admit we are wrong.

To be more specific, if we find that men have certain anxieties and perhaps engage in bizarre activity under conditions of insecurity, we might fruitfully posit the need for security and see where it leads us. If we find or observe the same thing when individuals are alienated or seem t lose their identity, we might talk about a need for identity; and if we observe that people suffer from boredom, we might talk about a need for stimulation. (Sites, 1973, pp. 7–8)

Burns (1977) consciously employs needs as his navigation point: he is interested in the nature of leadership and observes that we lack a general theory of political leadership. Yet the phenomenon is clearly universal. He, therefore, seeks a central variable, rather than to be content with yet another description of leadership behaviour.

> Such a variable conceptually would have to cut across a wide range of cultures and classes and politics, for it is a *general* theory of leadership in social causation that we are pursuing. . . . Where do we start? . . . The primal sources of political leadership lie in the vast pools of human energy known as wants, needs, aspirations and expectations.

Later:

> Wants and needs and the elements into which they may be transformed may all be considered examples of motivation, a blanket term that has come to mean all variables from innate biological drives to the most refined and developed attitudes. It is these motivations, whether in their more individual or collective manifestations, that the leaders tap on the basis of their own motivations as well.

So, too, in other fields of behavioural inquiry. This reference point, this goal of human endeavour that can be checked empirically within social and biological behaviour, takes the place of personal value systems and ideological orientations. It should provide the basis of a science of behaviour, thus overcoming the methodological problems and ideological debates that have characterized thought and politics.

HUMAN SOCIETAL NEEDS

What, then, are human needs, these universal drives that influence all social behaviour in all societies?

There has been an endeavour over the years by philosophers and political sociologists to tackle the problem of conflict between social and individual values. The early political sociologists were less concerned with needs and their definition than in the forms of social and political structures that would, according to their own personal value systems, meet the requirements both of societies and its members. The idealistic literature of the fifties and sixties was characterized by condemnations of capitalism and faith in socialism; but it showed no clear understanding or knowledge of human needs. The concern was with structures: not directly with people. For example, Heilbronner (1959) traced the transformation of capitalism to socialism; Fromm (1961) was interested in the international system from the same point of view; and Niebuhr (1963) dwelt on the morality of political institutions, a theme developed by him in the thirties. Human needs were implied as being the reason for these interests, but they were not articulated. Consequently, the implied and stated prescriptions were suspect: too much faith was placed in an ideal 'socialism' without sufficient consideration of the needs that had to be met.

A little more than a decade later a different emphasis was reflected in the writings of Nisbet. For him, the issue was not capitalism or socialism, but 'the identification of functions, processes and membership which do *not* belong to the state and whose protection from the state and its bureaucracy should be a first order of business' (Nisbet, 1976, p. 242). He invited consideration of private and not public organization, human and not institutional needs and aspirations.

This shift from institutional to human concerns was a significant one. It was stimulated by developments in the totality of world society, in relationships at all levels, the family, industrial, national and interstate: i.e. a more conspicuous, less ambiguous and positive assertion of human needs. What was noted was that human needs were not generated by events: they were a constant. Altered conditions gave rise to their expression.

While there have always been assertions of human needs—described broadly by reference to 'rights', 'independence', 'participation', 'dignity' etc.—in recent years very large numbers of situations scattered over wide areas have drawn attention to them. Behind this development has been the postwar breakdown of former authority systems, feudalism, colonialism etc. and, more importantly, an explosion in education and in communications that ensures that the assertion of needs anywhere is noted everywhere.

In this political and social climate it is not surprising that many writers are basing their thinking on a list of needs, either implied or specifically mentioned. These are needs that are significant, not for the individual primarily, but through him for society. While Gurr was greatly concerned with relative deprivation, he saw the necessity of defining this in terms of needs. 'In psychological terms, values are the goal objects of human motivation, presumably attributable to or derived from basic "needs" or "instincts".' He employs a three-fold categorization that includes welfare values, power values and interpersonal values (Gurr, 1970, p. 25).

Implicit in the thinking of most political and social scientists has been a hunch that there are some fundamental human needs that must be fulfilled if social institutions are to be functional. For example, the literature on industrial relations abounds in implied assumptions regarding the needs and motivation of workers: participation, justice, self-respect etc. (see, for example, Blake *et al.*, 1964). In the field of deviance, many writers imply that a causal factor is a denial of needs such as identity relationships, opportunities and expectations (see, for example, Box, 1971). Indeed, a characteristic of twentieth-century thinking on social problems is this concern with individual fulfilment as a source of conflict: yet the particular needs are not often articulated. Galtung developed the notion of 'structural violence' by which he meant the gap between the actual and potential of individual development. He was implying some drive, urge or potential that was being frustrated by social and political conditions, particularly those that led to rank disequilibrium. His notion of structural violence could have had meaning only if he could have hypothesized certain basic conditions of life that required fulfilment (Galtung, 1969, pp. 167–91).

Most social scientists deal with human needs as a by-product of their interest areas. Burns (1977) is concerned with them in order to determine the nature of leadership and its purposes. Nisbet (1976), whose concern is the freedom of the individual, refers to the need for stimulation to offset boredom and its consequences, the need for kinship and a sense of belonging, and the need for security, amongst others. Rokeach (1976) argues the need for a belief system about both self and the total environment. Enloe (1973) is particularly concerned with development and points to ethnicity as a vehicle for need satisfaction.

Not surprisingly, some of the earliest attention to human needs from the point of view of society was given by social workers. They work within a political environment that accepts an integrated or coherent society as a goal and are, therefore, confronted by the conflict between the demands of the social environment and human needs. A book by Charlotte Towle (1973), commissioned by the United States Bureau of Public Assistance, had the title *Common human needs*. It set out to be a guide to those engaged in public social services and dealt with those problem areas that fall within the field of social work, the needs of children, the aged, the sick and disabled. It dwelt on security (through love and valued relationships), the opportunity for creativity and the attainment of skills. The National Association of American Social Workers (1958) dealt with 'human needs common to each person' and asserted the recognition of such human needs as one of its six philosophical concepts on which to base the practice of social work. In the particular area of child welfare, Mia Pringle (1974) of the (British) National Children's Bureau, asserted certain specific needs of children: love and security, new experiences, praise and recognition and responsibility.

This concern with human needs calls attention to the conflict between institutional and human needs that pervades not merely social work, but many areas of law, sociology and politics. Social work—along with law—is plagued by such a conflict: it is the everyday experience of social workers that their duty to their clients and their duty to authorities and to society are frequently at variance. The more thought and attention given to human needs, the greater precision in defining them, the greater and not the less this conflict becomes. The established view is based on the general proposition that the primary purpose of socialization is 'to provide individuals who will not only conform to socially prescribed rules (and roles) of conduct but will, as members of society, accept them as their own values' (Maccoby, 1968). In this view, the role of the social worker is to assist those individuals who have failed to come to terms with these rules or who have failed to use them sufficiently to their own advantage. It is not to change the rules or to encourage clients to change the rules. Consequently in the established view, the role of the social worker is to help the individual who cannot cope in his society. It is concerned with people 'at risk' who without assistance have little prospect of adequate welfare or normal behaviour. However, social work also reflects the same behavioural pressures experienced by all behavioural studies and has persistently moved in a problem-solving–needs direction. In 1958 it was argued by Boehm (1958) that social work has a problem-solving function; that it is an art with a scientific foundation; that it seeks to meet human needs and aspirations; that while the goals sought should not be incompatible with the values held by society, these values are often conflicting and social work is based on a selection of these; and that social work often adopts unpopular positions as it serves as the conscience of society. She argued, furthermore, that basic philosophical propositions include that an essential attribute of a democratic society is the realization of the full potential of each individual and the assumption of his social responsibilities through active participation in society and society has a responsibility to provide ways and means in which obstacles to this self-realization can be overcome and prevented. Later similar transformations in industrial studies are noted.

Those working directly with people and social problems are the most responsive to the behavioural environment. Theorists explain at a later date, perhaps in more depth, this empirically-observed behaviour. The school of 'control theorists' has given attention to needs, both what they are and what are the consequences of their not being met. Sites (1973, ch. 2) postulates eight, all of which require fulfilment and, therefore, none of which is necessarily more important than others.

The first is a need for response and, furthermore, consistency in response. It is only by consistent response that there can be learning and consistency in behaviour. Response is reaction to the actor's behaviour—whether it be an individual or a group. Second, the other side of the coin, is stimulation, i.e. an input into the actor, no less required in learning, for example, of language, custom and skills. The learning process requires a third need, security: without it there is withdrawal from both response and stimulus. The fourth need is recognition. It is by recognition that the actor receives confirmation that reactions to stimulation are relevant and approved: recognition provides the encouragement factor in learning, whereas responses can be positive or negative.

Out of these four needs others develop which make a qualitative difference to development, though learning may be possible in their absence. The fifth is distributive justice, i.e. not merely a consistency in response, but an appropriate response or reward in terms of experience and expectations. Sixth, there is a need to appear rational and to develop rationality. This follows from the need for consistency of response. However, the separate mention of rationality draws attention to the fact that the need is for consistent behaviour in others: rationality is a function of the behaviour of others. Inconsistent responses bring deviant and inconsistent behaviour—irrationality. Seventh, there is a need for meaning to be deduced from consistent response. Unless the response is meaningful to the actor it is interpreted as an inconsistent response. Even consistent responses can be interpreted falsely and, therefore, lack meaning. This need is stated to direct attention to problems of communication and perception in social relations. Eighth, there is the need for a sense of control. Control is a defence mechanism: if other needs are fully met then there is no need for control. But this is never the case: an ability to control rather than merely to react to the social environment is consequently a need.

All of these lists of needs are made from the point of view of the 'inferior' in relationships: attention is directed to the individual's struggle for security, control, identity, etc. Perhaps they could all be grouped together within the conceptual notion of 'role': the individual attempts to secure a role and to preserve a role by which he acquires and maintains his recognition, security and stimulation.

This thought directs attention to those who already have achieved roles, who have achieved a satisfactory measure of these needs and who act to preserve their role, i.e. the 'superiors'. If there are needs that are universal they must be experienced by elites, authorities and the privileged in a society as much as by anyone else. The whites in Africa have needs to satisfy and to be preserved, no less than others, particularly security and recognition. The para-militaries in Northern Ireland could contemplate a cease-fire and a peaceful solution to their majority–minority dispute only at the sacrifice of roles that cater for needs such as those which Sites lists. Consequently, we must add to the Sites list and to those mentioned by others, 'role defence' or the protection of needs once they have been acquired.

Whether or not we happen to be in sympathy with those defending roles, such as in South Africa, is besides the point. No explanation of a conflictual situation or the behaviour of individuals, groups and authorities is complete without consideration of role defence as an important need. It is a need for which biological evidence is available, for it explains the behaviour of dominant members of packs and the main fighting within species that takes place. Without the notion of role defence there cannot be a complete explanation of industrial conflict, the behaviour of management in preserving we–they relationships, of union leaders in seeking to maintain their own positions by reacting against management. Nor can we explain continuing communal conflict, the excesses in behaviour of some dictatorial leaders who in practice have a monopoly of violence or the behaviour of politicians who indulge in forms of corruption to maintain themselves in office. Family, matrimonial, pupil–teacher conflicts all invite the inclusion of this role dimension in their analysis.

Adding this dimension helps to focus attention on prescriptions that are more realistic than those suggested by coercion and value theories. Processes are necessary that allow the costs and consequences of role defence to be considered. When we return to discuss processes, role defence must be taken into account.

If there are human societal needs that are universal and necessary to the existence of societies, then it could be expected that some evidence would be found of them in all species that form societies or functional wholes. The sociobiologists—have been examining biological evidence from this point of view.

Wilson has taken a first step, by empirical studies, towards a theory of sociobiological human motivations. In his view purely sociological studies of human behaviour have been intuitive and concerned only with social structures and non-genetic factors. In his view, 'much of what passes for theory in sociology today is really labelling of phenomena and concepts . . . ' (Wilson, 1973, p. 574). Certainly, when one looks at some current treatments of man and his social problems, there is evidence that this is so. For example, the table of contents of Zawodny's (1966) important book is confined to labels: 'Frustration—anxiety; Fear and anger; Hostility; Aggression; Conflict; Behaviour under stress; Social maladaptation'. Wilson believes that human needs can be determined by taking into account evolutionary influences. He is impressed, for example, with the functional similarity of the social systems properties of termites and monkeys.

> Both are formed into cooperative groups that occupy territories. The group members communicate hunger, alarm, hostility, caste status or rank, and reproductive status amongst themselves by means of something in the order of ten to a hundred nonsyntactical signals. Individuals are intensely aware of the distinction between groupmates and non-members. Kinship plays an important role in group structure and probably served as a chief generative force of society in the first place. In both kinds of society there is a well-marked division of labour, although in the insect there is a much stronger reproductive component. . . . This comparison may seem facile, but it is out of such deliberate over-simplification that the beginnings of a general theory are made. (Wilson, 1973, pp. 4–5)

Overall, Wilson's findings give strong support to the list of needs and desires put forward by Sites, with its emphasis on identity, recognition, security, rationality and control. These are the sociopsychological and sociobiological needs that finally underpin, modify or destroy institutions. They are the needs institutions ideally help to promote: group integrity, identity, freedom from 'structural violence', legitimized relationships and others that some writers now choose to place under the heading 'liberation' (see Goulet, 1973) and which are described by creative writers who endeavour to depict the lives and drives of peoples and social groups living within institutional frameworks.

While Wilson may have written the most comprehensive review of the biological literature, others have come to similar conclusions. For example, Ardrey (1966) points to 'territory' as evidence of the need for security and identity; Eibl-Eibesfeldt (1971) to the need for positive relationships that contribute to respect; Nance (1975) to evidence that security through isolation eliminates aggressive behaviour. It is an inconclusive yet developing literature that could reveal in detail that which is as yet only conceptually known.

For the purposes of this study it is not necessary to enter into any argument whether such needs are genetic or environmentally induced. A theory could be developed that such universal needs are universal for neither biological nor environmental reasons. They could be systemic and occur merely as a result of the individual in society being a unit in a social organization. In this study universal human needs, such as Sites lists, that have a societal significance, are asserted as a hypothesis; in Popper's terms, this is a personal as distinct from a scientific assertion. The testing of the hypothesis, how it helps to explain unsolved problems, whether it is a reliable base from which to predict is the scientific interest.

THE UNCONTROLLABLE NATURE OF NEEDS

An empirically based list of needs would not alter analysis or advance policy if it were still assumed that their satisfaction were controlled by environmental and normative conditions. Such a list would have limited practical significance unless accompanied by empirical evidence that such needs cannot be suppressed and will inexorably be pursued. It has always been agreed that there are human needs, even though what precisely they are has not been agreed. It has also been accepted in traditional thought that needs can be achieved or satisfied only to the extent that conditions allow: if not so satisfied they are required to be suppressed by self-control, by acceptance of law and custom and by moral obligation. However, implicit in the hypothesis that there are certain human needs and desires that are universal is the view that they *will* be satisfied. Altered environmental conditions, changed political and social relation-ships and altered differentiation of power, give opportunities for the overt expression and pursuit of needs. As a consequence there was an explosion of latent drives towards independence and participation in the decades after 1945. However, even without such environmental changes, needs are satisfied either by deviant or pathological behaviour when other means prove futile. In the view of Sites, social norms are used as a means of satisfying needs. Many, if not most members of societies, find some or most norms useful to them. However, norms will not be observed if they are not found useful. They are tools and useful only to the extent that they accomplish what is sought. The individual in society—any society—*will* engage in deviant behaviour despite the possible consequences, if needs and de-sires can be satisfied only by these means. 'Society, then never completely conquers the individual' (Sites, 1973, p. 11).

This represents a significant change in approach to the study of behaviour and, consequently, to social policies. The emphasis is no longer on the ability and necessity for the individual to adapt to his social and political environment, to be socialized, to conform; but on his ability to use the system for his own purposes. If this is a valid interpretation of behaviour, there are some significant implications for education and other means of socialization. It could be that societies are endeavouring to guide and to control behaviour by means and along lines that cannot succeed, towards goals that are behaviourally irrelev-ant. There are similar implications for the fields of crime and deviance generally: no amount of deterrence and 're-training' permanently alters behaviour while conditions prevail that continue to frustrate needs. Herein lies the irrelevance and invalidity of traditional coercion theories and the notions of integrated societies.

Furthermore, such a theory offers an explanation of the 'inhuman', 'mindless' behaviour associated with communal murders, mugging or other forms of violence. 'If acting in accordance with one's beliefs does not produce sufficient control, the individual will typically change his behaviour even though his new behaviour goes against his own beliefs at that particular moment' (Sites, 1973, p. 21).

This is a sufficient explanation of why deterrence by threat is a weak control of behaviour. It justifies the conclusions reached by Niemeyer and more recent international and civil law scholars. 'International order, in the proper sense of the term, cannot be established by organizing an agency of power over and above the separate states, or through any other collective accumulation of force. . . . The effectiveness of international law rests fundamentally on its own merits, not on the assumption of some pressure behind it' (Niemeyer, 1941, p. 21). In the domestic field, in cases where the socialization process has failed: 'The harder we try to induce conformity to the law where conformity does not exist, the more we seem to fail' (Pepinsky, 1976, p. 2).

It is of political significance that universal needs are not treated as such. Even where it is generally accepted that the need for participation in decision-making or the need for recognition is a human 'right', the exercise of this right by others is none the less often resisted within and between groups. Other values or institutional norms of behaviour are invoked, such as values associated with particular forms of law and order. They are held to be overriding and to justify the suppression of these social–psychological needs. The drives and motivations of people are thus suppressed by institutional and cultural values. The reason for this conflict between human needs and institutional norms is not hard to find. Specialization in social exchange leads to loss of independence and to relations based on bargaining and power (Blau, 1964). Institutionalized norms then serve to legitimize and preserve the resultant social structures. Normative sanctions emerge as the means of controlling power relationships. In these circumstances the motivations and responses of others—even though they are identical with one's own—come to be regarded as a threat to existing institutions and positions of privilege. Indeed they are: there is a latent conflict between needs and institutional norms so established.

The pursuit of their needs by some actors is interpreted by others as ideology and even irrationality. In historical and political writings needs are sometimes treated as being among influences that should be curbed and against which institutions of restraint should be directed. The pressure to achieve, to be accorded recognition, to obtain security and control, result in a variety of behavioural patterns. There is rarely any mutual recognition that different patterns are evidence of the same motivations. The activities of professionals and others favourably placed to dodge tax, to use office facilities for private purposes, are held by such people to be acceptable patterns of behaviour, while petty thieving is held to be not merely beyond the law, but unacceptably antisocial. Similarly, the petty thief condemns the tax dodger and the maker of money by financial manipulation.

One reason for this ambivalent attitude to human societal needs is probably that while their existence is recognized in social investigation, it has not yet become a part of conventional wisdom. In 1964, a Nobel Prize winner for Chemistry wrote:

> What are human goals? Basically man seeks freedom from hunger and want, adequate warmth and protection, and freedom from disease. Added to these he wants reasonable leisure and recreation and with these the freedom to seek an understanding of the workings of the universe in which he lives. These seem to me the main goals of humanity in 1964 as they were in 1864 or 1064; I have no reason to doubt that they will still be its goals in 1984 and they will still seem far off for many people. (Todd, 1964, p. 9)

We arrive at the position that the individual in society will pursue his needs and desires (some of which may be programmed genetically and may include some elements of altruism) to the extent that he finds this possible within the confines of his environment, his experience and knowledge of options and all other capabilities and constraints; he will use the norms common within society and push against them to the extent necessary to ensure that they work in his interests; but if the norms of the society inhibit and frustrate to the degree that he decides they are no longer useful, then, subject to values he attaches to social relationships, he will employ methods outside the norms, outside the codes he would in other circumstances wish to apply to his behaviour. In so doing he will be labelled deviant by society; but this is the cost he is prepared to pay to fulfil his needs. He will act this way, pay this cost, because in terms of human behaviour there are no options. Threat of punishment, punishment itself, isolation from society will not control his behaviour: already there has been a loss of identity, of a sense of control and of other needs that led to the deviance and further loss will not constrain.

POLICY IMPLICATIONS OF NEEDS

The interest in human needs in the behavioural paradigm does not reflect an ideological or sentimental interest in the individual as is the case in the conventional system of thought. On the contrary, the pursuit of human needs and the sacrifice of the individual are not necessarily incompatible goals: altruistic behaviour, Wilson (1973) has argued, is genetically programmed. The interest in human needs is an interest in properties of actors behaving in a social system, the recognition of which is required for system survival. The behavioural interest in human needs is not in making the individual happier, though this may be the outcome. It is in determining the conditions necessary for social organizations to survive harmoniously. Problem-solving at the social level—be it the small group, the nation-state or interactions between states—is possible only by processes that take the needs of the individual as the basis for analysing and planning. Any settlement of a conflict or attempt to order society that places the interest of institutions or even of the total society before those of its individual members, must fail—unless, as rarely is the case, institutional values happen to coincide with human needs. The legitimized status and authority of institutions is finally derived from behaviour at this sociological–biological level.

Traditionally social problems have been tackled within the existing social structure and the general aim has been to preserve it. The emphasis has been on the need for the individual to adjust to social norms: society has been the unit of analysis and its norms the reference point in deciding whether behaviour is conforming or deviant. The problems posed have seemed to be how to persuade the units within the system—be it a society, an industry or a school—to cooperate in achieving its goals. The interest has been in the preservation of the system by minor adjustments in its structure and by persuading actors within it to adopt its goals. This approach assumes that human behaviour is or can be controlled by 'will' or some such influence that can ensure social conformity. Certainly social–psychological values change with altering conditions and different environments; cultural, religious and ideological values are evidence of this. Social–biological needs have the same appearance of alteration or of emergence, but this is probably due to altering environmental conditions that allow them to find expression. It may be that we have mistakenly regarded these needs as evolving or being created over time instead of merely coming into evidence as social and political changes have permitted. Feudalism and slavery, even the 'happy slave' phenomenon, do not demonstrate that needs for recognition and participation did not exist. Indeed, the collapse of these systems suggests they did.

We have had difficulty in explaining the widespread and apparently spontaneous nature of independence movements, political revolutions and social rebellions, that have been recorded in history. A hypothesis that there are social–biological needs that are fundamental particles, parts of the information content of biological organization, serves to explain the historically evident phenomenon of continuity of social and political change in certain directions, as for example, the continuing struggle for participation and freedom to develop personality within a social environment. Aggression and power drives may be no more than manifestations of frustrated needs and evidence of the existence of more basic drives. At a political level, such a hypothesis serves to explain the persistent demand for independence of nations and for identification of groups within states. These manifestations of nationalism have biological origins and protective functions.

There is a supposition here that, in the course of social evolution, basic drives and motivations have been suppressed by institutional restraints, initially of a purely social or communal character and later by those resulting from economic specialization and organization. In accordance with this supposition, the overt expression of needs that characterizes every level of contemporary society is a reaction against this institutional overlay. In other words, there is a supposition that social–institutional development includes an interaction between the expression of needs and their control. In relatively stable and satisfied political communities the process of political socialization effectively channels and controls social–biological drives. Where, however, there are ethnic communities that feel threatened, economic groups that feel prejudiced or minorities that have no means of effective participation in political decisions, there is reduced political socialization. This applies as much, if not more, to highly developed industrial societies as to underdeveloped ones where the problem of alienation is also becoming acute.

It is ultimately an empirical question whether solutions to authority problems can be achieved on any basis other than that of human needs. However, an answer to the question can be deduced from the proposition that needs *will* be pursued. The emphasis on human needs as the basis of analysis and problem-solving is orientated towards the stability and progress of societies: the human needs of the individual that enable him to operate as an efficient unit within a social system and without which no social organization can be harmonious.

The handling of social problems requires problem-solving techniques that take into account the total situation, including the goals and frustrations of the actors. However, the attempt has been made to make a puzzle out of serious and complex problems by positing social goals: law and order, control of inflation, new towns and re-housing, integration of communities and ethnic groups and others. The goals, thus stated, are pursued as social goals requiring the cooperation of people and units within society, apparently on the assumption that they have the same goals and the further assumption that the processes of attaining them are compatible with their interests. There is always an answer to a puzzle: given powers of coercion, finance and techniques, most social goals can be pursued to a conclusion. New towns can be built, ethnic groups can be bussed and mixed, inflation can be controlled, law and order can be enforced. The result usually is that these immediate social goals are achieved; but the social problems they were supposed to solve become more complicated, other problems are created and even the immediate goals are finally given up or changed.

The alternative is to take individual needs as social goals and adopt the relevant strategies. Re-housing within altering kinship groups and without threatening ethnic identity, using instruments other than unemployment to control the money supply, tackling deviant behaviour in its social context and not merely by the coercive application of social norms: in short, applying the tests of recognition, security, stimulation, distributive justice and others to the strategies adopted in solving social problems.

There appears to be a linear trend in the relation between institutional and human needs. There are many continuous trends in the development or growth of societies. For example, there appears to be a persistent tendency for labour to be concentrated initially in primary and extraction industries then for diversion into secondary industries, followed by the growth of tertiary industries and subsequently by diversions into welfare, research and environmental control as economic development proceeds. Some degree of prediction in development of societies is possible as a consequence. To take another example, there are trends in social mobility, in the declining power of central authorities after a certain peak, in the concentration of populations in cities, in the increased use of energy, in the growth of communications and in the availability of education and welfare services. We have postulated a continuing conflict between human and institutional values. If this is valid then there should be evidence of a continuing trend in the evolving forms of social structures and in authority relationships. Evidence of pressures for independence, participation and other human needs should appear in institutional changes over a period of time. Slavery, feudalism, colonialism and other hierarchical forms of authority are associated with successive periods of time. It is more likely that each is part of a continuum which would include also current we–they attitudes in industrial relations, class and cultural barriers to and inequality of opportunities. The increase in the last thirty years of the number of states following the success of independence movements may well be part of this trend towards greater political participation and greater opportunities for identification with language and cultural groups.

The problem we are investigating—deviant behaviour generally—relates to such a linear trend: it is part of a continuing erosion of coercive authority. It could be that the longer-term trends and the immediate deviance problems societies face, have some common origins and causes. Demands on authorities and society have extended from immediate working and economic areas, to political and to aesthetic areas where freedom of expression is more and more demanded.

To the present day we have perceived each point in this linear trend—the challenges to slavery and colonialism—as a challenge to social stability and as a problem of law and order. We have failed to ask why it has occurred, just as we today are more concerned with preventing terrorism than investigating and dealing with its causation. The emphasis has been on preservation, law and order, defence of institutions, the promotion of morality in terms of the observance of social norms. Educational curricula, legal systems, religions and rewards for achievement have been directed towards the preservation of institutions and the observance of norms, commendable in itself, save to the extent that the development of the individual is sacrificed. The linear trend has now reached the stage at which the emphasis is on individual development, even at the cost of institutions and of respect for authorities.

For these reasons we must conclude that if an attempt is made to subordinate individual values to social values, then, because it is not possible to enforce social values that are inconsistent with human needs, there will be responses that are damaging both to the individual and, through him, to the social system.

Once we move from the integration of society to the satisfaction of human needs as the goal of social organization and of authorities, we can give some meaning to the otherwise emotive phrase 'historic processes'. It was suggested on p. xiii that solving social and political problems may be hastening and, possibly, even giving direction to this process. The 'historic process' is the end-result, over time, of the conflict between institutional values and human needs, between the structures and norms created and supported by powerful elites and the human needs that must be met at the individual level if societies are to be functionally efficient and harmonious. This definition of the historical process, in turn, points to the significance over time of role defense, being an important reason for the lag that exists between human aspirations and their achievement. This problem is considered separately in Part Three.

CHAPTER FOUR

Control Mechanisms

We have argued that the pursuit of human needs cannot continually be constrained without serious social and personal consequences. This raises the issue of control: assuming that social norms are promoted by legitimized authorities (a condition to be examined in Chapter Six), and are widely supported, by what control mechanisms can their observance be ensured?

COERCION

The classical basis of authority relationships on which conventional thinking is founded in Western societies (and probably no less in others) has been set down by Lloyd thus:

> What is entailed in the notion of authority is that some person is entitled to require the obedience of others regardless of whether those other persons are prepared to find the particular order or rule enjoined upon them as acceptable or desirable or not . . . there is something which we may call a peculiar aura of mystique investing the lord, the policeman, or the judge which arouses a certain response on the part of the other party, namely that he feels that superior party (for so we may call him for this purpose) can legitimately give orders which he, the inferior party, feels in some sense obliged, willingly or unwillingly, to obey. This feeling of legitimate subordination is clearly one of great significance in law and calls for further explanation.
>
> Why should one person in some curious way feel himself bound to acknowledge the authority of another person and so constrained to obey the orders of that person? Or, to put it another way, what is the source of the obligation which is apparently imposed or assumed to be imposed on the subject party (the obligee)?

One preliminary answer which may be suggested is that fundamentally the obligation is a moral one, in the sense that what the obligee really feels is that he is under a moral duty to obey the behest of the lord, the policeman, or the judge, as the case may be. (Lloyd, 1964, ch. 2)

It will be noted that this classical view corresponds with the view advanced by coercion theorists: Dahrendorf (1959, p. 167) used the terms 'domination' and 'subjection' meaning 'endowed with authority' and 'excluded from the exercise of authority'.

Classical thought not only postulated rights of authorities to expect obedience, but also the right to ensure obedience by deterrence and coercion. As Lloyd interprets: 'What then does experience show? Surely that at all levels of society human law has depended for its ultimate efficacy on the degree to which it is backed by organized coercion'. In explanation he continues: 'Psycho-analysis has taught us of the unconscious factors in man's psychological make-up. Among these unconscious factors are to be reckoned, not only forces which make for social cooperation and which exemplify Aristotle's famous dictum that man is a political animal, but also powerful drives which require to be effectively reformed in order to subject man to the needs of social discipline' (Lloyd, 1964, p. 4).

We are alerted to questioning the thinking and assumptions of this position by the difficulties and logical inconsistencies encountered. If man has antisocial propensities, why is it that some men can be trusted to govern and to control a monopoly of violence? One classical answer is that some men manage to control greed and aggressiveness and only some people are antisocial: some are inadequate because of moral, mental and physical characteristics due to inherited or environmental influences. This raises the question, how is selection made for authoritative positions—by tests of ability and morality? The conventional answer is that selection is by influence and power, not necessarily derived from ability or morality. It is sometimes based on inheritance and tradition. May it not be, therefore, that non-legal behaviour is not due to personal greed, aggressiveness or immorality, but that it is merely a response by some to the exercise of authority over them by others who happen to be in a position to impose on them unacceptable attitudes and values?

If this is the case, the law will clearly require enforcement, not because of any individual shortcomings, but because of the structural conditions created. Classical theory not only asserted a right by authorities to expect obedience and an obligation by others to obey; but, in addition and as a safeguard, a right by authorities to coerce. And herein lies the problem—this conventional thinking rests on the assumption that deterrence deters. Leave aside the argument that human needs cannot be for ever frustrated, save at the expense of social harmony. Indeed, leave aside behaviour involving human needs and focus on behaviour in relation to superficial social norms. Is it deterrence that leads members of a society to conform with social norms of behaviour?

Clearly, threat of punishment, threat of costs greater than satisfactions to be gained, has an influence on the decisions of individuals and groups. The rules of the road, parking rules, are obeyed in many cases because of threat. Often a deliberate costing is undergone; sometimes there is a calculated preference for a fine that is less costly than the gains to be made from defiance of the law in particular circumstances. It might be that some crimes are deterred by deterrents more costly than any gains, subject to calculations as to risks of being caught and the level of punishment. For the most part crime is not deterred—most crime is probably not even discovered. Can we deduce from this that societies are as harmonious as they are because of threats and deterrents: is coercion the explanation of social order? Are shared values, supported by coercion, the explanation of social order?

At first thought the assumption that deterrence deters is one that is axiomatic. Its validity is fundamental to our notions of social organization and law and order. When in practice deterrence fails it must be argued, on the basis of this view, that this is merely because the amount of deterrence and coercion and of risk of detection is less than required or that some different form of deterrence and detection is needed. No other explanation of the failure of coercion to contain deviance is possible within the framework of classical theory: to recognize the failure of deterrence as a control instrument would jeopardize a whole set of conventional notions involving rights, obligations, morality, values, the socialization process and the justice of institutions and legal processes.

So much is it an accepted assumption that deterrence deters that writers have focused mainly on its processes, e.g. how threats can be made more effective by ensuring credibility, by promoting accurate perceptions of threat and by maintaining a sensible relationship between crime and punishment. Other studies that equally accept deterrence as an effective instrument of control focus on the relationship between levels of punishment and degrees of risk in being apprehended. Rarely is the effectiveness of deterrence seriously questioned. Raser (1966, p. 313) introduces his analysis of the literature on this subject thus: 'Deterrence is a means of controlling others' behaviour by the threat of punishment. It is a ubiquitous phenomenom which obviously works ...'. Yet the empirical evidence in crime statistics suggests strongly that it does not. 'We have tried to induce reasonableness, rationality and compliance by surgery, corporal punishment, humiliation, confinement, labour, training, supervision and other 'rewards' and 'punishments'. The harder we try to induce conformity to the law where conformity does not exist, the more we seem to fail' (Pepinsky, 1976, p. 2). In conventional thinking, reasonableness and rationality are still equated with conformity and with behaviour as dictated by law; yet daily reasonable and rational citizens defy the law just because they are reasonable and rational in the pursuit of their goals. Frequently these are the undeclared goals of their society, such as achievement or the declared policy objectives of their governments, e.g. participation, adequate housing, etc. However, these cannot be pursued successfully within the norms of their society.

As is so often the case, experience at the stark interstate level of behavioural relations forces re-thinking about relations at other levels. We cannot dodge this re-thinking by the rationalization that experience at such a level is not relevant to small group and to interpersonal relations. The notion of deterrence is applied at the interstate level on grounds that 'the principle of deterrence can be generalized across levels of systems' (Raser, 1966, p. 313). The assumption that deterrence deters is clearly articulated at the strategic level. National defence strategy is merely a special case of the belief that adequate negative sanctions prevent the 'rational' decision-maker being 'aggressive'. NATO officials argue that if it had not been for NATO there would have been aggression in Europe from the East. Warsaw Pact officials probably use a similar argument. 'How do you know' is regarded as an irrelevant or unnecessary question. In practice there cannot be an answer because there cannot be a test. The only possible answer is in a belief system. A belief system that assumes aggressiveness and the effectiveness of deterrence leads to the view that deterrence deters. One that questions this assumption regards the question as relevant and necessary. In the pre-nuclear age the empirical evidence is clearly that strategic balances and military threats do not deter 'aggression'. There is no evidence that the nuclear threat is any more of a deterrent than was the mighty power of the United States against Japan when the latter bombed Pearl Harbour. The failure of capital punishment as a deterrent to those engaged in organized fighting and killing in a communal conflict would suggest that 'rational behaviour' includes in some circumstances the acceptance of the risk of paying the highest possible price—which means that there is no deterrent. On these purely formal and logical grounds the assumption needs to be questioned whether deterrence is, in any but the most trivial circumstances, an effective control mechanism.

It is to be noted that some legal thinking has moved away from a reliance on deterrence and merely argues that the actor has freedom of choice, to transgress and pay the price or to conform. This thereby avoids the need to take any position on whether deterrence deters; but in doing so attributes control to nothing more than a market mechanism.

RELATIONSHIP AS A CONTROL MECHANISM

There are probably reasons why some persons are conformist and others are not, quite apart from coercion and shared values. Box (1971, p. 104) answers the question, why do not all people break the law, thus: '. . . *we all would*, if only we dared, but many of us dare not because we have loved ones we fear to hurt and physical possessions and social reputations we fear to lose'. In other words, the effective control of behaviour is not, in this view, coercion by authorities to observe legal norms or morality, but a value attached to relationships which would be threatened by antisocial (legal or non-legal) behaviour. In explanation, it is interaction with parents that leads the child to conform because whatever other satisfactions he may seek, he experiences satisfactions from the continuing parental relationship. So it is throughout social life: the observance of etiquette and social norms is a direct response to interactions and affiliations. In due course, the consequent behavioural patterns become habits and are internalized, so that conforming behaviour frequently continues even in the absence of rewarding satisfactions or unrewarding disapproval. It follows that if circumstances occur which deny to the actor in any area of his behaviour the opportunity to interact, there are decreased incentives to conform in addition to decreased opportunities even to know what is required of him in that area of behaviour. Thus the child, deprived of a relationship with a parent, a teacher, a peer group or authorities—or the adult similarly deprived—cannot be expected to conform to social norms. The original reason for the deprivation may be that there is no parent or substitute parent, for some reason no link with the parent, no relationship with the teacher because of poor performance or a personality clash, no links with authorities and society for some environmental reasons or maybe because the actor is retarded, physically handicapped or rejected on racial or religious grounds. In every case, there is an absence of positive or negative inducements relating to the maintenance and development of relationships—an absence of relationships effectively— and therefore no learning or internalization of social norms. There is no self-imposed control because there is no motivation for it; there is no value attached to any authority.

Modern industrial society tends to destroy and not to build relationships. Technological developments require shifts in occupation and changes in living environment. There is little identity and few relationships, on a personal basis, with a nationalized industry, a large company or the society as a whole represented by the tax gatherer and police. There being no relationship, there is no motivation for observing the rules. The 'outsider', the 'alienated', the 'drop out', now comprise a growing subculture. At the same time, industrial society makes greater demands on its members; it is competitive, its luxuries become necessities and its inequalities provide a motivation for types of behaviour which defy its property-based norms. Where there is conflict between, on the one hand, cultural expectations, such as acquisition and status, measured by wealth and role and, on the other, social norms, then, as Merton (1957, ch. IV and V) has observed, the technically most efficient procedure, whether legitimate or not, becomes typically preferred to institutionally prescribed conduct. Theft, blackmail, sharp financial practices, are an efficient means of attaining culturally accepted goals.

The two factors, the absence of relationships that, if present, would promote conformity and the presence of pressures that motivate deviance, together ensure an increasing level of organized crime, for relationships can be developed within a criminal subculture, thus satisfying a basic human need. The norms of this subculture are policed, as in the wider society, by the value its members attach to relationships within it. Thus all its members are required to observe norms, such as violence against the wider society from which they feel rejected.

Having thus deviated, having not observed the norms of society, the actor is required, on the basis of classical theory, to experience a form of negative sanction. Punishment, even physical punishment, by a parent is usually in the context of a relationship. It is not the physical hurt that has effect. Within a system of relationships, physical or any other punishment is a means of communicating disapproval. What is at stake is the relationship and to preserve this the child is prepared to conform if necessary. Etiquette must be most unimportant to a small child, as is unselfishness; but if relationships can be secured by conformity, then some degree of self-discipline is worthwhile. However, punishment by a parent, teacher or authority with whom there is no valued relationship rests entirely on the physical pain or the deprivation inflicted, with which the human organism has a physical and mental capacity to cope. It is this form of punishment, unassociated with valued relationships, that the court, authorities and society inflict. Behaviour is not altered by it in the direction intended: on the contrary, the behavioural response is to damage the person or property of that parent, teacher, authority or society as soon as opportunity offers. Furthermore, the form of punishment is usually exclusion from society and, more seriously, from the few kinship and other relationships which remain, thus aggravating the initial causal condition of non-conformity. Punishment deters only to the extent that the avoidance of crime and punishment is necessary to maintain relationships; remove those relationships and no threat or risk deters. It is deprivation of relationships that is the intolerable deprivation; once they no longer exist there is nothing further to lose, except the relationships of prison. Further crime, followed by punishment and prison become the only means of securing these.

Thus, conventional theories lead to policies that are self-defeating. Indeed, Pepinsky (1975, p. 6) makes the assertion: 'that a pattern of popular response dictated by the form and substance of the written criminal law in the United States is a necessary and conceivably sufficient condition for the growth of crime rates in the American social system'.

We are here considering a matter that may be most important in helping to solve social and political problems. It may be that threat and deterrence are subject to limited boundaries of effectiveness, being relevant only in relation to the daily rules of social relationships that rest on mutual convenience, such as rules of the road. It may be that they have only marginal relevance for behaviour that is destructive of social harmony, e.g. violence against the person, corruption, exploitation, robbery, revolt, etc. The degree of social harmony that societies do experience may be due mostly to different influences, such as values attached to transactional relationships. If this were to be the case, quite fundamental changes would be required in the explanation of harmonious social relationships and policies designed to promote these. Not even the most ideal social system we can imagine can avoid a measure of disharmony due to structural and institutional constraints on behaviour; but unless attention is given to values attached to relationships, it is likely that deviant behaviour may be more pronounced than need be the case and punishment of deviance more likely to increase than to decrease it.

However, our main concern in considering unsolved social and political problems is with behaviour that is not controlled either by deterrence and threat or by values attached to relationships. We are concerned with types of behaviour that appear to defy all controls. We are, therefore, not primarily concerned with control mechanisms, though these clearly have their place. We are concerned with avoiding the conditions that lead to behaviour that calls for control. This leads us to consider social and political structures, that is the environments to which subjects respond and in particular relationships between controlling authorities and subjects.

CHAPTER FIVE

The Settlement of Disputes

Control mechanisms may reduce the incidence of conflict—interpersonal, intergroup and between persons or groups and authorities; but they do not eliminate it. Consequently mechanisms for handling disputes or conflicts of interest evolve in all societies. Generally they include third-party decisions based on conventional rules and norms of justice or fairness as defined in the particular culture. However, as with all evolved processes there are many hidden assumptions involved in contemporary settlement procedures which may or may not be valid now and may never have been valid. There are some that appear to be particularly relevant to contemporary unsolved problems.

THE ASSUMPTION OF SCARCITY

Dispute settlement processes assume scarcity. Traditional thought is greatly concerned with scarcity: economics has been defined as the study of how best to make use of scarce resources; politics has been defined as the authoritative allocation of resources; political philosophy has wavered between the liberal tradition based on the primacy of individual preferences and the authoritative tradition based on man's conflicting interests within societies that seek equality—both pre-suppose scarcity. The contemporary concern with resource scarcity, accompanied by population increase, has led sociologists to focus not primarily on liberty and equality, but on fraternity by reason of the need to deal with the problem of scarcity in a fair and harmonious fashion (see Hirsch, 1977; Halsey, 1978).

In this traditional view there is a fixed amount of satisfaction to be shared: there is a cake of a given size to be divided in some proportion. The 'cake' need not be a physical property: it can be security, fear, a sphere of influence or responsibility for decision-making. Accordingly, in this view, the outcome of conflicts of interests must be such that any given gain in satisfaction by one side results in an equal loss to the other: relationships are win–lose or zero-sum. The conflict can be ended by victory by one side and an ability to impose its terms on the other, by compromises made between the parties perhaps with the help of a mediator, by acceptance of third-party decisions or by third-party enforcement of some conditions of settlement.

Contemporary conventional wisdom has it that conflicts of interest are mostly, if not always, of this fixed sum type. They are thought to occur as a result of competition for limited resources and struggles to fill unique positions of influence. A common view is that violent conflict is probably inevitable because competitive activities regarding the possession of cakes of a given size or incompatible claims on parts of them, cannot be resolved except in a win–lose context, the actual result being determined by the relative power of the parties or norms that reflect power.

This assumption of scarcity has, logically, far-reaching consequences. Allocation becomes a major decision-making problem. While societies develop norms as guide lines to authorities and courts for making allocations, nevertheless power dominates, being the source of many norms. Theories of power, power politics and change by processes of revolution underlie conventional thinking—all logically deduced from the assumption of scarcity.

In recent years there have been many attempts to refine the notion of power, reflecting an intuitive feeling, backed up by empirical observations, that suggests that power is not the only or perhaps not even the main organizing influence in societies. The defeat of a great thermonuclear state in a regional struggle for influence, the growth of communications and the spread of ideas, difficulties in defining any point along the spectrum influence to power, have required some re-thinking of the notion. However, given scarcity, societies must have power relationships as their basis. For this reason alone power must be something that is endemic in all social relationships.

As a consequence, decision-making institutions have developed which reflect, even though they try to control, the power relationships that have been assumed to be the organizing element in societies. For example, there are adversary institutions in which the relative power of opposing parties can be channelled and controlled by rules. The party parliamentary system is by its nature adversary politics: it is the duty of the government to propose and of the opposition to oppose. Judicial procedures involve debate by prosecution and defence in which tactics and legal debate can be as important as is evidence in determining the final outcome. Industrial relations in free enterprise economies are characterized by bargaining and by threat of withdrawal of labour or capital.

The adversary processes govern relationships widely even outside these formal institutional arrangements. Majority–minority relations in multi-ethnic societies and class relationships are conducted on the same basis. It is argued—as it was in Cyprus and Northern Ireland—that the minority has an obligation to observe the 'democratic' processes by which the majority has a monopoly over decision-making. Different arguments are used when the power faction happens to be a minority, as in South Africa and other countries in which there are minority governments. In both cases the form of argument is used merely to justify or to rationalize a power position.

If power relations and the norms that develop out of them—such as majority government—are generally accepted as the organizing influence in social relations, then justice, stability and the avoidance of revolt require institutions to apply these norms, to adapt gradually these norms to changing values and generally to mediate power by tempering it with 'justice'. Justice is, consequently, another notion that defies precise definition and can be regarded as yet another logical extension of the assumption of scarcity.

THE SETTLEMENT OF DISPUTES

The assumption of scarcity and of the consequent need for authoritative allocations of resources give rise, logically, to a particular approach to the settlement of disputes. The traditional means of settling disputes is by direct power confrontation (war) or negotiation (bargaining); but other means, e.g. judicial settlement, arbitration, mediation, conciliation and good offices, are required if deadlock and its consequences are to be avoided. These means are the direct consequences of a set of assumptions: first, that conflictual relationships are win–lose—there is a cake of a given size to be allocated; second, that relationships, being based on scarcity, must be controlled by judicial settlements based on social norms and precedents when negotiation and bargaining fail; third, that decisions by such processes can be enforced; fourth, that there are rights and obligations, respect for authority and legal norms, that underwrite these settlement processes, even though they reflect power positions and elite values. A fifth completes the set: that revolution, including violence, is justified when other processes fail. (See Johnson, 1966.)

The practices of negotiation, power settlements, authoritative decisions and coercion, have been pursued to the point at which they are recognized, accepted and incorporated into political philosophy, ideologies and policies generally. A group of lawyers (concerned primarily with international law) reviewed the processes available to parties to a dispute and came to the conclusions that they were adequate. What was lacking was the will to use them (Davies, 1966). This is hardly satisfactory as an explanation of the failure of these traditional means of handling processes of change and conflict.

A more reasonable explanation is that these means, far from being adequate, are not effective or not seen to be relevant. The scholars concerned could not consider any other processes because they were thinking within the conventional paradigm and were bound by the assumptions inherent in it. What applies conspicuously at the international level applies no less at all other levels. The processes of bargaining, mediation and law governing social behaviour and deviance, industrial relations, communal and race relations, may be thought to be adequate in terms of the legislation and penalties implied. However, they are not effective and the question is raised whether they are any more relevant at the national than they are at the international level.

For these reasons it is necessary to examine the assumptions—including the assumption of scarcity—on which traditional decision-making and settlement procedures are based. Before doing this a more analytical look at the processes that fail is necessary: it should reveal the nature of the problem.

There are three elements in a traditional adversary settlement process, whether it be in relation to an international, an industrial, a communal or person-to-person dispute. There is the role of the third party, the participation by the parties involved in the dispute and the adversary communication between them.

An actual conflict, whether it be war or a street mugging, does not immediately involve a third party. There is some adversary communication between the parties, even though this be limited to acts of violence or abuse and obviously there is participation by them. The conflict 'profile' is one that shows no third-party activity, little communication between parties (and this adversary) while there is total participation.

Processes of 'peaceful settlement' seek to avoid or to terminate conflict by substituting for direct confrontation by the parties some ritualized forms of conflict settlement. The ideal in traditional thinking is a settlement within the framework of accepted norms: judicial settlement. The profile is very different from the conflict one, the third party (a court) playing the dominant role, with very little actual participation by the parties to the dispute or communication of any kind between them. The argument is on the basis of legal norms, not the goals, interests and responses of the parties.

This process is often not acceptable to states, to unions, to members of minority communities engaged in conflict and charged with law breaking by the majority 'establishment'. It is becoming less and less acceptable to those whose duty it is to promote the interests of individual offenders, especially juveniles, who are brought before the courts. The reason is that when important interests are at stake, parties to a dispute are not prepared to allow their future to be determined by interpretations of imposed norms by precedents and by decisions taken without reference to their wider behavioural and environmental needs. They wish to be in control of their own affairs right up to the point of final decision: if the final decision were acceptable, then the process would be acceptable. However, the legal process is such that the final decision is unknown until made, making the process unacceptable.

Quasi-judicial processes, such as arbitration, suffer from the same defects. There is little more participation and communication between the parties: even though parties nominate arbitrators, they cannot have control of or confidence in the final decision.

Mediation, where the third party endeavours to suggest compromise outcomes, is more acceptable in the sense that the parties are less bound to accept recommendations; but the obligation to accept what appears to be a 'reasonable compromise' makes acceptance of the process difficult. In any event, mediation which is usually employed when parties refuse to meet face-to-face, fails because the mediator is seen by parties to identify with the position of opponents as soon as he endeavours to explain the position of the opposing parties.

Good offices, an even 'weaker' form of third-party intervention, allows for more participation and communication. The profile is far removed from the judicial profile: there is some third-party role and extensive communication and participation by the parties. Provided the conflict is at a low level and the parties will meet, good offices can be effective. This, however, does not deal with serious conflict situations.

The ultimate in participation and communication is direct negotiation. The profile is no third-party activity and total communication—of an adversary type—and participation by the parties. However, this is the profile of conflict! Negotiation is little more than transferring conflict from the battlefield to the conference table and is unlikely to do other than further escalate the conflict, as happened at the Paris conference on Vietnam in 1972 and as happens in industrial confrontations.

These processes arise out of the basic assumption that conflictual relationships are win–lose and that what is required, therefore, is some means of third-party decision or a power bargaining process. They all fail because parties engaged in a struggle cannot accept any processes that take away control over final decisions or impose obligations to accept decisions. The only alternative, on the basis of these assumptions, is a settlement that results from power bargaining. In summary, classical thought was concerned with degrees of authoritative control and degrees in the win–lose nature of relationships. Hopefully, relationships would be characterized by low coercion because of low potential losses: this was the test of a peaceful and stable society. However, classical theory could not embrace a situation in which high coercion was required to deal with conflicts of interest that appeared to be highly win–lose, except to regard such situations as power confrontations or revolutions, out of which developed an altered power elite.

There is an implicit assumption—or is it a historical rationalization?—that truth and justice are the outcome of such confrontations. Obviously, this need not be the case. Adversary processes are not efficient in arriving at decisions. Nor can they be supported by scientific methods that stress the need for testing.

> The success of the scientific enterprise has been the result of a view of the growth of knowledge which lays stress on the specific testing of particular propositions, not on the dialectic conflict of systems or of political and social organizations. In the pre-scientific age, man's view of the world was essentially ideological. These ideologies served to provide the basis for the integrative structure and the organization of separate societies, and the conflict among these societies largely determined the spread of the various ideologies. There was a testing process in all this, in the sense that societies which believed less non-sense had a better chance of surviving in this conflict than societies which believed more non-sense. What survived, however, was the total ideological package containing both sense and non-sense. The peculiar genius of the non-dialectical revolution of science has been the discovery of a way of increasing knowledge by separating out the components of ideological packages and testing individual propositions separately. The growth of knowledge, then, no longer depends on dialectical conflicts of total systems in which one system overcomes another, but on the testing of individual propositions and the gradual adjustments of the total systems as individual propositions succeed or fail in the testing process. (Boulding, 1970, pp. 73–4.)

THE ASSUMPTION OF OBJECTIVE CONFLICTS OF INTEREST

The traditional assumption that it is material goods and their scarcity that are at the root of social and political problems has led, deductively, to processes and institutions that have themselves created problems: bargaining, settlements based on power norms, confrontation processes, social values attached to acquisition, class differences based on wealth with which are associated norms for the protection of property and attacks on these norms and on property itself.

More fundamentally the resource scarcity hypothesis leads, deductively, to the notion of objective differences of interests. The conflictual image of society that has been put forward by coercion theorists rests heavily on this assumption. Within a problem-solving approach which questions key assumptions, this apparently obvious proposition invites examination.

For there to be objective differences of interest there need to be:

   (i) finite resources, that is, scarcity
  (ii) incompatible goals or conflict over the same goal
 (iii) a perception by each party of the value system of others such that it is believed that goals are incompatible
 (iv) a costing of the pursuit of these conflicting interests such that each party makes the judgment that it is in its interests to pursue them.

Finite Resources

We are examining the proposition that there are objective conflicts of interest that lead, not merely to the usual tensions and disputes, but to major problems involving class antagonisms, frustration responses damaging to the individual and to society, communal violence and wars. The assumption that scarcity is a source of conflict is self-evident. It would also appear axiomatic that scarcity of resources is likely to lead to major forms of conflict and be a root cause of unsolved problems at all levels—leading to theft, industrial disputes and violence at higher levels of social organization. Is this assumption valid?

Resources are of two kinds. There are material resources that are in short supply: scarcity is a reality in relation to these. In addition, there are non-material goods, social goods, that are not necessarily in short supply: indeed, in many cases the more they are consumed the more and not the less they are available. The more security and recognition one has, the more and not the less others are likely to have. At the international level, the more security one state experiences, the more and not the less security others experience.

These two types of resources are functionally related, which is one reason why scarcity of material resources has been the focus of attention even in cases in which the source of conflict is not scarcity. An industrial conflict can take the form of a demand for increased wages; but the real and experienced cause of the demand may be an altered differential in wage structures, giving rise to status claims. Status claims require quite different responses. Scarcity of material resources by itself is a reason, not for conflict, but for cooperation. It is scarcity and the need to make the most efficient use of resources that leads to specialization and exchange relationships. Scarcity and the naturally uneven distribution of resources are a source of transactions. However, the means of distribution of scarce resources can be a source of conflict. The problem area is allocation, not scarcity. It is the processes by which allocations are made that are the source of conflict, which is why participation and legitimization of authority are important behavioural considerations. When attention is directed to allocation of resources and not to their scarcity, the area of interest is that of non-material goods, such as security, distributive justice, participation and other human societal needs.

There is an important question raised here: which is the more important in motivating behaviour, especially that behaviour which is conflictual, scarce material resources or non-scarce non-material goods? The struggles for independence in economically underdeveloped countries were accompanied by declarations that, given the choice between freedom or prosperity, the former would be pursued. Communal struggles by small minorities are frequently prolonged at great cost in material living standards. The Eks chose starvation and an animal-like existence rather than move from a tribal area. We have no evidence that theft and muggings, while giving a material benefit, are initially motivated by a desire for this gain.

There have been attempts to differentiate material resources, for example the 'guns or butter' choice argued particularly in the late thirties. There has been little attempt to differentiate, in order to evaluate them, goods for having and goods for being. The assumption of scarcity is questioned immediately the idea is entertained that the source of conflict may not primarily be related to scarcity of material resources, but may be more particularly related to the availability of a type of resource that may be in infinite supply. Whether this idea is worth pursuing is a matter to be examined: only the logical point is made at this stage that the notion of objective conflicts of interests presupposes resource scarcity and that the resources that may be the main source of conflict and of unsolved problems may not be scarce.

There is, however, one type of non-material resource that is in short supply, i.e. authoritative roles. There are objective conflicts of interest in relation to these. This is an important special case which is dealt with separately in Chapter Seven.

Incompatible Goals

For there to be an objective conflict of interests, there would need to be, also, incompatible goals, such as elitism and egalitarianism, free-enterprise and total planning or a common goal involving a scarce resource, such as acquisition of a particular territory or a particular facility. Such a conflict of interests gives rise to a win–lose situation: the gain of one party is equal to the loss of the other and where compromise is possible it leads to some degree of dissatisfaction.

Frequently goals appear to be incompatible because there is a confusion between goals and tactics. The Golan Heights in the Middle East dispute, command of the seas in great power strategic relations, represent a cake of given size: they represent win–lose situations in a bargaining or negotiating framework. The security of one side is threatened by the possession of a territory or of control of seas by the other. However, possession of territory or control of regions is a tactic designed to secure a goal: it is not itself a goal. The goal is a relationship that guarantees security. Territory is finite and conflict over its possession in a win–lose conflict; but the security which the tactic is designed to secure is not of a given size. It does not present a win–lose situation. On the contrary, the more security one party experiences, the more cooperative will be its behaviour and the more security other parties will experience as a consequence, giving in turn more security to the first party. Security, like other social goods, is not finite. The arguments in a communal conflict revolve around tactics—how decision-making can be shared. The goal is the benefits to be secured from the decision-making process, including a sense of control and participation in the process.

Furthermore, goals change. As costs escalated for the United States of America in Vietnam, the declared goals changed: to preserve a local regime, to preserve American interests in South East Asia, to preserve the Free World. Mugging and robbery can commence as an alienation response and end up as a profession. Industrial disputes that are usually evidenced in wage claims frequently have unstated causes, e.g. conspicuous we–they relations among workers and management, and the relative priority given to these are revealed and alter during the struggle. The traditional bargaining and negotiation processes tend to cloak different and altering value systems because they tend to freeze declaratory positions: they give a false impression of definitive and incompatible objectives. The bargaining process includes negotiation from 'strength' and trading scarce resources or positions: it does not make relevant any considerations that would transform the argument from scarce tactical resources to expanding social goods. The bargaining requirement is to maintain a position of strength and the original definitions of situations. Any shift might be interpreted as a sign of weakness or willingness to compromise.

Goals are rarely singular, even though they are declared as such. There is a hierarchy of values and this is subject to change as situations develop, as knowledge and costs alter. It is unlikely that parties experiencing a conflict of interests would share the same hierarchy of values. Different priorities open up possibilities of agreement, thus eliminating incompatibilities. The fisheries disputes between the United Kingdom and Iceland in 1976–77, which appeared to be win–lose, was in practice characterized by values attached by each side to relationships with each other, with other states and with the international community. These induced restraints: there was no single overriding goal on either side. Furthermore, in the course of disputes, priorities alter: increased knowledge of the motivations of the opposition, changes in the attitude of the wider community, changes in role occupants, give rise to altered preference systems, opening up options and possible solutions not previously perceived.

The main source of objective conflicts of interest are widely thought to be structural situations that create conditions of privilege and underprivilege, inequalities of opportunity, relative deprivation and dominant and subject groups. Within a traditional system of thought, aggression theories and individual responsibility for deviance were dominant. During this century more attention has been given to 'violence' inherent in social structures. No clear distinction can be made, those who take this view argue, between hurt through direct violence and hurt through starvation or some structural condition of underprivilege. Violence of this order is defined as the evidence of the gap created by structures between individual or group performance and individual or group potential development (Galtung, 1969). Clearly, from such a theory of 'aggression' or 'violence' there arise questions of policy. The policy implication is that structural change is required. The study of conflict has thus led to the study of the problem of change.

Those developing the theory of structural violence are working within a tradition and a cultural consensus on several assumptions. Conflict, defined as incompatibility of objectives is by definition zero-sum or win–lose in its consequences; conflict is related to particular goals, i.e. it is single rather than multi-valued; the goals are essentially materialistic, involving goods and services in short supply; conflict must be dealt with finally by reference to social norms rather than the values of the parties concerned; and most important of all, the final outcome of conflict is determined by the relative power or influence of the parties, which is also reflected in the social norms being applied.

This set of assumptions set the stage for a major debate on policy. Some of those who hold that structural violence is the source of conflict at all social levels, tend to favour 'resolution' rather than 'management' of conflict; i.e. they favour change rather than merely damping down conflict by coercion or other authoritative means. They believe that this can be done by breaking, at some point, the vicious circle of conflict over incompatible goals, conflict behaviour and conflict attitudes, which lead to increased conflict over incompatible goals and so on. They take a 'subjectivist' view, i.e. they argue that only the persons affected can determine whether or not they experience structural violence. The happy slave, because he does not perceive the structural violence that prevents his full development, is not in a condition of conflict with his master. As a policy, then, what is required is structural change and at least to some degree, attitude change: if perception of structural violence were eliminated, there would be no conflict situation.

Others, in opposition to this approach, give full support to the theory of structural violence, but challenge the policy implications. In their view there cannot be structural change by peaceful means. Those who are in the best position to change structures are also those most committed to maintaining the status quo and in a position to prevent change. In this view, 'resolution' by structural change will come only through polarization of the conflict and by the resultant relative power of the parties. Those who favour attitude change are merely playing the game of authorities, giving them the tools of control. The 'objectivists' take the view that structural violence is an objective fact and that the happy slave suffers from lack of development even though he is unaware of the fact. He should be made aware. Social scientists should be shaping the tools of change for use by the underprivileged.

At one point in the seventies the World Council of Churches was caught up in difficult decisions about helping underprivileged in Africa to oppose 'structural violence' and were soon accused of financing violence. Some scholars declared their position to be that of the 'objectivists', even though the implication seemed to be support of violence as a means of change (see Curle, 1971).

Accordingly, scholars and practitioners have been engaged in this argument whether change can be brought about by altering attitudes of authorities and of those over whom they exercised their authority or whether confrontation with authorities is inevitable. Within the power paradigm the dilemma is clearly unavoidable: conflict and violence arise out of the existence of structural violence and structural violence can be removed only by violence against those who, because of their authoritative role, have a monopoly of state power.

A third position is that structural violence inhibits the development of those who are regarded as privileged, no less than those who are more conspicuously the casualties of social injustice (Goulet, 1973). Every actor in a society endeavours to maximize satisfactions and it can reasonably be assumed that those enacting authority roles will defend them and the structures of which they are a part. Power is the ability not to have to adjust to environmental circumstances and possessing power, those in elite positions will tend to use it to the full. However, elites, as actors within the wider society, experience some degree of conflict between their personal value systems and their role behaviour and also suffer 'structure violence'. The elite is no more responsible for the conditions that lead to his behaviour than the deviant. The differentiation of power process produces certain results, favouring some in particular respects and working to the disadvantage of others. In each case the actor behaves the same way—maximizing his satisfactions within the limits of the constraints operating. The malign influence is the differentiation of power, not the actors it creates as inadequate, defiant or socially deviant. Consequently, it cannot be assumed that change in social structures and norms is necessarily win–lose; there could be general gains and a maximization of actor satisfactions within a consensual and legitimized framework.

This third or intermediate view is strengthened by the reality that in any complex social organization each actor is in some segments privileged and in some underprivileged. The crude differentiations of class, income and role are not a sufficient basis for determining the existence of structural violence. This is particularly the case in developed political organizations in which most members enact a large number of roles, some supportive and some threatening to existing institutions and norms. Social mobility, communications, education, trade union strength and a multitude of factors lead to attitudes and interests that prevent most individuals falling into either a status quo or a revolutionary role.

Structural violence theories do not support the classical 'natural order' ideas that give elites a special role; but they appear to accept as inevitable the continued existence of institutions that reflect the adversary nature of social and political organization, even though the class basis for such confrontation was eroded. While institutions have an adversary structure, there is, nevertheless, an increasing level of problem-solving in practice. Parliaments, law courts and industrial processes have formal procedures that emphasize confrontation. However, parliaments have joint-committees, courts have the assistance of social workers and in industry many interests of employers and employees are commonly pursued, even though in the name of 'bargaining'. It cannot be assumed that elites are in the longer term likely to succeed or believe themselves likely to succeed in maximizing their satisfactions through endeavouring to maintain existing structures and the type of non-consensual society they dominate. There is an acceptance of the inevitability of structural changes that tend towards social order and consensual behaviour and to a greater or less extent offset tendencies toward antisocial elite behaviour. However, in the absence of institutionalized processes of change that avoid win–lose power confrontations and which seek positive outcomes for all parties, resistances to change are inevitable.

In these conditions it would seem misleading to refer to objective conflicts of interest, implying static situations, altered only by conflict and violence. Given a different hierarchy of values, altering values, common and compatible universal needs, objective conflicts of interest is a notion that may have no reality.

Perceptions

An objective conflict of interests would require, by those concerned, perceptions of incompatibilities, i.e. of conflicting goals or of the pursuit of the same resource for exclusive use. In practice, parties engaged in disputes usually perceive their relationships to be win–lose in this sense. In the Cyprus dispute the Turkish Cypriot community perceived a Greek Cypriot intention of union with Greece and threatened or demanded in response union with Turkey. Subsequent elections in which the President was opposed by an Enosis candidate convinced both sides that the real desire—which for internal and external political reasons could not at first be articulated—was for independence. In industrial, family and all other relationships, this perceptual factor is important in a conflict situation, raising the question whether apparent objective conflicts of interest arise out of perceptions and definitions by the parties of the nature of their conflict.

Class and cultural differences in language, values and immediate interests are conducive to misperception of attitudes to change. Having in mind the reality of altering value system, universal needs, multiple role enactments, overlapping classes and overlapping interests between classes and income groups, an inflexible structural condition is unlikely. In many cases, demands for change are articulated by persons from advantaged groups. Such demands are resisted by these same groups; but it is not always clear that there is resistance to change in principle or resistance to change as demanded without a process that is both acceptable and likely to lead to a structure in which there will be distributive justice. The only processes experienced by which major change has been brought about have been power processes, the end-results of which could not be envisaged except as winner-takes-all. The question must be regarded as an open one whether change would be resisted by those who are relatively privileged in a particular structure if the processes of change were such that outcomes were positive sum.

The one important exception that yet has to be dealt with needs to be noted once again: the case of role occupancy of unique or scarce authoritative roles. If this problem can be dealt with outside a power framework, then it can be assumed that the corporate defence problem involving resistance to change by privileged groups can also be dealt with without violence.

This study is concerned with social and political problems at all levels. Examples and references inevitably are drawn from particular systems levels and the general application is not always in mind. In this case, for example, perception of behaviour and of role behaviour is most readily understood by reference to relationships between conflicting groups, communities or states. One must constantly pause to reflect on the generality. The juvenile criminal who is not deterred by possibilities of punishment, who achieves in the social sense—accomplishes, makes money, acquires status—through unlawful gains, who defies society and its norms and invents his own or shares antisocial norms with others similarly engaged in unlawful practices, is enacting a role within his own social relationships. His way of life, his most valued relationships, his stimulus, his sense of control, his identity are all tied up in this role. He perceives himself and society sees him as being in a win–lose relationship: if caught he must be punished and he knows that attempts must be made to destroy his role. He will resist demands made on him to change his role. After punishment he will continue in the same role. This is the one he knows, the one from which he benefits, the one that gives him satisfactions of his human needs. Just as in the case of privileged classes, he will and can resist demands for change made within a power framework. However, there is no evidence that there is resistance to change when the processes of change are problem-solving ones in which the individual takes part, which have the outcome of satisfying his needs and not just those of society. The behaviour of groups and individuals is clearly different in many important respects: but when dealing with objective conflicts of interest—in this case between society and an individual—and the perceptions each party has of the other, what is important are processes by which situations and relationships are defined and redefined, processes by which change takes place. It is possible to generalize about processes by which change is brought about, even though it may not be credible to generalize about behaviour.

Costing of the Pursuit of Goals

Another influence relevant to objective conflicts of interest is the assessment of values in relation to costs. Costing is of two kinds. Within a bargaining framework costing of the pursuit of goals is always present: compromises have to be considered and weighed against losses likely to be incurred if agreement is not made. The view that 'all wars must end' has meaning only in the sense that in due course costs are experienced that will alter values. However, there is also a costing that involves changes in values, priorities and goals in order to take advantage of options that were not previously contemplated: this is a costing of changes, not for compromise, but for additional gains.

The costing process is constrained by declaratory positions that prevent or make politically difficult any alterations in goals. For this reason changes in leadership may be necessary in order to restore flexibility and to reflect the altered values that are present in elite groups and societies. The costing that takes place during negotiations between delegates is not readily communicated to those whom they represent, thus placing constraints even on delegates. Alteration in values, the costing process, is seen to be a show of weakness and compromise, which is often the case in direct negotiations. Processes are necessary that reveal costing as a process by which priorities can change in order to take advantage of options and possibilities not previously thought to have been possible. If the Golan Heights are initially defined as a high priority within a power bargaining framework and if problem-solving processes lead to a redefinition of security that reduces the strategic value of these Heights, then a re-costing and alteration in priorities is required to take advantage of possibilities of a wider security derived from relationships, previously not contemplated.

The question arises whether there is ever an 'objective' conflict of interests. If not, to what extent is conflict due to false perceptions of the motivations of the other party and to false forecasting of costs of pursuing the conflict in relation to values sought? Images of reality tend to create their own reality. An image of a party as a threat leads to defensive attitudes that finally persuade that party to adopt its postures—and the validity of the original image appears to be confirmed. A breakthrough occurs in the abilities of parties to manage their relations when means are found to change the game from one in which there are thought to be fixed or negative outcomes to one in which there are thought to be positive outcomes for all. This is likely to occur when, in the course of conflicts or in the course of settlement processes, it becomes clear that opposing parties have needs that are universal and, furthermore, inexorable. This, probably, is a more recent influence at the domestic level than it has been at the international level where the opposing parties have defined their conflicts in like terms, with an emphasis on security. At the domestic level, the failure to deter crime has pointed to explanations of deviance other than lack of discipline and morality. A society that attaches importance to achievement while failing to provide reasonably egalitarian means to that end, in due course has brought to its attention deviance that relates to alienation and absence of any sense of participation and control. The creation of a negative self-image in any system stimulates behaviour internally to redress the balance and externally to prove a capability. For example, the quest for black power, which gives rise to a variety of forms of deviance, may not be a phenomenon of blackness, but of alienation and non-recognition.

POSITIVE SUM OUTCOMES

The assumption of scarcity can be seen to create a dilemma. On the one hand it leads to the need for authoritative allocations of resources based on power and to adversary processes, on the other hand, allocations based on power confront principles of legitimacy even when the adversary processes are institutionalized. In any event they confront problem-solving principles.

It is useful to make a distinction between settlement, i.e. an outcome of conflict within a win–lose or power framework, by war, judicial settlement or mediation, and resolution, i.e. an outcome of conflict that is self-sustaining, not in need of any coercion, because it is positive sum in the sense that the parties concerned achieve their goals.

It was outside the bounds of classical thought to entertain the possibility of positive outcomes in which all parties to a conflict gained through its resolution and, therefore, the need not for coercive third parties, but for institutions that facilitated the transformation of what appeared to be a win–lose situation into a positive gain one. An alternative, behavioural paradigm or set of assumptions is synthesized, not around the notion of power and settlement of conflict by bargaining and relative power, but around the resolution of conflict by problem-solving processes.

A simple diagram depicts the different positions:

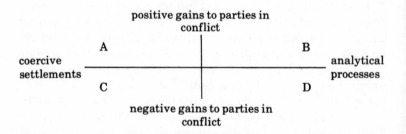

Segment A is the area in which third parties impose settlements that are favourable to parties in dispute (including authorities and the individual) in the absence of their participation (e.g. the Constitution imposed on Greek and Turkish Cypriots by Greece, Turkey and the United Kingdom in 1960). Segment D is where the outcome is win–lose, but the rules are accepted—as in a game (e.g. changes of government by electoral processes). Segment C is the traditional area of thought, where it is assumed that outcomes are win–lose, requiring third-party coercive settlements (e.g. industrial, interstate and most other conflicts). Segment B is the area in which both parties gain as a result of their interactions and require no external coercive decision-making; their conflict can be resolved as distinct from settled (e.g. agreements to exploit shared resources or to define security in terms other than geographical). Classical thought does not deny the existence of segment B interactions, even between authorities and the individual. Indeed, the absence of the need for enforcement was evidence of legitimized government. However, political realism decreed that significant decision-making and social control fell into segment C and this justified the institutions of law and order and coercive settlements.

Segments C and B are of immediate interest to us: C is power politics, bargaining and coercive settlements, giving rise to win–lose outcomes; B is problem-solving such that there are positive gains to all parties. It is at once apparent that a problem-solving process avoids the features of traditional means of peaceful settlement that make them unacceptable to the parties involved and, therefore, unworkable. In a problem-solving process there are no commitments or obligations in advance and decision-making continues to be within the grasp of the parties until the problem is solved to their satisfaction. There is no requirement to agree to parts of a settlement, to negotiate or to compromise: there is a final package deal in the form of a solution to the problem arrived at by the parties. If no solution, there is no package to accept or to reject. It is no less apparent that problem-solving requires the transformation of a perceived win–lose conflict into one that is perceived to have a positive outcome.

Problem-solving is a process not well understood and not researched, because it is outside the boundaries of conventional thinking. In so far as it is researched, it deals with 'real' problems, i.e. the practical problems of the physical world and symbolic problems associated with them, the construction of a dam or a bridge and the associated mathematical problems (see Wickelgren, 1974, p. 10; Polya, 1945, p. 149). In Chapter One it was argued that this notion of problem-solving is closely associated with puzzle-solving, where there are specific goals and answers or results following upon the application of rules and procedures. It deals with closed systems: there are no behavioural interactions with an environment.

Problem-solving as a means of resolving a conflict situation is an open-ended process that is likely to end in solutions that cannot be anticipated and it opens up possibilities that may not relate to the original bargaining stances of any party. The problem at issue has arisen out of systems of thought: it is not a 'real' problem. War and mugging are realities; but the problems of war and of mugging arise out of thought systems, ideologies, belief systems and interpretations of behaviour. The origins might be inequalities, scarcities, ambitions and responses to these; but these are separate problems with solutions that do not necessarily involve war or mugging, even though the parties concerned believe they do.

In this sense problem-solving as applied to conflict resolution is concerned with paradigm change. No 'solutions' are found on the basis of sets of assumptions each party makes about the conflictual situation. Communal and interstate conflicts end in power solutions. Mugging and robbery are not controlled by the policies that reflect the assumptions of authorities concerned with law and order and who consider that no solutions are possible except those that reflect the relative power position of the parties. Problem-solving is, therefore, directed towards these assumptions, towards redefinitions of the situation, towards a set of assumptions that appear to be more realistic. The processes by which the original assumptions, perceptions and definitions of the situation are examined and reappraised are the processes of conflict resolution.

The question, therefore, is whether conflict, which is perceived by the parties concerned as having a fixed outcome, can be transformed into a positive sum one. Every system behaves in identical fashion in pursuing its interests by responding to the perceived environment in the most appropriate fashion in the light of knowledge available to it. Is the nature of conflict such that conflicts that appear to have fixed outcomes can be transformed into conflicts that appear to have positive outcomes by the alteration of goals and perceptions? Is the re-perceived relationship closer to 'reality' than the conflictual one?

At the level of interstate conflict, Waltz has classified philosophical thinking on the origins of conflict by reference to those who attribute responsibility to man, the state and the interstate system (Waltz, 1959). Each one of these notions has its corresponding remedy—conversion and coercion, less or more intervention by the state in the affairs of its peoples and institutions for the control of the exercise of power by states. Since he made his classification there have been other developments in thought. A fourth image is a communications or cybernetics one, promoted by Deutsch (1963). In this image the origins of conflict are in the inefficiencies of decision-making. The nature of man and the state remains as the early philosophers thought it was. Conflict could be avoided by steering processes and response to the environment. The remedy would be, therefore, better training for the management of political affairs. Another image was introduced in the sixties by Rosenau (1954) and this attributes conflict to political and social change within states and the tensions that spill over into international relations. The remedy in this case would be non-intervention by states in the domestic affairs of others. A sixth image now beginning to emerge in more recent writings such as those of Gurr (1970 & 1976), Kelman (1977) and Enloe (1973), is one that postulates values and needs that are widespread if not universal, that cause conflict within and between states as peoples assert their independence and demands for equality and participation in decision-making at all levels. The solution of conflict in this image is in a recognition that each system—from individual to nation—is pursuing similar objectives and that aggression and other attributes can be interpreted in terms of basic values and needs.

All of these images have their corresponding third-party activity or means of resolution of conflict once it occurs. The images of man, the state and the interstate system, clearly require compromises and perhaps third party enforcement. To a lesser degree this applies to the fourth image; but the last three require mediation to be of a supportive type. In these cases the mediator is required, not to find compromises or to arrange for an enforced settlement, but to endeavour to interpret the motivations and origins of the conflict to the parties concerned. If we could find which one of these images or which combinations, represented 'reality', then we would know what form of resolution of conflict would prove appropriate and effective.

An image of man and the state as the cause of war leads to defence measures by each state and an image of the interstate system as being responsible for war leads to collective action. The game is being played on the assumption that man and the state are aggressive by nature. The decision-making, the spill-over and the value images provide the basis of another game, in which conflict arises out of inadequate knowledge, false perceptions and internal political struggles. A breakthrough occurs at the point at which parties to a dispute see the possibility of changing the game and of creating that reality which occurs when action is based on assumptions that man and state have similar motivations and purposes that can be achieved most effectively by cooperation.

Fixed outcomes suggest the relevance of judicial settlement, mediation and conciliation and other means by which to arrive at compromises and they suggest the ending of actual hostilities because of escalating costs. None of these means resolves the conflict. However, once the idea is entertained that there could be positively beneficial outcomes, then other processes of ending conflict become relevant. These are related to ways and means of becoming aware of options and satisfactions not previously considered.

Whether or not there are objective conflicts of interest is, finally, an empirical question. It is not difficult to demonstrate that in some cases what were initially thought to be objective conflicts of interest were found to arise out of false perceptions, were found to be avoidable by changes in goals or were found to be resolvable by outcomes beneficial to both parties. By bringing parties together in conditions in which the required analysis can be made by them of the perceptions each has of the other, of options and satisfactions in relation to costs, the empirical question in respect of any particular relationship can be answered (see Burton, 1969).

THE ROLE OF THE THIRD PARTY

The interstate level draws attention also to circumstances in which apparently objective conflicts of interest induce cooperation: a simple alteration in the definition of a situation transforms the conflict from a seemingly objective one into one that requires cooperative problem-solving as values and costs are re-assessed. Soviet Union–United States relations were once defined in terms of 'coexistence' (conflictual competition) and then 'detente' (a lessening of tension as more tolerance of each other's position was displayed). Now there is a common realization that many problems, the solution of which may be literally vital to their relationships and their existence, cannot be solved by either acting alone. Problems of development in the Third World, problems of social and economic change almost everywhere, problems of finance and international transactions, problems of ecology and pollution, ethnic identity problems, all require common problem-solving solutions. This means a redefinition of the previously considered competitive relationship. There has to be a re-thinking of 'dialectics', 'objective contradictions', 'coexistence', 'free enterprise' and many other notions that have arisen out of an assumption that there are objective contradictions and differences of interest and could be determined only within a competitive and power framework. The relationships can no longer be defined in win–lose terms: they are more and more appearing to be win–win or lose–lose. The power paradigm has become an anachronism.

This same phenomenon occurs in domestic conflicts at all levels. Deviant behaviour, e.g. theft and mugging, has the same elements of values, perceptions and costing, both on the part of the deviant, who is one party to a dispute, and on the part of authorities, who are another. Problems of deviance, industrial problems, classroom problems cannot be solved either by deviants acting alone, by protest, by strike, by violence against the person or by authorities coercing and endeavouring to apply social norms and to enforce 'law and order'. Yet their solution is important to both. The active cooperation of both in a problem-solving framework is required.

The act of deviance is a symptom of behavioural problems: an inadequate self-image, resentment, a plea for attention, etc. What precisely these are we do not know. Certainly they cannot be differentiated and determined in any particular case by an observer and the parties themselves may not be aware of them. This, however, is not important. It is not necessary to have such knowledge: what is necessary is to recognize the existence of complex subjective elements and to devise processes such that the outcome of conflict resolution will reflect all subjective influences, even though they may not be recognized even by the parties. The judicial process is particularly bad at doing this: it is symptoms of behaviour, acts, that determine assessments and judicial judgments. The problems that give rise to action remain. A process is required that reveals to the parties as many of the relevant behavioural aspects of the relationship as is possible, the motivations of each other and their perceptions and definitions of the conflict situation. In addition, the process must leave them finally satisfied that the outcome is acceptable and meets their needs in so far as they are presently aware of these.

The process of conflict resolution must, therefore, be an analytical one and, furthermore, one that involves the parties in a direct relationship in which they can test out their assumptions regarding the motivations of the opposing parties. It is in this way that there can be value changing and costing of objectives such that no compromises are required that would leave parties in a state of continuing conflict. It is an exercise in which adversary communication gives place to analysis. Referring back to the set of profiles above, problem-solving includes a major role by a third party; total participation by all the parties involved; an absence of adversary communication; and an analysis or definition of the situation arrived at by all interested parties with the help of a third party.

The role of this party in such an exercise has little relationship to the traditional notion of a mediator or judge. We are here concerned with problem-solving. The approach is deductive. Rather than work from ascertained 'facts' in a particular situation, the attempt by the third party is to apply generalizations about conflict to the particular situation being examined, thereby helping to analyse it. Its role is confined to feeding-in information about conflicts in general and is not concerned with suggesting 'solutions' or arriving at assessments. There is an implied assumption that the analysis of a particular conflict, within this analytical framework, itself leads to the resolution of the conflict. There is a hypothesis that once the relationships have been analysed satisfactorily, once each side is accurately informed of the perceptions of the other, of the alternative values and goals, of the alternative means and costs of attaining them, the possible outcomes acceptable to the parties are revealed.

The third party has an initiating and structuring role. Tentative assessments must be made as to which are the parties and which are the issues relevant to these parties, that are to be discussed. Typically deviant behaviour involves many parties in addition to those engaged in the deviant act. Juvenile crime involves parents, schools and peer groups, not just as parties that can assist the deviant in returning to conforming behaviour, but as causes of the deviance and as means by which the environment of the deviant can be altered. In many cases, authorities concerned with living and working conditions may be parties in this sense. So, too, in wider conflicts. An industrial conflict involves many unions and many different levels of organization within unions, each of which experiences conflict within its organization and this applies to management also. It is the role of the third party to ascertain which parties are those that are most directly concerned, and to arrive at a tentative schedule of analysis that will ultimately take into account all parties and all issues. Traditional settlement tends to dwell on those parties that appear to be powerful, rather than on those directly concerned, as in the case of a communal dispute in which more powerful states are involved. Structuring communication between parties is an important role, requiring some tentative analysis and perhaps some tentative judgments regarding the nature of the conflict and its probable origins. (See Burton, 1972, for further discussion on process.)

The parties themselves must play the main role—unlike that which occurs in judicial and quasi-judicial processes. It is their dispute and it is their perceptions and knowledge that both create it and make possible changes in definitions of the relationships and give rise to options not previously considered. For this reason, attention is given to 'communal' processes in handling deviance (Pepinsky, 1976).

There is thus a significant paradigm change in the handling of conflict situations already taking place at many social levels of interaction. The role of the third party in relation to an international dispute clearly demonstrates this. The following is a list of some dichotomies that emerge (listed during some discussions between diplomats, lawyers and problem-solvers):

(i) Mediation is an art; there are 'born' mediators who cannot pass on their techniques; success is measured by the reputation of the mediator as diplomat or lawyer and not by his performance, for this is determined by the complexity of the situation.

Mediation is a learned technique and performance is measured by success and failure.

(ii) The personality of the mediator is the important consideration.

Personal temperament is relevant to all occupations, but the presence or absence of learned techniques is the important consideration.

(iii) 'Time is of the essence': at some stage, which cannot be defined, conflicts can be resolved; at others, not.

Conditions under which conflict can or cannot be resolved can be determined: if 'time is of the essence', then conflict is like the common cold and will cure itself, making the mediator irrelevant.

(iv) No two cases are the same: conflicts are like road accidents; they just happen.

There are common patterns in conflicts, making them essentially the same and subject to the same techniques.

(v) The mediator requires power support from an international institution, powerful states or financial institutions.

There is a difference between enforced settlement and resolution of conflict and the latter is accomplished without support except respect for the professional knowledge and status of the mediator; authority is derived from the parties and not from external institutions.

(vi) It is the duty of the mediator to suggest solutions.

It is only the parties that can arrive at solutions and the mediator should never prejudice his position by suggesting them.

(vii) The mediator's genius is in suggesting reasonable and workable compromises.

No party should ever be asked to accept a compromise and the mediation exercise is to arrive at alternative goals or means that do not require compromise.

(viii) The interest of greater powers and world society as a whole must sometimes be placed before the interests of the parties.

In any conflict, the relations of the parties most directly concerned take precedence and are then subjected to the resolution of any conflict they have with interests at other levels.

(ix) Relations between states are relations between authorities within them and mediation must be between authorities involved in a conflict situation.

World society is not comprised of states as separate entities, but of transactions of all kinds that cut across state boundaries: mediation must be at different levels involving parties and different issues, sometimes parties within parties and not only legal authorities.

(x) International conflict is separate from domestic conflict.

International conflict is usually a spill-over from domestic conflict in which parties seek foreign assistance and mediation must involve domestic consideration of ethnic and other groups and not be confined to international conflict.

(xi) Parties 'should' accept processes of arbitration and mediation.

No party can be expected to submit to third party judgments or be involved in processes which place it in a position of having to accept a consensus view. Failure to accept some form of arbitration or mediation is a reflection on the mediation process and is not evidence of a party's unwillingness to resolve the conflict or to cooperate in world society.

(xii) Some decision-makers behave 'irrationally'.

Parties to a conflict are responding to the situation in the ways that appear most beneficial to them in light of the knowledge they have of the motivations of others and the options open: 'irrational' behaviour is behaviour not understood or not approved by others.

| (xiii) No fixed procedures are possible. | A disciplined adherence to rules of procedure is desirable once they have been tested. |
| (xiv) The mediator should be one person. | The mediator needs to be a panel of specialists in the field of conflict. |

A similar shift is observable if the roles of the parties are analysed or the processes of conducting a settlement process and a resolution process are compared at all levels of transaction. It is in this sense that the handling of conflict situations synthesizes thought systems and brings into sharp contrast different approaches to solving problems.

CHAPTER SIX

Legitimacy

So far this study has discussed the traditional assumptions that societies are integrated social systems—or that it is the goal of authorities to make them so; that the social or collective good takes precedence over individual values; that coercion is an effective control mechanism; that disputes require settlement procedures by which resources or positions are allocated authoritatively. In the course of this examination various modified or alternative propositions have been suggested: that societies are characterized by functional relationships that do not depend either on coercion or shared values; that certain universal human needs require satisfaction if societies are to be harmonious; that values attached to relationships may be more significant as control mechanisms than deterrence; that disputes can be resolved by processes based on the assumption that the satisfaction of human societal needs may be more important as a means of solving problems than some particular distribution of scarce material resources. It has been noted that the processes by which distribution of material resources and authoritative positions are allocated relate to some of these needs: the process may be more important than the actual allocations.

This leads to a consideration of a set of assumptions in traditional thought that may be the most important sources of social and political problems. Assume, for argument's sake, that the criticisms of traditional assumptions and the alternatives suggested are valid, i.e., assume that problems affecting members of a society can be solved by problem-solving processes and that these lead to positive sum outcomes. Is there any reason to believe that such processes have any relevance in dealing with problems that relate to the status and the power of authorities and elites who may place the preservation of their interests and structures above the solution of problems such as dissidence and deviance generally?

The traditional argument drawn from the assumptions that have been examined is that the differentiation of power through social exchange ultimately leads to 'superiors' and 'inferiors'—elites and others—who, by the use of their influence and power, create institutions, structures and norms that promote their interests and that the monopoly of power they hold enables them to socialize and to coerce non-elites into accepting these. Any disputes can be settled on the basis of these norms and within the institutions and structures that exist. In short, the traditional argument is that problem-solving techniques are irrelevant to problems of fundamental social and political change and, therefore, not relevant to fundamental social and political problems. The only means of such change is revolution. This occurs when there is extreme disparity between elite interests and those of non-elites; it is, like war, the legitimate instrument when all else fails (Johnson, 1966). Before such revolution takes place, all manner of social and political problems occur, frustrations, robbery, destruction of property, kidnapping, assassinations, dissident behaviour of many kinds. Following the revolution there is a consolidation of power, a new structure that is protected by the same use of power by those in authoritative roles, leading in due course to the same sequence of frustrations, revolt and revolution. In support it could be argued that this was the case before the Russian Revolution and is the case in contemporary situations such as in Africa where white minorities are dominating black majorities in such a way as to preserve their privileged positions. It could be argued that these are examples of power confrontations that have only power solutions, making problem-solving irrelevant.

If this view is valid, then defence of authoritative positions and structures against the types of changes that are continually required as values and conditions alter, would appear to be one of the significant causes, if not the main cause, of social and political problems, both social and civil: solutions to problems usually require alterations in roles, in role behaviour and in the norms associated with roles and the institutions that emerge as the outcome of role occupancy and behaviour.

The term 'role defence' is an appropriate label to give to resistance by occupants of authoritative roles who employ the advantages associated with their roles to protect themselves, their institutions and structures. It refers not merely to defence of official positions, but also to infighting in management, in unions, in families, in schools and universities and in all walks of life.

For this reason it is important to determine whether problem-solving techniques are in any degree substitutes for power processes in overcoming this problem of role defence. This issue is dealt with in Chapter Eight. In preparation there are many aspects of power that require examination: the nature of the process of differentiation of power, whether it leads inevitably to elites and inequalities, the nature of legality and legitimacy and the role of authorities. The prescriptive question to be examined is whether problem-solving is a means of breaking into the vicious circle implied in the traditional view referred to above, legal and institutionalized authority, traditional authority, resistance to change, frustrations, charismatic leadership, revolt, rebellion and revolution, a new elite and structure, coercion, legal and institutionalized authority and further resistance to change.

DIFFERENTIATION OF POWER

The classical position, as reported by Lloyd (see p. 85) assumes that 'superiors' and 'inferiors' are differentiated in all societies, implying a universal and an inevitable process. The processes by which those emerge who are 'superiors' are generally held to be those initiated by relative power, reflecting relative abilities, differences in command of resources and in opportunities.

Societies in the form we know them today and authority roles in them, are largely the result of a continuing process of differentiation of power through social exchange (Blau, 1964). Rarely are exchange relationships, even social relationships, evenly balanced. A good turn carries with it a social indebtedness. In the economic world the imbalance accumulates, because those who have resources and skills that can be exchanged favourably acquire advantages in exchange that place them in an even more favourable position in a future exchange. Without having to assume 'individualistic' elements, greed or aggressiveness, we can formulate a structural theory that rests on nothing more than the fact that in societies and communities there are exchange relationships that are not always balanced in their consequences.

All societies, all cultures, exhibit inequalities, relative power positions, privileged and underprivileged. The formulation of the rules of social relationships and the structures of societies have been, traditionally, within the power of those who have acquired influence by these and related means. Consequently, the structure and the authorities in control are 'natural' and attract explanations of natural order. Entailed in the traditional notion of authority is, as has been said, the belief that some people are entitled to require the obedience of others, who in turn have a moral obligation to acknowledge this authority. This relationship can be applied at all levels: the individual and the state; the child and the parent; the pupil and the teacher; the small state and the large one; the colonized people and the colonial power; the employee and the employer.

Earlier philosophers who arrived at this view were observing and reacting to a social and political environment in which authority so acquired was recognized as a fact of life. They sought to explain its general acceptance in terms of charisma, tradition or legality. The need for coercion or power was not questioned in any of these forms of authority. In the event of successful defiance, as in a revolution, a new power structure was established and the monopoly of power by the state was re-established and, again, accepted as a fact of life. Violence by the state was readily justified. In this formulation there could be no major or seemingly insoluble problems of deviant behaviour, there could be no challenges to basic theory: there was no consideration of the circumstances in which the moral responsibility to obey would not apply or in which there may be claimed a moral responsibility not to obey. No clear distinction was made between what was legal and what was 'legitimized'. They were not asking the question whether what they observed was compatible with human aspirations such that it could persist in social organization. They assumed that because social exchange led to power differentiation, this was an inevitable condition and would persist.

It will be seen how the various assumptions were pieced together into an integrated and convincing theory of social organization. Furthermore, it was and still is an attractive theory when applied to societies in which structures reflect the outcome of power differentiation through exchange. There are scarce resources, relationships are consequently win–lose and, therefore, there must be legal norms and authority with power to allocate resources and to coerce compliance. However, an insoluble problem is posed, at least insoluble within the set of assumptions made. Power differentiation is inevitable, authority roles resting on power lead to non-participatory organizations, these require coercive controls; coercion provokes resistances, requiring more coercion. In short, unacceptable behavioural responses are provoked by the structures which are the inevitable outcome of exchange relationships. The theory required the hypotheses that in fact authorities can coerce, that deterrence does deter and that power is the monopoly of authorities and is effective. Without these untested hypotheses the theory is incomplete. When deviance occurs, this can only be because there has not been sufficient deterrence and coercion. Within the theory there can be no other explanation of deviance.

However, the differentiation of power through social exchange does not result in a balance or a static condition. On the contrary, a differentiation of power is the stimulus to a reaction and to further differentiation of power. When imbalance occurs in any behavioural system—unlike some mechanical systems of balance—the consequent compensatory processes do not return the system to the original state. On the contrary, system change is likely. The response to structures created by the differentiation of power by social exchange is organized opposition and a further differentiation of power by functional cooperation among those over whom power is exercised. This is clear in industrial relations in modern societies, but applies no less among former colonial peoples in their opposition to powerful industrial states. Hence there is a reactive or secondary diffentiation of power that, far from creating a consensual society, seeks to establish alternative structures that provide alternative forms of privilege and elitist opportunities.

Look in particular at industrial relations. Union organization is now sufficiently powerful in modern industrial societies to counter the influence both of management and the state: an altered differentiation of power both nationally and internationally is emerging. Resort to legislation or any form of coercion by the industrial firm or by the state is not an effective means by which to prevent collective bargaining through which unions exercise influence. To be effective coercion would involve a level of enforcement which would destroy the nature of society and perhaps lead to widespread civil strife going beyond the bounds of the immediate problem.

Nor is it sensible or realistic to expect unions and workers generally to forgo their positions of strength and the gains which they can make within a collective bargaining framework. Contemporary industrial relations have their origins in a system of landlord–peasant relationships in which direction was a mix of paternalism and coercion and in which grave injustices touching upon basic human needs were widespread. It was only when communications among workers and concentrations of workers in small industries made organization possible that the paternalistic and coercive one-to-one, owner–worker relationships was avoided. Craft and other organizations of workers created conditions that made collective bargaining possible. Consequently, industrial relations have from their inception been on a bargaining basis, first between owner and groups of employees and in modern times between management and unions, both organized nationally and internationally. What has occurred is a 'natural' process of power differentiation that previously placed management in an all-powerful position.

There are many other examples of secondary differentiation of power: class, communal and race relations—and more recently terrorist relationships—are providing evidence of the same processes at work. In traditional terms there is 'change in balances'; but the explanation is differentiation of power through social exchange in conditions of technological, economic and population change and in conditions in which altering values, attitudes and philosophies strengthen and weaken the relative positions of competing groups.

Once exchange theory is modified to include the consequential processes of secondary and subsequent differentations of power, the permanent basis of superior–inferior, we–they and authority relationships is upset. The defence of the status quo can no longer realistically be an objective of social policy; the basis of the rights of some to control and the obligation on others to obey is destroyed and the political notion of 'elitism' is irrelevant. Classical philosophers were probably justified by the empirical evidence of the time in assuming stable authority relationships and the existence of a ruling elite and the inevitability of elitism. In contemporary times the continuing conventional view that inequalities and elitism are inevitable cannot be sustained.

Some processes in secondary differentiation of power are labelled deviant by those whose power is threatened; but this is deviance only within the norms that are associated with the existing differentiation of power. There are more extreme forms of deviance, including violence against people and property that occur during attempts to erode the existing differentiation of power and more especially when there is frustration experienced in attempting this. The struggle is to obtain a role in society, a sense of equality in the systemic sense that units have a role to play that is necessary to the operation of the system, no matter how mundane the role may be.

Far from creating inequalities, power differentiation through social exchange leads over the longer term to equality, to the rocognition of individuals as members of a society each with a role of systemic significance. In terms of 'historic processes' differentiation of power through social exchange leads to equality of role power as the conflict continues between values attached to structures and the requirements of human needs. That there must be authorities is not questioned; what is being questioned is the belief that authorities have some special endowment that makes their role occupancy permanent within the norms of society and that they are justified in the employment of power, even violence, in its preservation. The probability is that power through role differentiation is not inevitable, that is is deliberately preserved despite processes that tend to erode it. If this is so, there is here an important source of conflict and of unsolved problems.

'LEGALITY AND LEGITIMIZATION'

The classical position in jurisprudence argues that the law is what the legislature and the courts say it is: there are 'superiors' and 'inferiors' and the latter are obliged to obey. More recent approaches by some lawyers, who take into account the political realities, assert 'that there is a natural law springing from man's own humanity which must be incorporated into the positive law of the state: under the first approach revolution is invariably unlawful, but under the second approach revolution can be justified as lawful, if the existing positive law of the state offends the natural law . . .' (Scarman, 1977).

This observation brings to attention an important distinction between legal authorities and norms, on the one hand and legitimized authorities and norms, on the other. Furthermore, it focuses on the nature of legitimacy: that which serves 'man's own humanity'. Authority, whether it be coercive or based on relationships, is effective only to the degree that it is accepted and regarded as 'legitimized' by those over whom authority is exercised.

Conventional thinking appears not to make any clear distinction between that which is 'legal' and that which is 'legitimized'. In traditional thinking the legality of authority has its sources in effective control, heredity, constitutional processes, foreign recognition and other such tests. 'Legitimized', by contrast, refers to authority that is derived from those over whom it is exercised. This, however, should not be construed as applying only to the constitutional processes by which subjects select authorities. It is a notion that applies to the decisions of authorities when once placed in authoritative positions; it implies perceived satisfaction of human needs by those over whom authority is exercised. In some cases constitutional processes can achieve this or at least help to achieve this; in some cases constitutional processes give no real choices and do not achieve legitimacy in these terms; in some systems there is legitimacy even in the absence of electoral and constitutional processes. The test is performance in satisfying needs rather than the processes by which authorities are selected or self-selected.

It could be argued that the authority of a charismatic or traditional leader is derived from those over whom it is exercised and is, therefore, 'legitimized' in the sense that they accept it or at least do not reject it. However, more than this is required. In practice many authority relationships, perhaps most if we take all social levels into account, do not fall into this classical framework. For example, on the football field the captain can be changed every match by common consent, as can the chairman of a meeting: it is a matter of agreed role enactment. It is convenient to all concerned to have a captain or chairman and to select one of its members to enact that role. Parents have a role by dint of being parents. Their authority role, however, must rest on an accepted role differentiation. So with a teacher: his legal authority is derived from his teacher status. His legitimized authority is based on his differentiated role: pupils accept him as a teacher because he, as a person in his teacher role, has something to contribute to them in their role of pupil. So with the police, managers and all authorities in a legitimized relationship. There are no inferiors, obligations or rights in this notion of authority. There is a reciprocal relationship in the sense that in exchange for benefits expected, people give alliance to role occupants. This can be expressed in another way: loyalty of people is to values identified with roles and institutions, not to leaders enacting these roles and to instutions as such. The values are those of the people giving the loyalty, those over whom authority is being exercised. If there is 'power' invested in legitimized authorities it is the power or influence of those over whom the authority is being exercised.

There is, therefore, a source of authority in addition to charismatic, traditional and legal, namely the authority which is consequent upon agreed role behaviour. There is no implied sanction of force attached to this authority. Classical theory was confined to coercive authority and appears not to have included this fourth type.

What appears to be the empirical position, in terms of social evolution, is that charismatic, traditional and legal authority have gradually eroded, giving way to a condition in which only role-differentiated authority is acceptable. In behavioural terms, only non-coercive relationships constitute acceptable authority relationships—and classical power theory could not accommodate this notion.

Reference has already been made to values attached to relationships as having a significant influence on behaviour. The implication is that there are reciprocal gains to be had by reason of relationships. This is the essence of 'legitimized' authority relationships: authorities are required to accomplish, to solve problems, to observe social standards of behaviour. The role of legitimized authorities is not primarily to preserve law and order. It is to demonstrate an ability to accomplish planning and problem-solving, to disseminate knowledge and generally to perform the roles of leadership. effectively in the pursuit of values and needs. Attempting to solve financial problems by means that in practice create unemployment, thus depriving people of recognition and stimulus, endeavouring to settle a communal conflict by the imposition of 'law and order', dealing with mugging, theft from open display counters and corruption by officials by punishment without removing causal conditions, are authoritative behaviour patterns that reduce legitimacy because they do not solve problems.

Once this distinctintion is made between authorities that are 'legal' and 'legitimized' and between particular acts or policies that may be 'legal' but not 'legitimized', it no longer necessarily follows that the imposition of 'law and order' by coercive means can be justified. On the contrary, if coercion is required in a significant number of cases or against minorities which are politically significant, the implication is that authorities lack 'legitimized' support.

However, goals and values sought by people do include values attached to the preservation of existing societies and institutions, with all their weaknesses. The party parliamentary system in many countries, such as the United Kingdom, is generally valued. More than fifty per cent of people are prepared to be governed by representatives of less than forty per cent of people with whom they strongly or mildly disagree. However, there occur circumstances in which the immediate goals of minorities appear to them to be of such overriding importance that they are prepared, if necessary, to attack institutions in order to achieve them. This is frequently the case as, for example, in a communal conflict in which the opposition is a minority one with no prospect of being an alternative government. In the view of this minority, authority does not have a legitimized status, consequently there is no moral obligation to acknowledge it. So, too, the child respects family and social institutions, but in some circumstances they are found to be repressive or remote and do not attract allegiance.

POWER

These observations lead to a consideration of power. In the area of conventional thought there are few, if any, notions as widely accepted as that of 'power' as the controlling element in social relations at all levels. Hawley (1963) reflecting this view in his discipline, states that: 'Every social act is an exercise of power, every social relationship is a power equation, and every social group or system is an organization of power.' Power theories have dominated international relations throughout the history of the study of this topic (see Morgenthau (1948)—the most widely read text on this subject) and sociologists place power at the centre of their analyses (see, for example, Olsen, 1970).

So much has 'power' been assumed to be the core topic that there has not, until recent times, much questioning of its meaning. Where it is now questioned, it is still on the basis of the notion of power being on the continuum from influence to physical coercion. It has been looked at from the point of view of those with power; i.e., it has been defined as the ability to affect social activities, to overcome resistances and the ability not to have to adjust to the environment or to change—the ability to impose the burden of adjustment on others, namely the less powerful. The topic has not included the responses of those over whom power is exercised, the manner in which they have been damaged, deprived of development, the manner in which they respond, either within social norms or by deviant means. Consequently, a degree of surprise seems always to be registered when power comes 'unstuck'. When the United States of America failed in Vietnam, it was a surprise; when minorities rebel and cannot be controlled in multi-ethnic and politically developed societies, there seems to be no reasonable explanation. In the area of conflict it has generally been assumed, even by many contemporary scholars, that conflict is settled finally by reference to a relative power. This view is questioned because in many cases power in any form is not merely unimportant, but not even present. Where it is present it does not necessarily control.

The traditional focus on power reflects a preoccupation by scholars and administrators with the problems of society as experienced by elites and authorities, both within their societies and at the international level. What is now being realized is that there is another aspect—the needs of members of societies—that affects the whole notion of power in any particular situation and generally the responses of those being coerced. As a consequence, a body of literature on the nature and problems of compliance has begun to develop, both within the fields of law and of sociology (see, for example, Krislov, *et al.* 1966). Krislov in his paper, 'The perimeters of power' has gone so far as to say that it could be more profitable to define politics as 'the study of the uninfluential and the powerless'. It is their responses that determine the perimeters of power. Cowan (1971, p. 590) asks: 'Could not our jurisprudentialists boldly assert that force and law are basically and essentially incompatible. . . ?'

In every social organization there appears to be a conflict between, on the one hand, effective participation and pursuit of needs by the individual members of the organization and, on the other, the efficient use of resources and the administration of public policy. Traditional and conventional thinking has tended to rest at the power or public administration end of the spectrum, while acknowledging that the efficient dictatorial and totalitarian state could prove inefficient, ultimately because of public responses. In contemporary conditions, practice is forcing policies that tend more and more to rest on participatory and related goals. As a consequence, power as the main organizing force in society is being challenged. What ultimately causes change and determines structures are demands for satisfaction of needs at the actor level. One could rationalize and say systems are becoming subsystem dominated, i.e., power is now in the hands of those who are organized into unions and other interest groups, rather than in the hands of central authorities. However, this is so extending the meaning of power as to make it quite a useless notion. It is more useful to acknowledge that power, as defined, is not an organizing force but, on the contrary, a force created and employed to curb and to suppress those elements in social organization that ultimately do organize societies. In this perspective power, far from being an integrative force, must be regarded as a liability: its possession leads to policies and strategies that are likely to be successful only in the short term. Its absence leads to a search for policies that may be more difficult to administer, but ones that are more likely to survive.

THE ROLE OF AUTHORITIES

If the role of authorities is a legitimized one, if authority is a function of role differentiation and if the law-and-order activity is not primary, what then are the goals of authorities?

The need for an active role is evident if the problem of deviance is looked at from the point of view of the deviant and his impact on society. Deviance is to some degree, perhaps in some cases to a significant degree, a dynamic input into social change. It is protest, it is a vote of no confidence on social and political systems, it is the warning that structures and institutions require consideration, it is the signal that rates of change and stresses are greater than actors can tolerate and it is in many ways both by itself and by its influence on authorities the reason for change. Deviance does not, however, necessarily take forms that would suggest the directions change should take. It is negative protest and reaction. While it may be associated with some ideology or belief or a condition of unwarranted inequality, injustice or deprivation, it does not suggest solutions to problems. The deviant may know why he is deviant—though this is unlikely; even so he may not know the social, economic and political conditions under which he and others would not be deviants or under which his behaviour would not be defined as deviant. It follows that for deviance to lead to changes in society such that individual behaviour leads to social harmony, it must be mediated by some agent. This agent can only be authorities—leaders, planners, problem-solvers. Leadership, therefore, is a necessity, some would argue, a genetic need. However, what is required is a particular type of leadership, one that reflect more an agreed division of labour than the acquisition of power and privilege. What appears to be objectionable—and the reason for ideologies that discount leadership—is the exploitation of leadership roles in the interests of the role occupants.

In considering the role and activities of authorities it is useful to make a distinction between 'restrictive' and 'constructive' intervention by authorities—once again, authorities at all social levels. 'Restrictive' intervention is defensive, protective of existing conditions against internal change and external influences. It characterized state activities and policies when the prime function of princes and rulers was to defend the realm against internal and external threats. It characterized state policies between the two world wars when depression conditions that were worldwide induced governments to adopt protective economic policies as a means of maintaining employment. It was clearly self-defeating as it was seemingly politically necessary within each state. It was the kind of activity that *laissez-faire* economists most opposed—interventions into the national and international market that destroyed the controlling forces of the market. It ultimately led, not merely to increased unemployment and depression, but finally to aggressive action by countries, such as Japan, that had no option but to try to acquire a co-prosperity sphere under their own political control. After the Second World War, in the period of reconstruction that followed, there was a general recognition that such policies were self-defeating in terms of economic and political goals. An obligation to maintain high levels of employment was accordingly included in the United Nations Charter and many international organizations—the ILO, the Food and Agriculture Organization, the International Monetary Fund—were designed to cope with this problem. In the recession of the seventies, governments throughout the world generally resisted pressures to impose protective duties for fear of these self-defeating repercussions. Externally, countries with strong trade balances were persuaded to modify their import policies and, internally, active steps were taken to re-train labour, to encourage investment and to adjust the economy to the wider world environment. In short, the role of authorities was, perhaps for the first time, to intervene 'constructively' in the sense that the aim was, not to break world trading patterns and world systems of transactions, but to adjust to them and to promote further international transactions.

At the level of social transactions the same developments have occurred. The activities of authorities have increased, but their nature has also altered. The power of authorities has been exercised less, because the activities of authorities have not primarily or even mainly been concerned with law and order and the enforcement of regulations. Extensive redistributions of income through social services, such as education, health and social benefits, require little coercive authority. The promotion of investment, interventions into conciliation and arbitration in industrial disputes, positive steps to promote better relationships between ethnic groups, are activities that fall into the category of legitimized role differentiation rather than coercive power. Some first steps in dealing with social and political problems, including deviance problems, by constructive rather than restrictive means, are being taken. The development of social work as a profession, the handling of juvenile delinquents outside prisons and direct measures to improve living conditions that lead to social problems, are examples. Legislation seeking to alter the climate of opinion and thus discourage discrimination on grounds of sex, race and religion is a long-term but constructive means of solving a difficult social problem.

However, such policies do not extend to more serious problems, such as terrorism and other forms of revolt or to communal conflict. Restraint, punishment, coercion by violent means still prevail. If a 'constructive' approach is seen to be required in one area, logically it might be applied in others. Experience is that para-military organizations involved in major communal conflict or independence movements cannot be repressed, yet little if any attempt is made to use means other than repression. This appears to be politically impossible: it seemed to be impossible for the Greeks in Cyprus and for the authorities in Westminster when dealing with Northern Ireland. Why has it been possible for authorities to behave on the basis of legitimized role behaviour in relation to one set of problems but not in relation to others? Why is it that there are authorities that are autocratic, even terrorist in respect of some minorities, corrupt and little concerned with the welfare and development of their subjects? Is there a connection between the restrictive behaviour of authorities in developed societies and the similar behaviour by leaders in less developed political systems—i.e. are there situations that occur within developed systems, e.g. communal conflicts or secession movements, that provoke the same kind of responses as less threatening situations do in less developed societies? Are the reasons for coercive and non-legitimized behaviour wherever it occurs a function of personality? Do they reflect a universal response on the part of leaders to threats to their status and roles? There appears to be a connection between levels of repressive behaviour and levels of political development, a connection between personalities and the use of violence to defend roles. Each of these requires some examination.

An answer to these questions is implied in the research carried out by Gurr (1976). He made a comparative analysis of public order in four countries and he differentiated between crime and civil strife. The two cannot logically be separated, but they form different categories at any one time. For example, in the nineteenth century in some countries labour organization was a crime and later, while organization was accepted as legal, consequent disturbances were issues of civil strife. This categorization enabled Gurr to point out that while theft, personal assault for non-political purposes, crimes of violence, generally, are acts against person and property, civil disturbances and riots are directed against authorities. Having made this distinction, he argues that marked increases in crime in Western cities are most pronounced in offences that are commonly held to be the most abhorrent. 'One would expect this kind of commonly perceived problem to stimulate concerted public demands and programmatic official response. In fact the elite and governmental response has been relatively tolerant.' The explanations he gives are, first, that governments do not know what to do about widespread crime. 'Second, elites and officials are in fact relatively little concerned about these kinds of crime because their costs—unlike the costs of civil strife—are sustained mainly by ordinary citizens, who are most likely to be assaulted and who bear, directly and indirectly, most of the costs of personal and commercial theft' (Gurr, 1976, p. 99). Later he refers to the 'decriminalization' of theft, abortion, drug-taking and other acts that previously came within the area of crime. In Sweden shopkeepers are required first to warn a thief where it appears to be a first offence: police are concerned only if theft is persistent (Gurr, 1976, p. 103). No such down-grading of civil strife occurs.

The answer to the questions by this analysis is that authorities believe that they can afford to be tolerant of crime that does not affect their roles and institutions. In respect of crime they are prepared more and more to accept problem-solving techniques; but where their own interests are affected they keep to the tried and traditional means of coercive power and punishment. This conclusion directs attention to a more specific question: are problem-solving techniques relevant in situations that are perceived by authorities in any way to threaten their positions and the economic, social and political instutions on which their roles depend or are there only power solutions to role defence problems?

CHAPTER SEVEN

The Problem of Role Defence

THE SPECIAL CASE OF 'POSITIONAL GOODS'

Reference has been made to the special case of scarcity of positions, especially of authoritative positions, as a source of conflict. Unlike many social and collective goods such as recognition and identity, positional goods are frequently in short supply relative to the number of persons who, in most societies, appear to seek them. Furthermore, unlike other goods that are in short supply, such as material goods and services, increases in supply of positions tend to increase conflicts of interest. The reason is that the importance attached to positions decreases with the creation of others which reduce the prestige and authority roles of the original ones. In this special case the demand is for prestige and authority in role behaviour: competition and conflict for positions cannot be resolved by creating more of them because the extra ones reduce the status of each. A breakaway group in a political organization creates new positions to be filled; but both the new and the old ones then carry less prestige than the roles associated with the positions in the previously integrated organization. For example, political movements that are frustrated, such as independence and revolutionary movements, are characterized by in-fighting that leads to breakaway groups under rival leadership. Despite the additional roles so provided, there is bitter fighting as each occupant of leadership positions endeavours to arrive at an ascendancy. This occurred in Northern Ireland para-military organizations, within the Palestine Liberation Organization and within the black nationalist forces in Zimbabwe. It appears to be a general phenomenon. Factions within criminal gangs, within professional and trade union organizations, evidence the

140

same dynamics. The in-fighting between such rival groups, despite the fact that they have common objectives and differ mostly on tactics, can be more important to those concerned than the conflict they have in common with external interest groups. As is the case with the incidence of murder in kinship groups, the highest levels of violence are associated with in-group fighting.

In most conflict situations, therefore, there are two levels of positional goods: those associated with the initial challenge to established structures and those that emerge when existing leadership fails to attain group goals. The additional roles increase conflictual relationships. The handling of the initial conflict is made the more difficult by the in-group fighting; the solution of the former is probably dependent on the prior solution of the latter.

The question posed in this chapter is whether problem-solving as a peaceful settlement process is relevant in such cases or whether situations in which there is role challenge necessarily rely for their settlement on power or violence against role occupants, their structures, institutions and values. This is the worrying question facing scholars and practitioners concerned with questions of human rights and others who endeavour to improve the lot of the mass of peoples who are ruled by dictators, minorities and parties that have no legitimized status and who rule in the interests of small elites. In contemporary times the consensus is that violence is probably the only remedy, a consensus that includes many of those who are deeply committed to non-violence. This dilemma invites a careful analysis of the proposition that conflict over positions is a special case and as such is not subject to resolution by problem-solving processes.

This issue relates less to an assumption contained in classical and traditional thought than to an omission. While there is an extensive literature on major forms of resistance and revolt against authorities, there is no significant literature concerning the defence of authoritative roles, either government or private. Within a traditional framework there was no call for such a consideration: there were assumed to be those with rights to govern and those who had obligations to obey and the former were assumed to have a monopoly of power with which to ensure obedience. Interest was only in resistance, how it could be avoided or overcome, the nature of revolt and the legitimacy of revolution once it had succeeded. In some contemporary writing, however, there are passing references that acknowledge that a problem exists. Blau, whose interest was in the differentiation of power through social exchange, was led to observe that: 'Institutional restraints are needed to protect these opportunities and freedoms because groups whose social standing and power is endangered by the economic and political endeavours of others cannot be expected to look upon them with tolerant benevolence but are likely to meet these threats to themselves with intolerant opposition'. His only remedy lies with non-involved citizens: 'It is the duty of those citizens of a democratic society who are not immediately involved in particular power struggles to help safeguard equality of opportunity and political tolerance, since the involvement of the participants makes them incapable of doing so' (Blau, 1964, p. 142). Friedrich draws attention to the problem when he observes that rules in the restraint of power are defined by the rulers and enforced by them against themselves. 'On the other hand, there is the belief in the corruptibility of all men when entrusted with power and the consequent need to check and control them continually if abuses are to be avoided. The latter belief leads to the notion that power should be divided and carefully circumscribed' (Friedrich, 1963, p. 271).

These advices, however, make no great contribution to the problem of role defence and the sufferings and conflicts that it occasions. They go little further than the admonitions contained in classical thinking which never failed to point out the need and obligation for restraint in the exercise of power. The problem is that in traditional thinking that rests on power, the authority equation is unbalanced. On the one hand those with obligations to obey can be coerced into obedience; but those with rights to command operate under no such constraints. The question now posed is, therefore, whether problem-solving processes provide means by which this unbalance can be avoided, thus making possible change in role and role occupants as and when this appears to be necessary in the pursuit of human needs and in the interests of a harmonious society. The question could be posed in many other ways. Can there be 'permanent revolution' by means of institutionalized processes of problem-solving rather than by outbreaks from time to time of violent conflict with authorities? Does problem-solving make possible revolution by evolution? Is change necessarily the outcome of a dialectic process or is it possible to bring about the desired result by analytical means that preserve those features in the present that are required as part of the future?

CONDITIONS PROMOTING ROLE DEFENCE

There are many reasons why role occupants are led to defend their positions even in the face of evidence that they have no legitimized status. These relate both to needs and to the systematic conditions in which the individual operates.

Role Acquisition

Reference has already been made in Chapter Three to Sites, Box and other control theorists who have pointed to the way in which interests and needs *will* be satisfied, if necessary by dishonest and illegal means, despite individual preferred values and social norms and constraints (see p. 75). The social norms that are useful are employed; but if these are not adequate in achieving that which is expected by society or that which seems to the individual to be his needs, other means are employed. In the political field, i.e. in the seeking of authoritative roles, this is particularly so. A candidate seeking election to an office requires support by a party. It is necessary, therefore, to go along with a party platform whether he agrees with it or not and to pay lip service to pressure groups that are influential. This can be justified by arguing that this is the only means to office and once in office he will be of more service to the community than others. Once elected he finds that he still needs the support of pressure groups in order to remain in office and to be re-elected. The rationalizations and corruptions necessary to obtain office are necessary to remain in office. Political parties as a whole adopt similar expedients, especially in the adversary type of party systems of government. A conflict develops, therefore, between the intentions of providing adaptive and educational leadership and the acceptance of the processes necessary to remain in office. The Watergate Scandal lent support to this view. What was revealed dramatically there may not be different from practices that are widespread at all levels of social interaction in which there are authoritative roles to be enacted. While the process is sometimes more apparent at the political level, role defence of this nature is probably a general phenomenon. It is, in this sense, a systemic phenomenon, one that arises out of the institutional structures in which individuals act, rather than a feature of individual behaviour as such. The remedy is a structural change, especially one that removes the adversary nature of the decision making process and reduces authority to the bounds of role differentiation (see p. 131).

Role Defence in the Absence of Rules

It has also been argued that in so far as role acquisition reflects the pursuit of needs, so does role defence (see p. 73). Where the rules of role change are well defined, where role change can take place without the loss of needs of security and recognition, as is usually the case in a party parliamentary system that has long been established, there is likely to be readier acceptance of change. Where, on the other hand, there are no accepted processes, no expectations that security and recognition will be accorded, then the position is perceived as a win–lose one evoking the strongest possible resistances. In practice the most violent role defence situations are where there are no acknowledged processes for change: a power confrontation seems inevitable. While demands are made for change on those occupying authoritative roles, they are not accompanied by any recognition of the legitimate human needs of those to be displaced. In 1978 in Rhodesia—Zimbabwe—some national leaders acknowledged the fears and the needs of the white minority and arrived at an agreement on the transfer of power calculated to take these into account. Other national leaders who had already adopted the view that violence was the only possible means of bringing about change were committed to the belief that there was a 'cleansing effect in violence' and continued to press for a win–lose outcome, thus ensuring further defensive responses from the white minority. These considerations raise the important dilemma inherent in the need for change, namely to secure peace in conditions in which violence is the only apparent means of change. This is discussed on p. 173.

Personalities

It has been argued above that the behaviour of persons in roles is influenced by the pressures imposed by the institutional framework in which they act, a systemic influence on behaviour. At the same time it is clear that role occupants in adversary systems, such as party political systems and other authoritative positions that are derived from processes other than role differentiation, are to a large degree self-selected. There is probably a particular type of person who seeks political office, industrial leadership, administrative responsibility or authoritative positions. For most people the needs for role and recognition are met within the ordinary interactions and associations of a society, membership of organizations of all kinds, local bodies, recreational, kinship, etc. There are those who, in addition, seek authoritative roles with wider influence. If, therefore, role occupancy of high level authoritative positions is associated with a high level of role defence by personalities that could be judged more assertive or more devious than the average, then this must be treated as a systemic feature, part of the problem to be solved, not a reason for moral censure or punitive action. Personality may be an important influence in bringing about role defence; but sensibly the remedy is not one that is directed against the person. The remedy is an alteration in institutional structures and selection processes.

Whether personality or role demands are more important influences in decision-making has been studied by many scholars. It seems clear that in some circumstances role attracts to it certain loyalties regardless of personality and this tends to give a greater freedom of action, including increased opportunities to defend the role and its occupant (Rosenau, 1968). When the role is a new one and when circumstances are changing rapidly, when for any reason expectations of role behaviour are not widespread or well defined, the personality of the role occupant can influence behaviour in the role (Greenstein, 1969). In authoritative positions role behaviour is restrained and controlled in the long term by an ability to give the required leadership and to solve problems (Burns, 1977). Failure to achieve acceptable results leaves the role occupant in an unfavourable position, requiring a measure of external support, including repression and violence. At this stage there is an important interaction between personality and role, some occupants being more

apt to accommodate to circumstances than others. A role occupant who has attained his role by force is more likely to attempt
to retain it by the same means.

Admission of Error

It is the nature of scientific inquiry that propositions should be
falsifiable and it is no reflection upon the scientist if he succeeds
in demonstrating that a proposition he favoured and set out to
test is false. In decision-making, especially authoritative
decision-making, error in judgment is regarded as reflecting on
the leadership abilities of those concerned. Mistakes are not
admitted: the failed policies are justified on some grounds. This
is particularly so where the political institutions are of an
adversary type in which oppositions set out to discredit those in
power. For these reasons the ordinary feedback processes,
through which policies change, do not operate effectively and
contrary policies put forward by oppositions have to be avoided.
In these circumstances problem-solving processes are not relevant. Authorities are in a position in which they are required by
the system in which they operate to pursue policies that are not
achieving their goals or to make modifications that fall short of
the measures that experience dictates. Such a situation invites
defensive responses that sometimes go beyond mere verbal
argument. Many African countries have endeavoured to introduce some elements of planning without the necessary administrative infra-structure, resulting in inefficiencies and corruption; but radical changes in policy seem not to be possible. In a
major communal conflict situation such as the United Kingdom
experienced in Northern Ireland and the United States in
Vietnam, altered definitions of the conflict and altered policies
were not possible from within administrations. Leadership is
associated with the successful handling of situations, not necessarily with problem-solving and the feedback processes and
alterations in direction that this might imply. Authorities are,
therefore, faced with the dilemma: admit error and resign or
rationalize error and endeavour to press on with the same
course, resisting all pressures for removal. This is a structural,
systemic problem, rather than an individual one, that can be
resolved only by structural change and alterations in decision-
making processes.

Altered Role Requirements

One of the main difficulties leading to role defence is that circumstances and requirements change such that altered role behaviour is relevant. For example, a charismatic leader is required within a society that seeks independence for there must be a united opposition to colonial rule. Having won independence the leading role occupants needed are the planners, organizers and administrators who win allegiance, not through charisma, but through performance and achievement. The charismatic leader and his particular following cannot readily adapt to the new role, nor do they wish or see the reason to step aside. There are many cases in recent history in which a charismatic leader has lost support after independence and then endeavoured to remain in office by appeals to religion, to nationalism, by corruption and the use of force. In due course they have usually been removed by violence when their failure as leaders became widely apparent. Once again it should be noted that they were operating in a political environment of adversary politics in which the institutions for role change were absent, except those of violence.

The Resistance of Bureaucracies

The form role defence takes in developed societies is changing as the result of changes that are taking place within them. In the industrial period the struggle was between capital and workers, any role defence being by those representing capital. Many industrial societies now seem to be entering a phase which has been described as the 'post-industrial' era in which the struggle appears to be between, on the one hand, technologists—including the bureaucracy, trade unions and other elites associated with bureaucratic decision-making—and consumers generally on the other. The role defence is by the former. The latter comprise workers but include many others in addition. These developments have caused some Marxists to question whether the leading role of the working class can any longer be assumed, whether the Marxist conception of 'laws of social development' is any longer valid. Furthermore, the emerging society will not be the harmonious one of ideal socialism, but will generate new conflicts and new strug-

gles, not along class and power lines, but in attitudes to change
and to science (see Bell, 1973).

The old freedom and control dilemma may have missed an
important aspect of this authority problem. The dilemma may
not be freedom versus control in the interests of those wishing to
be free: it is more likely to be a conflict between freedom and
certain types of authorities and bureaucracies that place above
all other objectives the maintenance of the system they control
and their roles in it.

Elites represented in bureaucracies tend to be self-
perpetuating. The role defence problem inherent in this development cannot be overcome by direct confrontation and
violence for this merely overthrows one elite and replaces it
with another. Revolution, therefore, is not the appropriate
process in these new circumstances. A more likely response is
individual expression of dissent by behaviour that challenges
the norms of society or, alternatively, by behaviour that is little
more than frustration aggression, an expression of alienation or
even boredom.

The Nature of Change

There is always change affecting role performance and expectations of it: changes are required in behaviour within the role
and in the role itself. Some changes are accommodated, while
others lead to defensive and protective responses. Why?

Organisms and societies have a range of abilities to accommodate to change: this is the reason why some survive and develop
while others fail. The study of behaviour—biology, psychology
and related disciplines—is the study of this adjustment process,
consequently there is an extensive literature on it. By comparison the nature of change has been neglected: problems of
adjustment have focused primarily on the extent and discontinuity of change. In the social and political areas resistance to
adjustment has been attributed to those types of change that
threaten the interests of elites and cause widespread and discontinuous alterations in structures, norms and social values.
However, the magnitude and discontinuous nature of change
may not be the decisive reasons for failure to adjust or for active
resistance.

It is convenient to differentiate between primary and secondary change. Primary change is that which occurs without any deliberate initiative: changes in the weather, cyclones, changes in techniques brought about by discovery, alterations in tastes and values, changes consequent upon population increases or exhaustion of resources. Secondary changes are the deliberate responses to these, sometimes accommodating and sometimes resisting by means of placing the burden of adjustment on others. Which occurs in a particular case depends not necessarily on the magnitude or type of change, but on how it is perceived. Damage to property on an extensive scale as the result of a cyclone does not usually give rise to aggressive responses against others; but far less damage as the result of the deliberate decision of others is likely to promote retaliation against those thought to be responsible. Poverty in backward societies, in which there are no examples of or expectations of higher living standards, is typically accepted with resignation. Unemployment, poor housing, lack of opportunities generally in socially and politically developed societies are rarely perceived as being accidental or inevitable: authorities are thought to be responsible and to have the means to alter these conditions. A decline in an industry due to a change may lead to adjustments, whereas a relatively smaller decline due to 'unfair' trading leads to demands for protection or retaliation. It is this secondary change factor that creates conflict: the underprivileged perceive their condition as being induced deliberately by powerful elites who shift the burden of adjustment to change on to them, while the privileged perceive demands for equitable change as an attempt to force on them a disproportionate burden of adjustment to whatever primary change—such as a change in values—that has taken place. Both sides to the change–adjustment interaction perceive their relationships in a bargaining adversary and win–lose framework. Challenges to roles and to role occupants and defence of roles are symptoms of this perceived conflict of interests.

Once conflict emerges, once there is failure to adjust to change, cumulative factors operate at an ever increasing rate. The frustration reaction of those seeking change in structures and institutions, including crime and civil disturbance and the anxiety response of those threatened by change, are themselves changes in social relationships that promote further change. The longer adjustments are resisted the greater are the perceived and experienced injustices. Finally a situation develops in which, on the one side, change at any cost seems better than acceptance of the present condition and, on the other, defence at any cost seems better than acceptance of the changes demanded. Even the origins of the problem, the primary change that led to the need for adjustments in the first place, become lost: the conflict has a momentum of its own. This is typically the case in a communal conflict where minorities and majorities commence by arguing their respective positions, perhaps within the same political institution. In due course this adversary process leads to a walk out, to competing institutions, to fighting, to war aims that are far removed from the original demands made by the minority. The conflict creates roles and the separate parties enjoy some of the needs of rocognition that they sought initially. Fighting itself provides an answer to the original problem.

THE RELEVANCE OF PROBLEM-SOLVING

The question posed earlier (p. 139) why it was that 'no fault', problem-solving processes were being followed in relation to many types of crime, yet in relation to others, authorities—at all levels—chose to apply more traditional law and order coercive techniques. The question was asked in the context of evidence that problem-solving processes were gradually increasing due to a recognition of needs. As argued by Bodenheimer (1971, p. 662) and quoted by Zetterbaum (1977, pp. 988-9):

> On the basis of modern psychological evidence and 'a look at the contemporary scene' that the most important values that the structure of law is designed to protect and promote are security, liberty, and equality, and seeks to demonstrate that these values 'have not been arbitrarily singled out as lodestars of legal regulation but that they have deep ontological roots in the constitution of human beings'. . . . The needs described (which form the 'link to social and legal goal values') are 'empirical traits of men which are not deemed to be subjective and idiosyncratic'.

Gurr's observations that authorities show less concern for criminal offences that affect only other citizens than they show for civil offences that threaten social and political structures and values, provides part of the answer (see p. 138). However, it is necessary to look deeper, for no clear distinction can be made between crime and civil strife. Crime on an extensive and increasing scale is a symptom of the need for changes in the environment and, therefore, a warning that a type of change is being demanded to which civil strife is directed. Gurr does not mean to imply that there is a difference in behaviour reflected in crime and civil strife. On the contrary, referring to social-structural theories of strife, which he supports, he observes that:

> A premise common to a number of theories is that strife is a collective response to discontent, which arises from discrepancies between peoples' expectations and attainments. To explain strife it therefore is necessary to identify the social conditions that increase men's expectations or frustrate their attempts to obtain satisfaction. (Gurr, 1976, p. 166)

Certainly the dictator appears to appreciate the close connection between crime and civil unrest.

> The essence of totalitarianism, then, is that it annihilates all boundaries between the state and individual personality.... Totalitarian leaders are incredibly fussy about all sorts of inconsequential aspects of life—like the most anxious and demanding parents; and this is precisely because they, like demanding parents, want to shape human materials in their own image.... Totalitarianism is the ultimate in role defence: all human relations are subsumed to government. (Eckstein and Apter, 1963, p. 433)

If a problem-solving approach is relevant to the one, it is no less relevant to the other. However, if civil strife is differentiated from crime on the grounds that the threat to society is more immediate, necessitating more urgent intervention, then the reasons why force rather than problem-solving techniques is employed are understandable.

If this view is valid it would suggest that only those authorities that do not experience threat can afford to adopt a less urgent attitude toward social deviance, to accept the proposition that deviance may to some degree be due to environmental circumstances and to support 'no fault' and problem-solving processes even though these may lead to institutional and structural changes. The more successful they are in dealing with social deviance by adaptive responses, the less likely they are to be faced with civil strife and demands for fundamental changes. Logically they have a clear choice: either introduce coercive controls, deterrents, punishment or make alterations in structures, income distributions and norms that are required to remove motivations for the deviant behaviour, including the activities of those who are more privileged and who act on behalf of those who are underprivileged. However, it seems that authorities are usually reluctant to acknowledge the need for adaptive changes other than those that are consistent with the basic structures of society. Even changes that would modify, but not radically alter, social and political institutions are made only slowly. Having delayed they are finally confronted with situations where, apparently, there are no options but to use force. As a consequence criminal acts merge into behaviour defined as social strife. A minority claim for participation in decision-making starts with minor acts of frustration, damage to property, assault, theft. Soon a pattern is discerned indicating that this behaviour is associated with class, race or religious divisions. Simultaneously political demands for change are made by minority leaders and the one feeds the other. Compromises are made that do not remove grievances and eventually confrontations with authorities occur, leading to open communal conflict and long-term structural changes of a more fundamental character than either side initially sought. While this process is apparent in major communal clashes, e.g. in Northern Ireland and in Cyprus, it occurs in industrial relations and in most large organizations where frustrations are experienced.

There is much controversy over this reformist–revolutionary argument. While reforms are a deliberate attempt to make those alterations that appear to be required to maintain legitimacy, revolution is an unplanned and uncontrolled discontinuous change that may not achieve the legitimacy and the goals of need fulfilment which are sought. The revolutionary view, on the other hand, is that changes that radically alter the system will not be subject to reform—role defence will prevent this happening—and that sudden, violent revolution is inevitable. This argument has taken place within an ideological framework: in a needs–problem-solving paradigm it can be assessed less subjectively.

The reluctance or hesitation of authorities in making changes may be due to role defence, a refusal to take any action that would change social values, the economic structure and the role of those who conduct the political system. It may, on the other hand, be due to institutional constraints over which authorities have little control. There may be systemic reasons for hesitation and failure to respond as required, leading over a period to an accumulation of actions and changes needed that goes beyond the capabilities of authorities to implement and of the system to accommodate without widespread disruption.

The analysis so far suggests many reasons why policies are not adaptive. The decision-making processes that are universal in Western political systems are a major reason for procrastination and the continuation of policies that are not achieving their goals. Policies advocated by oppositions are resisted, mistakes are not admitted. Because electoral support has to be taken into account, including sources of funds, pressure groups that arise out of adversary processes, e.g. competing unions and management or minority and majority communities, frequently determine policies. The specialization of departments of government is another reason. Problems are treated as though they are puzzles by excluding the variables that would be taken into account if a broad view were taken of them. For example, financial, trade balance and related matters are the concern of treasury departments of governments. Policies are put forward by them to remedy inflation, trade deficits and other economic conditions without due consideration of the consequences that are the concern of less influential departments of government, such as social welfare, health, education and housing. These are spending departments and in the context of economic problems their calculations as to the long-term social and political costs of cuts in these services are not influential. Nor does a treasury take fully into account, for it is not equipped to do so, the consequences of unemployment that some of its policies are likely to create. Unemployment has far-reaching social and political consequences because, more than any other condition in an industrial society, unemployment destroys human needs that have a social significance. There are also the delays, hesitations and consequent frustrations associated with large bureaucracies.

These systemic conditions are less significant within a modern industrial society than they might be because there are already high living standards, fluctuating economic conditions that relieve unemployment from time to time, social benefits, changes in government that give rise to expectations and generally a high level of needs satisfaction in social life, if not at work. However, when these systemic processes are analysed in a majority–minority situation, in a repressive military regime or in a society in which a charismatic leader has lost his legitimacy, the process is a sufficient explanation of role defence. The government leading a white minority or the industrial manager employing labour in a multiracial society is bound by interests and pressures that are irresistible. Even though authorities, as persons, might wish to alter conditions, they would be powerless to do so. The adversary processes would ensure their defeat.

Coercion theory that is so deeply ingrained in political thinking, itself creates systemic conditions. There is an absence of institutionalized processes by which deviance, that is a sympton of civil strife and civil strife itself, can be dealt with by means other than coercion. Over many years, successive British governments refused to bring around the table representatives of the Catholic minority in Northern Ireland who had taken the military initiative against authorities: they were defined as gun-men, terrorists or criminals and on these grounds could only be outlawed and eliminated. While there were some private meetings and while politicians were impressed with those whom they met, for political reasons the official definition and policies had to remain. However, when such a situation is defined as an international one, as was the same type of revolt in Cyprus, it is politically acceptable for a mediator (who is never a national) to bring the parties together. In the same way, institutionalized processes by which domestic strife could be tackled without authorities appearing to sanction rebellion could be helpful. While there are these systemic sources of role defence, there are reasons to believe that those in a defensive position would prefer to find means by which they could bring about a legitimized system so that the problem could be avoided or in some way find a way out of conflictual relationships which they know finally to be destructive of their interests.

Elites as individuals are not responsible for the evolutionary processes that create their roles. As individuals they have the same human needs, including recognition and approval by those whom they dominate, as all persons. They operate within a system dominated by power differentiation, over which they have little control. All social organizations have within them the seeds of their own transformation or even self-destruction as power differentiation processes continue. An altered power balance creates new elites. Societies can be stable, in the sense of avoiding the disruptions of discontinuous change, only if there are deliberate inputs designed to offset or to eliminate the consequences of power differentiation. These deliberate inputs must be initiated by elites. They have the choice whether to allow the power differentiation process to operate without con- trol, except to the limited extent that adversary processes manage to temper the decision-making of the power elite or deliberately to ensure the satisfaction of needs. Societies to the present do not have the institutional processes by which to do this except in those limited cases already noted, such as juvenile and matrimonial problems, which in any event are a recent development not fully explored. The institutional processes required are those that have needs as their goals and the processes that are relevant are problem-solving ones which substitute positive outcomes for win–lose ones. As Bodenheimer observed, 'man has a biological essence, consist- ing of physiological, psychological, and noetic constituents which cannot without peril be discarded in the legal regulation of human affairs'. These 'ought to be taken int⌐ account by law makers in the interests of the health of ⌐he social body (Bodenheimer, 1971, pp. 679–80). That these inputs are not deliberately initiated may be as much due to absence of know- ledge and processes as to a determination to defend roles and structures.

Whether problem-solving techniques, as distinct from viol- ence, are relevant in overcoming role defence is finally an empirical question. Experience to date would suggest that they are not. However, historical experience is only that which has occurred within a power orientation. Deductively there are grounds for believing that problem-solving processes are relevant to situations characterized by role defence provided that institutions and processes are not such that elites are required to operate within an adversary and win–lose context. The empirical evidence will be available only when attempts have been made to deal with acute situations of violence attributable to role defence by problem-solving processes.

PART THREE

The Alternative
Paradigm

CHAPTER EIGHT

The Two Paradigms

PARADIGM SHIFT

When societies tackle their social problems there is a set of givens, a paradigm, that together form a generally agreed approach. Situations are defined and problems are dealt with on this basis. Shifts in conventions, social values, attitudes, new discoveries, altered environmental conditions, give rise to shifts in thinking and in policies. However, these shifts occur within an essentially unchanged set of givens or conventional assumptions about the nature of human behaviour, of society and of the norms to be observed. A high degree of failure in policies in relation to major situations, leading to widespread and persistent conflict, social disruption and violence, gives rise to more radical questioning of assumptions and policies. More than a modification of thinking and policies within the same system of thought takes place. There is a movement towards an alternative system of thought, to an alternative paradigm, as observers and policy-makers begin to analyse contemporary rather than past events, current behavioural patterns rather than accepted norms. Others follow once the alternative is seen to be convincing, to explain better and to be a basis for more reliable prediction. During this process the 'reality', i.e. the problem, does not change; its definition alters because of an altered perception of the situation, reflecting an altered system of thought.

Successive development of schools of thought is part of the continuing process in which some generally accepted theories are found not to explain behaviour as it emerges over a period of time, giving rise to modifications and sometimes to radically new theories. The changes in thought are not adaptations made

159

necessary by new or different human motivations and new or different problems. They are changes which occur because altered conditions allow behavioural patterns to surface and to be observed that previously were submerged under the weight of social, political and economic conditions. Resistance to feudalism and slavery, industrial unrest, independence, nationalism and identity struggles are all manifestations of the same human drives. At each stage analysts are forced to take into account different symptoms of a continuing struggle and are led to theories of behaviour that are progressively more comprehensive. Policies accordingly change over time from policies based, for example, on the view that, in the interests of social stability, more coercion and control is required, to policies that acknowledge the need for greater participation and control by the actor and less coercion by authorities.

In the course of this process it is the role of the analyst to observe and to articulate what is occurring and to formulate systems of thought accordingly; he points to motivations that are incompatible with accepted assumptions. Then earlier definitions of behaviour alter and in due course policies are adapted to the new definition of the problem.

Such revolutions in thought have occurred in particular areas in the natural sciences; the flat earth theory was proved to be false and a radical change in thought was needed to explain unexplained phenomena. It took time: rationalizations justified retaining the original theory until the falsifying evidence was overwhelming and the alternative theory was widely accepted. Such revolutions are rare in the social and political sciences and resistance to change is even greater. Conventional thinking is the product of leadership thinking and lends support to leadership values and to the preservation of existing social structures and institutions. Situations are defined and thought about and policies are formulated within this existing set of givens. It takes a major revolution in observed patterns of behaviour to induce a revolution in thinking. Over centuries there has not been any such major revolution in respect of the type of assumptions examined in Part Two: society being an integrated system, coercion being the means of social control, social values being more important than human needs. There have been social and political revolutions and changes in thinking; but these have taken place within the same power paradigm which has characterized thinking and practice from earliest times.

Yet it has been argued in Part Two that there is now evidence of a paradigm shift. Criticisms have been made of the assumptions that are inherent in conventional thinking on the grounds that they do not explain observed behaviour and that they do not lead to solutions to serious and widespread problems. What is the justification for treating the present as a unique time of paradigm shift?

There are many influences and together they have created a fascinating intellectual challenge; but more importantly they have created an opportunity for solving problems that have always plagued human societies and have become especially acute since modernization. Of these influences five are significant. First, there have been widespread reactions—culminating in wars of defence, independence struggles, communal and social conflict, and deviance of many kinds on an increasing scale—to the original differentiation of power that was based on the global and national distribution of resources and the unevenness of evolution of human societies that were exploring and exploiting these resources. This reaction was made possible by industrialization and population concentrations and in modern times was facilitated by an explosion of communication of ideas and events. Second, there has been a spread of knowledge beyond elite groups, both at international and domestic levels, such that the processes of socialization and defence of elite systems of thought have been challenged; and such that reactions to the existing power differentiation have been analysed, articulated and communicated. Third, the types of social and political problems that persist have drawn attention to relative deprivation, inequalities, exploitation, the absence of participation, which are now no longer perceived as inevitable conditions and are now translated positively into needs, thus cumulatively promoting demands for and acceptance of change. Fourth, in these new circumstances elite groups (whose composition in any event has been widened) are in many societies more ready to accept that the solution, as distinct from the containment, of major problems is ultimately in their own interest also. Fifth, greater sophistication in methodology, in particular less reliance on description and on inductive processes and validation, in favour of greater attention to deductive processes and falsification, have provided the tools whereby to sharpen the attack on ideological and normative systems. Without this substantial revolution in thought, conventional sets of ideas could not effectively be challenged. Indeed, there have been two related paradigm shifts in thought, the one in relation to content and the other in relation to methodology. The coincidence of the two, the causal interactions of the two, are probably the significant explanation of the contemporary revolution in thought.

However, even though one were satisfied by the empirical evidence that called conventional givens into question and even though good reasons were given as an explanation of paradigm change, it would still be necessary to demonstrate that the alternative provided an improved perspective in which to view, analyse, interpret and control behaviour in and between societies.

The assessment of the relative value of a system of thought is not an exercise for one or a few people. In the longer term it is an issue of consensus. However, there are some obvious applications in the context of social and political problems. It has been argued that the authority problem cannot be resolved within a conventional paradigm, but can be tackled within the alternative suggested. To demonstrate this would make a limited assessment of the value of the relationships paradigm.

In making an assessment of the relative value of these systems of thought it is necessary to ask, as a first step, whether the alternative paradigm helps to give more meaning and more precision to conceptual notions that have been quite vague and not particularly useful as tools of behavioural analysis: identity, law and order, legitimacy, integration, conflict, violence, development, morality, justice etc.; second, whether it helps to explain actual situations and to solve problems that were previously resistant to explanation and resolution; and third, whether it helps to describe and explain the present and to predict future trends in more detail and more reliably.

Some Conceptual Notions

The alternative paradigm throws light on many conceptual notions that in the traditional paradigm are vague and controversial, leading to policies that are divisive and self-defeating. By way of example some consideration is given below to several conceptual notions that have a different orientation in the alternative paradigm and which are significant in relation to unsolved problems. Amongst these are integration, human rights, the alleged functional nature of violence and justice. As must be the case, an alternative set of assumptions, an alternative approach to problems, gives a different perspective to most thinking: these are merely some examples.

Integration

The first conventional assumption that was examined was that societies are or ought to be coherent or integrated systems (see p. 44). When human needs were considered, recognition, identity, control (including participation) were emphasized as being necessary for a harmonious society (see p. 62). The alternative paradigm, therefore, would seem to place integration in a perspective that is incompatible with conventional thought.

Integration is acclaimed as a forward-looking goal for societies at all levels, one that is expected of thoughtful and progressive people. In the United Kingdom one of the major appeals by supporters of the Common Market was based on the idea that the issue was finally one to be fought out between the sophisticated and the backward, those who favoured integration and those who took an insular view. In this particular case the argument was weak because the European Common Market, while perhaps leading to integration in Western Europe, caused barriers between Western Europe and the rest of the world. However, putting this particular aspect aside, there is good ground for questioning the desirability, the practicability and theoretical justifications for such integration.

Integration, be it at this level of high politics or at kinship levels, is not an end in itself. It is a means. The end may be security or material welfare. In some circumstances such ends could be promoted in the short term by some forms of integration; any form of integration that decreases a sense of participation and control cannot be regarded as being practical in the longer term. Disintegration, leading to antagonisms and greater isolation, is likely to be the result. One has only to look at the history of integration attempts in South East Asia, the

Middle East, Eastern and Western Africa and Latin America to
come to this conclusion. The reasons are not merely irrational
attitudes and primitive behavioural responses by those concerned: there are fundamental deprivations at the root of these
failures. So, too, within states. The idea of integration of communities of different race, religion and language is widely
considered to be a desirable goal and one that should be promoted by education and by legislation. There are moral pressures
to this end. It fits in logically with the idea of majority government and human rights associated with majority government.
It fits in well, also, with ideologies that assert that race, religious and other divisions within societies are merely the consequence of middle class interests in preventing class revolution.
Ethnic minorities that fight to preserve their identity are, in
this view, 'backward'. In this view: 'It is not their identity that is
distinctive but their place in history. . . . The solution of ethnic
conflict therefore is to hasten the historical development of
retarded groups. As they are liberated from feudal backward-
ness they will lose their uniqueness and come to share the
proletarian class interests represented by the Communist
Party' (Enloe, 1973, p. 43).

An alternative view is that there are far more important
needs to be satisfied, far greater, even in poor societies, than
possible materialistic gain from integration within a society.

> It is conceivable that development and ethnicity are not
> inversely related. They may not be related at all. Under-
> lying this alternative proposition is a modified view of man
> and society—as well as modified notions of development
> and ethnic identity. This view perceives the adaptability of
> individuals to be limited not to the extent that people are
> irrational or 'slaves of nature' but at least to the extent that
> they have needs that cannot be sloughed off like passing
> fashions. Among these needs—which are no more mystical
> than environmental needs in ecological theory—is a basis
> of social relationship more enduring and less instrumental
> than occupations, status, and legal right. Ethnic groups
> may be one kind of collectivity that fills this need, and thus
> ethnicity survives long after its traditional functions have
> been taken over by more impersonal, secular groups.
> (Enloe, 1973, p. 268)

The consequence for policy of this alternative is far-reaching.
It touches on the handling of minorities, such as blacks in a

predominantly white society and catholics in a protestant dominated society, allowing members of a community the opportunity to live in the same location, while having equal work and
development opportunities in the wider society; it touches on
the handling of communal conflict, seeking solutions that are
based on identity needs instead of on the goal of integration
only; it touches on the invention of constitutional devices that
enable decision making at local levels, perhaps within a wider
federal system.

The establishment of 'ghettos' has been the result of felt
security needs and, more positively, a need for identity through
which there can be recognition. The 'ghetto' is merely the
physical or living expression of one form of community, kinship
groupings being another. There is a strong preference by those
concerned to live within their community, in a geographical as
well as a social sense. Attempts to prevent such cultural islands
within a state or to break up such communities by re-housing
and re-employment policies, lead to social and personal disturbances that are serious for the individual and for society. This
has been demonstrated frequently after the creation of new
towns, new housing estates and the re-distribution of populations into them. Psychological disturbances and increases in
crime follow. (See *The Times* (1977) for a report on experience in
the Manchester area.) The idea of a 'ghetto' was initially a
quarter in which Jews were required to live. It is misleading to
use this term, as it is widely used, to refer to ethnic communities
that have emerged by the decision of those who have migrated
to them by choice. There are undoubtedly economic and social
reasons why minorities migrate towards some particular locations that may be deprived areas; but this should not draw
attention away from the felt need to form kinship and ethnic
communities that arises out of identity, security and recognition needs. The tragedy associated with ethnic communities
living in the one area is not that they live in the one region and
keep to themselves to a large extent; their tragic circumstances
are in fact mitigated by the opportunity to live together. Their
deprivation is due to discrimination against them by the wider
society, limited employment, housing and educational opportunities and such factors that do not necessarily arise out of the
'ghetto' as such. Given a wider environment in which there is no

discrimination, given opportunities to explore beyond the community boundaries, given opportunities to experience the advantages of contacts across boundaries, the tendency will be to
work and ultimately to live in the wider community. The
probability is that closer social and functional relationships
between ethnic communities within states is more likely once
each community has an identity of its own, than it is when
attempts at integration are made by dispersal in living, school-
ing and employment. On a wider plane, cooperation among
tribal groups in African states could probably be accelerated by
secession and the creation of separate states more than by
coercion by central authorities dominated by one of the
communities. Federal systems cannot easily be imposed; feder-
ations occur as the result of a long process of functional cooperation.

There is an important distinction to be made, therefore,
between cooperation and integration. The objective of integration is essentially institutional. Authorities favour integrated
societies for national defence, administrative and prestige purposes. Integration has some implied normative overtones: it
implies a progressive approach to ethnic problems. It is almost a
moral notion: it reflects the-unity-of-man philosophy. A closer
look, however, suggests that its purposes are the preservation of
the society of the majority and that the structural basis of
integration is one that benefits more the majority than the
minority to be integrated. For integration to be achieved it is
required to be brought about by processes and within structures
that do not threaten or restrict the values and needs of the
members of the society that is being integrated. Forcing integration, by dispersing populations, by providing the one educational system, by discouraging cultural difference, is likely to
be self-defeating. Allowing integration to emerge as a result of
cooperation, in whatever form seems appropriate to those concerned, is likely to be a longer process, but also a surer one. The
convenience of the state, the preconceived notions of
educationalists and idealists, sometimes guide policies away
from the needs of those concerned.

This is not to argue that the process can be allowed to be one of
drift. The role of authorities is an active one: it is to marry the
longer term interests of the society with the needs of its members and to promote an understanding and acceptance of the

process of functional cooperation leading to closer personal relationships. Such a process also implies intervention by authorities to ensure unrestricted mobility in work and living conditions so that those who wish to explore across the ethnic divide are free to do so. It implies education designed for an understanding and acceptance of the exploratory process. In short, in the alternative paradigm attention is directed not to integration, but to conditions necessary for integration, while in the meantime making possible the satisfaction of human needs through their expression in ethnic identity and the security and recognition this can give.

The majority of violent conflicts in the modern world relate to sub-national movements. Consequently it is important to re-think attitudes and policies about enforced integration. There has been failure to bring about the integration of the two communities in Cyprus, leading eventually to partition. It would have been wise to have recognized the separation of the two communities from the outset and, from the security of their separate entities, to have concentrated on cross-ethnic transactions, leading to a higher degree of cooperation and to less fear and hostility. Similarly in Northern Ireland the attempts by the majority to impose integration on the minority failed and led to *de facto* separation of the communities.

In addition to the organized minority movements within states, there is the incidence of deviance at the individual level that is so often a direct result of loss of identity, absence of recognition, discrimination and deprivation inherent in majority–minority relationships. Organized violence and violence at the individual level that arise out of minority protest, including class minorities, are not conditions to be labelled deviance nor can they effectively be treated as such. They create socio-political problems, not conditions to be suppressed. Once we move from the perspective of the central authority that attaches most value to integration and law and order within an integrated society, to some means of achieving cooperation without loss of identity and the security and recognition that it gives, solutions are possible. It is in this sense that a clarification of notions such as integration within a human needs paradigm signals alternative diagnoses of problems and alternative policies and means by which to achieve stated goals.

Human Rights, Justice and Violence

The second set of assumptions examined related to human needs. One of the most interesting examples of the way in which perspectives change with altered systems of thought is in relation to what Scarman describes as the 'ancient and respected' notion of human rights. Originally declarations of human rights represented attempts to restrain rulers: the attempt to achieve 'justice for the individual when faced with the power of the state'. An interest in human rights reflects a reaction to 'the flat assertion that law is what the state . . . says it is'. A human rights approach to law asserts that 'there is a natural law springing from man's own humanity which must be incorporated into the positive law of the state'. (The comment on human rights takes as its starting point a lecture delivered by the Rt Hon. Sir Leslie Scarman, Lord Chief Justice of Appeal in the United Kingdom, on 18 October 1976 (Scarman, 1977).)

Within the traditional paradigm there is difficulty in defining human rights. Declarations such as the American Bill of Rights, the French declaration of the Rights of Man of 1789, the United Nations Charter Statement of Purposes and the Universal Declaration of 1948, focused on rights such as liberty, security of person and property, freedom from want and poverty, freedom of the press and many other civil, political, economic and social 'rights'. These largely reflect cultural values and in particular the values of elites in Western European free-enterprise cultures, in which security of property and freedom of the press, to name just two, are regarded as fundamentally important. In all cases they are subject to cultural and ideological interpretations. Cultures relate to economic structures in which there are inherent inequalities of power that arise out of the differentiation through social exchange, to which reference has been made (p. 125). The 'rights', therefore, are those minimum standards that are to be accorded to citizens to attract support for social and political structures. They are the concessions that have to be made to enable the system to survive. They are not necessarily available in the social and economic system unless provided deliberately. In Western-type free-enterprise systems they imply social services, income re-distributions, unemployment relief, non-discrimination on grounds of race and religion, which those who value the existing social, ecónomic and political structure are willing to contribute as part of the cost of maintaining the system and their roles in it. In centrally-organized societies dominated by ideological parties they imply degrees of freedom of association and expression of belief as required to prevent resistance to the system generally.

In practice, declarations of human rights are frequently advocated, not merely by men of good will, but also by those who take extremist views in support of existing structures that in practice threaten these rights. For example, an initiative for such a declaration in Northern Ireland came from extremist elements in the majority protestant side: these were the concessions offered in return for the observation by the minority of 'law and order' within the established protestant-controlled society. Similar provisions were embodied in the original constitution of Cyprus and offered by Greek Cypriots, in a revised constitution, to protect the rights of the Turkish minority.

This being the case it cannot be expected that human rights declarations will satisfy those who believe that existing political and economic structures are discriminatory, that make second class citizens of minorities and leave decision-making in the hands of a ruling faction. No concessions given by them can be regarded as being a substitute for altered structures such that would make these paternalistic concessions unnecessary. It can be expected that assertions of human rights by leadership in one culture or political system will be regarded as challenging and even aggressive by leadership in others.

The problem of definition of human rights that leads to declarations of this nature is overcome once human rights are defined in terms of human needs. Being universal, societies cannot continue to exist harmoniously without their satisfaction. There is a common interest across cultures and political systems to promote them. Declarations and legislative provisions that provide for consistency in response, stimulation, security, recognition, distributive justice, meaning and control as defined by Sites (see p. 72) require minor and major changes in institutions and policies: they do not merely represent a pay off to avoid them. In practice there is never effective legislative or judicial control in favour of the individual: the control that is effective is in structures and in relationships that arise out of them, not in agreed norms. Human rights is far less a problem of law and legislation as has been claimed and is far more a problem of structure and, in particular, a problem of bringing about changes in structures by peaceful means—hence, once again, the relevance of problem-solving, especially in the areas of role defence.

In many ways the notion of human rights as a judicial or constitutional issue is damaging to social and political development because it appears to provide a just solution to a structural problem. It diverts attention away from the fundamental reasons for the unrest that promotes the giving of human rights. It diverts attention away from the need to re-think structures and processes. For example, the goal of the Northern Ireland establishment was to preserve law and order within the democratic framework of a party political system. The argument was that in a democracy it is the duty of the majority to govern and of the minority to accept the decisions of the majority. Human rights were offered as a guarantee that there would be no discrimination against the minority in this democratic framework in which the majority by definition were the rulers. This in practice diverts attention away from needs which are experienced at the individual and social levels by members of the minority community. Whatever 'rights' are offered by a majority, they cannot satisfy these needs. Majority government is not necessarily democratic, ethnic integration is not necessarily desired by majority or minority. Other solutions, other structures require consideration; but this is impeded by the notion of 'rights'.

Related to the notion of 'rights' is the notion of 'justice'. Justice or fairness within the power paradigm is derived from legal argument. It is deduced from the notion of a social contract associated with the names of Locke, Rousseau, Kant—and some contemporary legal scholars who have tried to clarify the notion.

> The guiding idea is that the principles of justice for the basic structure of society are the object of the original agreement. These are the principles that free and rational persons concerned to further their own interests would accept in an initial position of equality as defining the fundamental terms of their association. These principles

regulate all further agreements; they specify the kinds of social cooperation that can be entered into and the forms of government that can be established. (Rawls, 1972, p. 11)

This is a formal definition of justice, remote from the life of the ordinary person except those few who enter into associations in a business or institutional capacity. Even so, as soon as attempts are made to spell out the agreed principles, difficulties are experienced. For example, the same author chooses two: 'the first requires equality in the assignment of basic rights and duties, while the second holds that social and economic inequalities, for example, inequalities of wealth and authority, are just only if they result in compensatory benefits for everyone, and in particular for the least advantaged members of society' (Rawls, 1972, pp. 14–15). This notion of justice takes little account for the needs of recognition and identity: it is small comfort to the unemployed and poor to receive 'just' compensations from the rest of society after authorities have decided that in the interests of the trading and financial system they should be made unemployed or kept poor.

This abstract and remote approach to justice is the best that is possible within the conventional paradigm that derives its goals from ideology and elite interests and value systems. There are no 'navigation points', no objectively based goals. Justice is a function of values, interests and culture. In the alternative paradigm justice is defined, not in terms of sharing scarce resources, positions and opportunities, but in terms of the achievement of human needs. These, because they are social goods, are not subject to scarcity. Recognition, identity, security, stimulus or the absence of boredom are not subject to scarcity. On the contrary, in many cases the more such social goods are consumed the more there are available for all. There are no problems of distribution involved and justice and fairness are not relevant concepts. Furthermore, the satisfaction of human needs is a societal requirement, it is not involved with balancing individual and social benefit: the social good is derived from the satisfaction of those human needs that require satisfaction for the sake of social harmony and without which there is social disruption. It is not justice or fairness that is leading industrial tribunals, courts, race relations commissions, local governments and welfare officers to give consideration to the requirements of the individual or groups that come before them: it is the societal interest that is being pursued through the satisfaction of the needs of the individual and group. While lawyers and men of goodwill are defining human rights and justice, even drafting conventions in respect of them, societies are in practice moving away from these power paradigm notions into a system of thought that makes them irrelevant.

There is, however, one element of justice that is relevant to the human needs paradigm, i.e. what has been termed 'distributive justice'. For purposes of growth and learning, the individual requires evidence of consistency, closely associated with rationality. If certain circumstances produce a particular result then it is to be expected that the same, or apparently the same, set of circumstances will produce the same results. The woman performing the same tasks as a man in the same factory requires the same reward—unless there are some special and agreed conditions that satisfactorily explain the apparent lack of distributive justice. The worker in one factory performing the same work as one in another expects to be treated the same. The child who has worked his hardest at school expects not to be streamed out of a class to which his friends have been promoted. The elite under threat from an opposing ethnic or class group requires a firm prospect of certain needs to be fulfilled before being willing to negotiate a change. This notion has nothing to do with scarce resources, allocations, levels of reward, balances between social and individual interests: it is a notion of justice that relates to rationality and consistency and has been set down by Sites (1973) among others, as an important human need.

This approach to human rights and justice has an important bearing on the handling of conflict situations, especially ones characterized by violent role defence. Human rights implies conditions that are required by or provided for underprivileged sections of a society, minorities, the poor and those not in elite positions who do not have opportunities for association and expression. When, therefore, a conflict situation is being analysed, such as an African–European conflict in South Africa, human rights are related to those conditions that should be made available particularly to blacks. The concentration on the rights of those seeking them places the authorities in a defensive position: the conflict is defined, by implication, as a win–lose one and in any such conflict no liberal initiatives can be taken without the danger of encouraging further pressures, leading to a final outcome of lose. If, on the other hand, a human needs approach is adopted there are implications that whites and blacks, authorities and others, have in common certain needs that must be satisfied if a harmonious outcome is to be achieved. The conflict is then perceived as a problem: how to satisfy the legitimate human and commonly held needs of all concerned. This still engenders resistance because elites in such circumstances enjoy privileges and advantages outside needs and many would persist in defending these. However, the prospect of an outcome that was not win–lose in human needs terms gives greater freedom of decision-making to elites: the possibility of a solution that would make possible a multiracial society or segregated societies rather than one dominated exclusively by the majority to the exclusion of the interests of all others.

In many regions of the world change is clearly demanded—the evidence being a high level of unrest and of repression. Defence by authorities, by forces at their disposal, of the institutions of society is such that peaceful change seems to be impossible in many cases. Some form of armed revolution seems to be the only means of change. At the meeting of Commonwealth Prime Ministers held in London in 1977 there appeared to be a general consensus that there was likely to be no change in Rhodesia and South Africa in the absence of an armed struggle. Even within politically mature societies, such as the United Kingdom, violent protest occurs as a means of change.

We have already noted (see p. 49) the observation of Johnson: 'True revolution is neither lunacy nor crime. It is the acceptance of violence in order to cause the system to change when all else has failed, and the very idea of revolution is contingent upon the perception of societal failure'. The argument seems to be that when other members of society accept the violence then it is revolution and that revolution thus has a legitimized status. This argument has far-reaching implications. To the extent that rebellion and revolution can be justified as response to a situation, so also can all crime: crime and civil strife cannot be differentiated analytically. They are treated differently only because of value judgments which give rise to definitions that legitimize the one and not the other. If revolutionary violence can be justified in this way so, then, can be the behaviour of minorities that believe they are being denied justice in education, jobs and social status and take to theft, mugging in the streets or other forms of frustration behaviour.

The weakness of this approach is in the phrase 'all other means'. The means that have failed are all variations on the same theme: relative power and coercion. Take, for example, the case of South Africa where a white minority is resisting demands from a black majority for equality of treatment and the end of discrimination. External support to the Africans is initially focused on helping them to strengthen their bargaining power, by assisting the development of trade unions, by giving training and experience in organization and by other peaceful means. Whites identify those giving such assistance as being not just in support of blacks, but in opposition to whites. The logical extension of such assistance is to supply other means by which the black majority can increase its bargaining power, including the means to take violent action against the white establishment. The justification is that by increasing the bargaining power of the weaker side, there is a greater possibility of a negotiated settlement. The reverse could be the case. The reaction of blacks would sensibly be to refuse to bargain until they have a superiority of power and the reaction of whites, no less sensibly, would be to resist increased pressures, using more and more coercion of which they have a great superiority. The stage is set thus for an escalation both of violence in role acquisition and in role defence. The costs to all concerned of this process and to the world at large are enormous and likely to increase. The reactions of the Palestine Liberation Movement to denial of their claims led to high levels of terrorism that spread beyond the Middle East. The Japanese Red Army, the Irish Republican Movement, German Red Army factions and Dutch Revolutionary Socialists have taken advantage of the training facilities organized by Palestinians: a terrorist culture and an international terrorist organization has developed among groups that have nothing in common other than that each has an establishment to fight. It was possible for the early philosophers to regard revolution and wars as a legitimate last resort; but in contemporary conditions the costs may be too high. It is necessary, therefore, to query whether some means of dealing with unacceptable structural problems, other than those included within the notion of 'all other means', should be explored.

Protest and defence of structures against which the protest is directed are not separate phenomena: both are responses to be analysed in the same framework. Those occupying authoritative roles are the objects of structural violence as are those who are the immediate casualties of a repressive regime. They seek the same goals of recognition and security and their tyranny is a means to these ends, just as is deviant behaviour within societies. All seek to maximize their satisfactions in the best way they know within the structural conditions existing and within the limits of their knowledge of options. The white minorities in Africa have no option, within the power framework in which they operate and in which they are opposed, but to defend their positions as best they can. There are no processes of peaceful change that would appear to preserve even their human needs: it is a zero-sum power situation. The same people operating within an established parliamentary situation would find no difficulty in accepting defeat at elections where there are accepted rules and processes and where the consequences of loss of role do not carry with them loss of human needs. Also in Africa there are tyrannical regimes that set upon members of other tribes within their national boundaries. They are caught up in a post-colonial situation in which boundaries cut across tribal boundaries and thus threaten ethnic identity and the security it gives. (The early decision by African governments after they acquired independence to maintain existing boundaries must give rise to violence and repression within many states and between neighbouring states and to constant accusations and fear of plots and counter-plots to overthrow leaders who are identified with opposing tribes.) All of these situations pose a problem that cannot be resolved within a conventional or power framework. If, however, the focus were on human needs, these situations would no longer be defined as status quo power versus revolutionaries.

They would become problem-solving exercises designed to find means by which the needs of all the actors could be pursued. Monopolies of power, positions of privilege and other structural conditions would require change; but not in a win-all–lose contest.

In a behavioural context it is process that is important. This has come to be the focus in recent thinking about development, for which term Goulet uses a substitute 'liberation'.

> For liberationists, success is not measured simply by the quantity of benefits gained, but above all by the way in which change processes take place. Visible benefits are no doubt sought, but the decisive test of success is that, in obtaining them a society will have fostered greater popular autonomy in a non-elitist mode, social creativity instead of imitation, and control over forces of change instead of mere adjustment of them. (Goulet, 1973, p. xvii)

Violence is a power response and as such is devoid of communication, feedback processes, exploration of options, analysis of behaviour or any problem-solving orientation. To argue that violence appears in some situations to be the only possible means of change is merely to assert that the total situation is not understood, that there are no known processes that can achieve the desired results more effectively. The alternative paradigm, that focuses on needs and processes toward them offers an alternative to the violence dilemma.

Other Notions

These have been examples of the way in which the alternative paradigm alters perspectives. Other examples could be given, the notion of deterrence that was discussed on p. 87, the differences between settlement and resolution and the different processes implied in each (see p. 112). Examples such as these demonstrate the argument put forward in Part One: unsolved problems are likely not to be solved within existing systems of thought, within 'normal science'. Their solution requires a re-examination of assumptions and the formulation of others. The alteration in meaning given to terms, the different content given to conceptual notions, is part of this paradigm shift, the provision of the tools needed to attempt afresh the solution of unsolved problems.

The natural sciences have usually specific objectives: to produce more crops, to harden steel, to find more efficient ways of doing specific things. The social sciences have similar specific objectives at the micro level: to reduce tensions in personal relations, to find guide lines for the distribution of resources. However, the social sciences have certain objectives in addition. These are to determine the motivating forces behind natural and social sciences with which natural sciences are not concerned. Why harden steel, why reduce interpersonal tensions? The answer must be in terms of human welfare, living standards, life satisfaction, development. However, the social sciences have never had any specific guides to these goals. What is meant by improved welfare, life satisfaction and development? In the absence of any reference point, there can be no answer to these questions except ones that reflect belief systems. Once human needs are defined, then these questions can be answered by reference to them.

Most terms used by social scientists relate to motivations and goals: development, progress, peace, order, stability, welfare, security, legitimacy, conformity. None of these terms can be defined without reference to an ideology, a belief system or a set of accepted norms. As a consequence the same terms are used in many different ways. The meaning given on any occasion can be determined only by reference to the relevant code. In practice there is a high level of communication possible by the use of these terms because there is a high level of consensus; but in practice it is not high enough to ensure precision in communication. Integration is a desirable objective to some, a damaging one to others. Precision in meaning and in communication is possible only when the use of terms reflects a common belief system and, in particular, a common definition of motivation. Greater precision on human needs and a consensus about human needs would provide this. Nothing else can.

There is no such precision and there is no such consensus. Science is always faced with this problem: it is necessary to work with what we have and make the best of it until there is some improved tool. To some degree we arrive at an agreed definition of needs through constant debate on the use of terms and the meanings that can be given to them. Recent debates on the meaning of development have forced consideration of values other than economic, implying a range of needs not previously taken into account. A direct attack on the definition of needs is likely to be more rewarding, to help clarify terms and concepts more rapidly.

It would be helpful to take a case study of a major conflict, e.g. an interstate or an intercommunal conflict, and a particular example of a social problem, e.g. theft or mugging, and demonstrate how each would be tackled within the two systems of thought. These would necessarily be extensive exercises, not fitting into the framework of this study. The Centre for the Analysis of Conflict (to which reference was made in the Acknowledgments) has undertaken such studies and their conclusions are reported by Burton (1969).

By way of example, however, the alternative paradigm suggests alternative approaches to a wide variety of problems by focusing on variables that would not normally be taken into account within the power paradigm. It directs attention to the Palestinians as party principals in the Middle East conflict, seeking identity and recognition and control—a focus it took many years for Western observers and mediators to obtain. In Cyprus it directs attention to independence as a major goal, despite claims for Enosis and double-Enosis—which the UN mediator failed to perceive (United Nations (1965)). It directs attention to identity and alienation as a background for the growing practice of 'mugging' by members of minority and underprivileged groups. It directs attention to boredom and absence of role in the social system in the pathetic attempts by football fans to identify with teams and with this identity to engage in violence against others. It directs attention to the mistake of trying to make the seas open to all-comers under licence rather than to allocate national and regional areas of responsibility and control which is necessary for conservation purposes. It directs attention to reasons for violence in schools and the sense of lack of recognition and control by pupils already lacking identity in their social environment. It directs attention to the need to eliminate we–they relations in industry.

A system of thought, a set of assumptions, an approach has its own logically deduced definitions of situations and these, in turn, determine policies. Implicit in definitions and policies are the labels given to behaviour—whether it be legal or deviant, revolution or terrorism, frustration or aggression. The alternative paradigm requires to be translated into labels attaching to behaviour—and this is discussed in Chapter Nine.

CHAPTER NINE

Labelling

Labelling has been widely discussed by sociologists interested in deviant behaviour. Some adopt the view that deviant behaviour differs from other forms only in that it is so labelled (see Box (1971, pp. 11–14) for discussion). This is a logical deduction from the proposition that deviant and conforming behaviour have the same theoretical and motivational base: the difference is one of definition. What makes the individual deviant or conforming is not his personality, but the total situation in which he operates. A deviant could be the businessman at work in a society that attaches importance to achievement as the means of recognition and security or he could be the deprived person experiencing a sense of loss of identity and control. Both behaviours can be explained by reference to the same motivations, even though the behaviour of the businessman, while sometimes antisocial, can be labelled as legal and the behaviour of the underprivileged, while sometimes illegal, can be regarded as having some measure of justice on its side. Labelling appears to be a device by which distinctions can be made between deviance and conforming behaviour and between deviant and conforming persons, despite the psychological and biological commonness of human behaviour. Cressy (quoted by Box, 1971) has drawn attention to expressions that help to maintain these distinctions between deviant and normal behaviour, between the criminal and the ordinary citizen: 'Honesty is the best policy, but business is business'. 'All people steal when they get into a tight spot'. 'The use of money temporarily is borrowing not stealing'. 'Assassinations for political purposes are not murders'. 'Robbery of the rich is a means of redistribution of income'.

However, labels are in practice useful and even necessary.

The criticisms that have been made of labelling are criticisms of a theory or an approach that leads to legal—right–wrong—labels. The alternative or needs paradigm suggests a different class of labels, descriptions of behaviour that are based not on legality or social acceptability, but on explanations of behaviour.

Deviance and Norms

Throughout this study the terms 'deviance' and 'norms' have been used in the way that they are commonly employed: deviance is departure from social norms, which themselves are the recognized guides or rules that are supposed to govern behaviour.

There are difficulties associated with this use of the term social or legal 'norm'. It implies a generally agreed and observed conduct, any departure being the exception, deterred or punished by legal and social sanctions. However, in practice some norms are not generally observed, sometimes leading to changes in the articulated rules. Does this mean that when rules are widely broken they are accordingly changed, as has been the case in some countries in relation to homosexual behaviour and the taking of some kinds of drugs? If this is so, is it a general proposition that applies, for example, to theft? Shoplifting and theft by shop assistants in the United Kingdom in 1977 amounted to an estimated £500 million. Even greater in terms of amounts and numbers of persons involved were abuses (not labelled theft) such as the use for private purposes of business and office cars, office stationery, telephones and stamps; the misuse of expense accounts; the stealing of tools and 'surplus' products from employers; tax evasion and others of this nature. While no figures are available, it seems likely that the 'norm' is theft of these kinds, observed by a significant majority of the society. Though illegal, many of these forms of theft have come to be accepted as legitimized social behaviour, sometimes with the knowledge and tacit consent of employers who indulge in similar activities in evading tax and consuming the resources of the business. The extent and nature of these types of law violation vary from country to country according to structures, conventions and opportunities, but the phenomenon is universal. Do the processes that lead to homosexual behaviour and some drug-taking becoming 'norms' apply to theft?

In the alternative paradigm the term 'norm' has its statistical meaning, that is the usual behaviour, the 'mode' or most frequent. If it is necessary to convey the notion of that which societies, through their spokesmen, believe should be the common patterns of behaviour, then 'norm' is inappropriate. For these reasons it is a term that is better avoided.

Similarly, there are some obvious difficulties with the traditional legalistic concept of 'deviance'. As sociologists have recognized, it leads to arguments as to whether the law is always legitimized and just; whether interpretations and applications vary according to circumstances such as class and profession; whether only those infringements that are detected—probably a small proportion of all infringements—are illegal; whether conduct must depart significantly from the rules before attracting the label 'deviant'; and whether deviant behaviour is no different from any other behaviour except that it happens to be labelled so, at the given time, due to certain social and political circumstances.

In the alternative paradigm the reference point is 'needs'. It has been argued that needs *will* be pursued. The individual in society pursues his needs and desires to the extent that he finds this possible within the confines of his environment, his experience and knowledge of options and all other capabilities and constraints; he uses the rules common within his society and pushes against them to the extent necessary to ensure that they work in his interests; but if these rules inhibit and frustrate him to the degree that he decides they are no longer useful, then, subject to values he attaches to social relationships, he will employ methods outside the accepted rules and outside the codes he would in other circumstances wish to apply to his behaviour. He acts this way because in seeking his needs there are no options. Threat of punishment, punishment itself, isolation from society does not control his behaviour: already there has been a loss of identity, of a sense of control and of other needs that led to his particular behaviour and further loss does not constrain.

The term 'deviance', then, cannot be applied to the individual:

he is needs-orientated, he is not capable of deviating from the pursuit of 'needs'. Meaning can be given to 'deviance' in the alternative paradigm only when applied to structures, institutions, conventions, rules, laws, policies or any administrative processes that run contrary to that which is required to ensure the highest possible attainment of human societal needs. Social structures that promote discrimination or inequalities of opportunity and economic policies that create involuntary unemployment are deviant in that they frustrate the attainment of needs. For these reasons, while the term has been used throughout this study, it is a term or label that says no more than that certain behaviour of groups and authorities is incompatible with the fundamental goals and requirements of society.

Behavioural Categories

In the alternative paradigm, in place of the questions why do deviants not conform with (power differentiated) social norms and what can persuade them so to do, the questions asked are what are the features and circumstances of consensual and legitimized behaviour; what occurs in authority and interpersonal relationships when there is departure from such features and conditions; and by what processes do such features and conditions evolve. In short, one question asked is not which members of society fit social structures, but what social structures fit human needs. A second and, in practice, more important one is what are the processes by which change in structures takes place.

All behaviour is a response by an actor—an individual or a group—to the environment. Behaviour cannot be analysed without reference to the personality of the actor. Nor can behaviour be analysed in isolation from the physical setting, the institutional structures and the legal and social rules of the society in which it occurs. It is the result of interaction between the needs and interests of actors and environmental constraints (including the needs and interests of other actors).

Consequently, rather than adopt the classical-conventional approach that takes social rules as givens and concentrates on control mechanisms that seek to ensure their observance, in this analysis human needs are the givens and the concentration is on the conditions that satisfy them. Possibly the two approaches could come to the same conclusions: some changes in structures and goals are necessary along with some constraints on the actors. However, experience is that the first approach—rules and their enforcement—is not leading to the solution of problems. The second approach—human needs and their fulfilment—may reveal acceptable social goals, prescriptive policies and control processes that can be incorporated into the first approach. Given the criticisms made of conventional assumptions, given the alternatives put forward, there is no option but to approach unsolved problems from a needs position rather than from a social rules one.

It has been asserted, as the fundamental hypothesis, that all members of a society have certain needs and aspirations in common. It can be deduced that the following conditions are necessary for the total fulfilment of such needs:

(i) Society has social and cultural values that give pride of place to human needs and social policies and institutions reflect these.
(ii) All actors, people or social units have equal access to sufficient resources and have adequate initiatives, skills and abilities relevant to the pursuit of needs within the rules of society.
(iii) The opportunities and conditions necessary for the pursuit and fulfilment of needs are deemed by the actors to be adequate or the possible optimum.
(iv) Authorities assist adaptive behaviour, discourage influences which mitigate against the pursuit of needs and promote those favourable to them.

Given such actors, authorities and environmental conditions, there would be maximum satisfaction of needs and, according to the theory implied in the second paradigm, minimum conflict in inter-actor and authority relationships.

Below are examined the consequences of movement away from this ideal condition and the manner in which social conflict and behaviour that deviates from the pursuit of needs and from the rules of society occur.

(i) Society has social and cultural values that give pride of place to human needs and social policies and institutions reflect this.
The first step in moving away from this ideal condition is to

relax the assumption that societies give highest priority to the promotion of human needs. The differentiation of power through social exchange (see p. 126) leads progressively to greater inequalities in resources and opportunities, thus destroying the mutually beneficial effects that are created, in theory, by exchanges based on comparative costs. More and more people are relatively disadvantaged and many do not find an acceptable role. As disadvantaged persons they are processed through an educational and social system that fails to compensate for underprivileged conditions and, indeed, reflects such conditions, thus increasing disadvantage. Having few valued relationships in educational, social, employment spheres, being without expectations that distributive justice and needs can be attained within social structures, membership is sought in an alternative society. (For an interesting account of the way in which young people in the United Kingdom form an alternative society attached to football clubs see Marsh *et al.*, 1978.)

In a society that values achievements and acquisition, dissatisfaction increases as the differentiating process continues. Society's dominant value systems make possible monotonous work carried out in a noisy environment, in institutional conditions that destroy human dignity by the segregation of workers and staff and in an absence of purpose and participation in decisions. Even where monetary rewards are high, the real rewards of housing, educational opportunities, cultural developments, status and role are not always available. A valued relationship with authorities, in the factory or in the wider society, cannot develop. Therefore, there is no effective social control of behaviour.

On the other hand, the differentiation of power through social exchange creates an elite that influences significantly the structures, institutions and social and legal institutions and rules. If socially approved behaviour and laws are designed to protect certain interests and structures, such as property and to tolerate inequalities in educational and occupational opportunities, then actors that are in a position to take advantage of these have little incentive to break the law. Consequently, societies include actors that have different value systems according to the level of resources, opportunities and attributes possessed. The elite value systems that are written into a legal code confront the value systems of more and more actors. More and more legal controls lead to more and more complexities and defiance until authorities are rendered powerless to control behaviour.

The modern 'welfare state' is designed to give protection against the poverty and hardship that the social exchange system generates, by provision of education, health services, housing and other benefits. This has not noticeably reduced the level of social protest evidenced in behaviour that confronts law and socially acceptable behaviour. The reason is that these are not measures that directly enable people to pursue their needs, achieve an acceptable role in society and the needs of recognition and security implied in role pursuit. A more radical re-distribution of resources, a more even distribution of educational and employment opportunities, a more fundamental alteration in the we–they relationships that pervade societies and their institutions, be they capitalist or socialist, is unacceptable to elites. Nehru once said, in justification of inequalities, that India had only poverty to distribute, meaning that re-distributions would make no significant difference to the way of life of Indians generally. The same argument is used to justify the approach to development in relations between wealthy and poor states and the inequalities that exist in industrial societies. However, re-distribution has political and social consequences and helps to reduce perceived injustice. The economic argument is probably false because there is a multiplier effect that transforms a small shift in demand for luxury goods into a large increase in the availability of necessities; but this aside, re-distribution has a political consequence and helps to reduce perceived injustice and the denial of need satisfactions.

The existence of different value systems, based on perceived distributive injustices, especially in societies that attach value to achievement and acquisition, is a source of class conflict and of opposition to the social conventions and legal rules agreed to by elites. Secondary differentiation of power (see p. 127) often accompanied by confrontations with power elites, finally creates additional privileged groups that share elite values, as when trade union leaders reach a position of influence in governments; but do not remove the incentives to illegal behaviour by the remaining underprivileged. Consequently, there is a category of behaviour that confronts social conventions and legal conduct that is based on a sense of frustration, even hopelessness, in the face of the obstacles to be encountered in the pursuit of needs. This accounts for the emergence of alternative societies, fringe groups, that have their own agreed rules that are observed and policed by the social communications inherent in any society. It accounts for the bulk of behaviour usually defined as 'deviant'. Galtung (1969) has used the term 'structural violence' to describe the structural conditions that lead to this type of behaviour (see p. 69). In the way he used this term it could mean anything anyone happened to disagree with. In this particular context it has a precise meaning: it refers to conditions in which individuals and groups cannot attain human needs, at least within the pattern of conventional behaviour dictated by society. In Gurr's analysis (1976) it is this kind of behaviour that is a warning of revolt and perhaps of revolution, certainly of fundamental change which could lead to revolt or revolution if elites are not prepared to adopt and to encourage the adaptive policies and changes that appear to be required (see p. 138). The label that is appropriate is one that attaches no blame either to the actors or to the elites in the system, focuses on the structure that is found to be frustrating, yet describes the behaviour of those who are frustrated. The label needs to embrace both the environmental conditions and the behaviour these conditions provoke in the context of need fulfilment. 'Need fulfilment' behaviour is not appropriate because all behaviour is of this type. It is need fulfilment behaviour that is structurally frustrated, causing the actor to indulge in behaviour he would in other circumstances not adopt. It was not the preferred behaviour of Iceland in the 'Cod War' to endanger the lives of English fishermen, nor was violence the preferred behaviour of the founders of the IRA in Northern Ireland. Nor is it the preferred behaviour of muggers, thieves, hijackers, terrorists and revolutionaries. It is the behaviour of persons and groups who live in societies in which needs are not the prime goal and are not deliberately provided for in the institutions and processes of the society. It is behaviour that results from deviant societies. It is symptomatic behaviour. The term that best fits these requirements and most conforms with conventional usage is 'rebellious behaviour'.

When such behaviour at the individual level becomes wide-spread, there are strong tendencies to find a solution to the needs problem by forming fringe or alternative societies, gangs, minority cultures, prison societies, football cults, terror groups, all of which are symptoms of alienation. This is further evidence that needs *will* be satisfied for in the alternative societies relationships are valued and a foundation for individual satisfaction within a condition of social harmony is provided. Violence at the individual level is a first symptom of social failure to provide opportunities for development; group activity is an escalation of this symptom, leading in some circumstances to wider disruption and unrest. Such group activity is better termed 'alienation behaviour'.

(ii) All actors, people or social units have equal access to sufficient resources and have adequate initiatives, skills and abilities relevant to the pursuit of needs within the rules of society.

The next step in moving away from the ideal situation is to relax the assumption of sufficient individual resources, initiatives and skills and to assume a normal distribution of these attributes. By normal is meant a smooth distribution about the average, resulting in some actors with some insufficient attributes. The statistically average actor finds the total environment conducive to the satisfaction of his needs; around him there are those that are within narrow limits more or less satisfied. In practice there is not an actual average actor as no one actor is likely to have all attributes at an average level. In practice, therefore, all actors have some high and some low need satisfactions. Overall each is satisfied to a greater or lesser degree. The ideal condition, in which total actor fulfilment is the relevant consideration, gives way to something less than this.

It has already been argued that values attached to relationships between authorities and subjects and values attached to interpersonal relationships generally are a controlling element in societies. In this near-ideal type of consensual society, in which all actors have attributes within the range of a normal distribution, limited differences in satisfaction do not lead to deviant behaviour because values attached to relationships are sufficient to constrain. There would still be a condition of social harmony despite actor differences in abilities and skills and in degrees of satisfaction. In the longer term, each actor can gain most—i.e. obtain the greatest average satisfactions—by working within the division of labour of society. Given mobility of labour, communication and other conditions necessary to exchange, actor A gains most by concentrating on those outputs in which it is most efficient and exchanging for the output of others, even though, relatively, A is more efficient than B in achieving the outputs of B. Logically this means that there is a valued role for every member of this society, no matter how relatively efficient or inefficient some are in achieving outputs required by others. Actor differences provide functional integration and harmony—subject to the important proviso noted on p. 129 about the social or status consequences of specialization.

Assume now that the distribution of resources and attributes is skewed: that there are some actors possessing high levels, but many are relatively poorly equipped. In such a society there is a higher proportion of disadvantaged actors: those that cannot find a role, that are inadequate in terms of output by reason of an inadequate share of resources, initiative, skills and other attributes. The more skewed the distribution, the greater the proportion of inadequate actors. As societies become more specialized and more highly competitive, the proportion of inadequate actors increases.

Inadequacy alone is not a necessary cause of extra-social behaviour: relationship values and internationalized social constraints can, even in these circumstances, control the interaction between needs and behaviour. However, because of a variety of influences—educational, occupational and environmental—the inadequate actor is likely to lack opportunities that give security and valued relationships that exercise constraints. The person who is inadequate relative to the demands made on him in pursuing human needs and who is devoid of the constraints of relationships, is prone to seek satisfaction of needs outside the conventions and rules of society: 'inadequacy behaviour'. This is to be distinguished from the special case of 'abnormal behaviour' due to physical and mental maladjustments, such that society can offer no role and such that the satisfaction of human needs like recognition and stimulation is less relevant.

(iii) The opportunities and conditions necessary for the pursuit and fulfilment of needs are deemed by the actors to be adequate or the possible optimum.

The third condition of an ideal state is adequate opportunities. By adequate opportunities is meant a condition in which environmental constraints do not present actors with a situation in which there is an unreasonable and unacceptable gap between expectations and aspirations, on the one hand, and realizations on the other. More precisely this means that the actors are not frustrated by social norms and expectations, by cultural sanctions, by institutional constraints and obligations, by over-burdensome competitive conditions, by inadequate participatory opportunities and by lack of opportunities for identification and isolation.

Now relax the assumption that there are adequate outlets for the fulfilment of needs and aspirations. Complex industrial societies reduce almost to extinction for the majority of actors any sense of recognition or role and any stimulus. High levels of frustration and boredom are a consequence and this leads to violence against person and property, to social withdrawal, drug addiction and related forms of escape. Potentialities are not developed and a poor self-image results: 'frustration behaviour'.

There is, also, behaviour that is damaging to the welfare and development of other members of society, yet defined to be within the legal framework, e.g. certain means of acquisition and manipulation of resources and finance. Cultural and social constraints, backed by relationship constraints, influence but do not always control this form of antisocial behaviour. Such behaviour is within the law because legal codes reflect the interests and practices of an achieving society. Associated with this behaviour is excitement, challenge, resourcefulness and courage—it is an alternative to frustration, boredom and underachievement resulting from lack of opportunities, but with similar origins.

There are, also, those who experience the same frustrations and set out to promote change, to ensure adequate opportunities for others and who experience stimulation and excitement in the process. They are prepared to confront authorities, to defy the conventions of society and even to risk legal sanctions in their endeavours. It is they who organize reforms, revolt and revolutions: 'reformist behaviour'.

There are, therefore, three possible responses to an under-stimulating society: withdrawal, excitement on the fringes of legality and reformist or revolutionary activities within and outside the law. Which is chosen probably depends on personalities and person value systems. All are in their own way evidence of social structures and institutions that are failing to satisfy demands for stimulus and recognition.

> *(iv) Authorities assist adaptive behaviour, discourage influences which mitigate against the pursuit of needs and promote those favourable to them.*

Once this condition is relaxed, in addition to those above, the problem of unsolved problems is defined. Societies are man-made. Differentiation of power leads to certain structural conditions that in turn cause problems; but there are always opportunities to offset these, to arrange inputs that lead to adaptive responses to change that ensure that the conditions listed above as ideal are pursued with every policy decision. However, this does not happen in practice. The reason is that societies are not aware of social goals other than those defined by ideologies and belief systems. Navigation points are found only by experience, by failure, by conflict—by which time role defence is institutionalized. The priority given to the defence of institutions, structures, privileges, the 'social good' and the 'national interest' over human societal needs, without the satisfaction of which there cannot be a harmonious society, is a sufficient explanation of most social and political problems yet to be solved. The individual is never deviant, using this term in the sense that deviance is behaviour that contradicts the pursuit of human needs. He pursues them by one means or another in all circumstances. Authorities are deviant in this sense— authorities at all social levels. The term 'deviant behaviour' is properly applied only to the systemic process of decision-making (not to decision-makers) that fails to give pride of place to human societal needs and fails to arrange inputs that offset any trends or tendencies in social evolution that mitigate against the pursuit by the individual of such needs.

There have been isolated above several types of behaviour

arising out of need fulfilment. Since this is merely labelling, it is not particularly helpful to differentiate such types. They are no more than 'ideal' or pure types: in practice there are many combinations of needs to be satisfied and, therefore, many combinations of these behavioural types. However, such a treatment does help to make the point that behaviour that creates social and political problems is explicable within the same analytical framework as any other behaviour: in all cases it is need fulfilment. These categories point to the desirability of structural changes rather than deterrence and punishment and, therefore, raise the core issue of means of change. Labelling in the traditional paradigm focuses on deviance from social norms and, therefore, on law and order and enforcement. This is attacking the symptom of problems and not their cause. The onus of responsibility for change, for solving problems, is not on elites, on authorities or on members of societies as persons. It is on all to adopt decision-making processes that are not orientated towards finding guilt and fault; but towards problem-solving processes. Process, not behaviour, is the objective of scientific concern because it is through process that behaviour is directed to solving problems. If there is any justification for labelling it is to emphasize that problems can be solved only by accepting people as they are, their needs and aspirations, to construct societies that meet these needs and to do this by processes that eliminate paternalism, ideologies, belief systems and cultural values and which involve those who are alleged to be the source of the problems to be solved. In practice, as is indicated in Chapter Ten, this is beginning to happen: experience and failure are leading civilizations to accept participatory problem-solving in the place of authoritative regulation and sanctions. The role of science is not to suggest solutions to problems, policies or prescriptions; it is to shorten the time lag between experience and practice by pointing out what is happening and why. Labelling, that reflects theory and explanation of behaviour, is a pointer to policy in this respect.

CHAPTER TEN

Process

SYSTEM LEVELS

This book is about human aspirations and values, individual underdevelopment, protest, the erosion of certain types of authority, deviant policies and role defence at all social levels from the domestic to the international and about the processes by which the associated problems can be resolved. It seeks to provide a framework, a set of propositions, procedures, in the framework of which those dealing with research, policy-making and administration can apply their specialized knowledge and skills.

It has been written as an extension of the special interest of the author—international relations. Once it was thought that such relationships were a special case, different from social and political relations within states. Some writers have made a distinction between international *societies* and national *communities*, the former being anarchic and lacking any central authority, the later being relatively orderly under the direction of governments having a monopoly of power. The studies of international relations and international law have endeavoured to draw on the domestic model, attempts have been made to create international authorities such as the League of Nations and the United Nations and to create a framework of international law and order on the domestic model of the state. This endeavour has failed except to the degree that international functional institutions have promoted order. Did it fail because interstate relations are different from domestic relationships and cannot be subjected to a supranational authority? Or did it fail because the domestic model is an imaginary one: that authority with effective coercive powers is little more existent there than in interstate relations? No statistical evidence is possible; but it could reasonably be argued that the international system is as orderly as the domestic, where the erosion of authority, leading to conflict and violence on a wide scale, is commonplace.

To the extent that this is so, the student of international relations may have something to contribute to the analysis of handling of domestic problems. Rather than start with a model of centralized 'law and order' and examine departures from it, it may be more rewarding to make an analysis based on a model of individualism and the individual optimization of needs. Rejecting, at both international and domestic levels, the ideal or ideology of law and order and normative solutions to authority problems, leaves us with no ready-made remedies for any undesirable situation, such as are provided within a law and order, coercive framework. However, in so doing we do not reject processes by which solutions are found. It has been argued that these processes are the same whatever the social or political level. For these reasons it it not surprising that there have been many references to international relations as a means of focusing on problems within societies: in many ways behaviour in the interstate scene is illuminating because we do not suffer in respect of it the distortions created by a law and order ideology. Through international relations a more realistic perspective of behaviour within societies can be obtained.

A methodological or philosophical issue is raised here that may have troubled the reader: what is the justification for applying theory developed at one systems level to problems occurring at others? Earlier it was argued that behaviour at all system levels was subject to analysis in the same theoretical framework (p. 17). Increasing numbers of scholars are finding it necessary to generalize across system levels as problem areas, rather than disciplines, become their focus: conflict, integration, rebellion. LeVine and Campbell dealt with this issue when they were considering ethnocentrism as the basis of conflict and group behaviour.

> Our point of view may be epitomized by the phrase *non-reductive congruence*. It is assumed that there are delineable multiple levels of analysis at which the collation of

empirical regularities and the proposing of laws might take place. . . . But it is also our position that theories at any one level will have inexorable implications for the other levels. In the asymptotic perfection of the theories, there will be a *congruence* among theories, so that the 'true' theories at any one level have no implications contradictory of the 'true' theories at any other level. (LeVine and Campbell, 1972, pp. 26–7)

THE ACKNOWLEDGMENT OF PROBLEMS

Most people are greatly inhibited in seeking an alternative approach to social and political problems. We accept and follow changes in fashion and living styles, we have little difficulty in thinking about technological problems and accommodating discovery, for example, in medicine and in communications. However, solving a problem in social and political areas affects us more directly—our roles, philosophies, values and interests. The pattern of thought which emerges from this study is challenging: it points to systems and policies rather than to people as being deviant and has far-reaching intellectual and policy consequences. It may be difficult to come to terms with it; but it does appear to answer some questions and provide an approach to problems that have not been answered or solved within the conventional system of thought.

Furthermore, our preference is sometimes not to solve problems, even though technically this may be possible. For example, some forms of antisocial behaviour and many problems of social concern, e.g. unemployment, could probably be dealt with effectively by altered allocations of resources—by providing more housing, education and jobs. There would, however, be a cost over and above the financial one: the cost of changing society. When faced with this cost, decision-makers, reflecting the interests of those who are articulate in society, find it easier to opt for repression as the means of dealing with protest behaviour and for unemployment relief to deal with unemployment. (For an appreciation of the social costs of unemployment see Green, 1977.)

It is particularly difficult to resist political pressures and vested interests when there are no clear policy alternatives.

Ruling elites are not devoid of ideals and values even though they may have positions of privilege to defend; but they tend not to consider alternative assumptions and policies unless the alternatives presented seem to solve problems reliably. It is as well that there is a degree of caution, otherwise trial and error and fashions in ideas would dominate. It is not sufficient to argue that the present is unsatisfactory: alternatives need to be explicit and to be shown to be practical. In considering social problems we need to discover under what conditions and by what processes changes in policies and restructuring of institutions can take place so as to achieve reliably agreed goals. Then pressures and interest can be resisted.

The growing acknowledgment that there are unsolved problems is in itself cause for elation: this is taking the first step in problem-solving. Moreover, the condition that creates the problem—challenges to non-legitimized authority and to legal norms—can also be welcomed. Protest behaviour is a symptom of the need for change and, also, a dynamic element in social development. While it creates problems it can be exploited as a resource. Complex industrial societies are young. The interaction between people and modern industrial society is new and intellectual curiosity is just being stimulated. How to harness dissent to the developments societies seek is a problem and problem-solving is a scientific endeavour. The despair reflected in the writings of some scholars and their complacent acceptance that little can be discovered in the way of solutions is a despair that arises out of failure and the failure arises out of inadequate methodological tools. The way in which these have developed over long periods of time has been recorded by Boulding (1956), and he has differentiated eleven levels of theoretical discourse, attributing to each a model. In so doing he has given a synoptic history of thought or history of how we have moved with the help of models from simple problem-solving to complex and abstract problems. He has listed frameworks, clockworks, thermostats, self-maintaining structures, plants, animals, humans, social organizations and abstract systems. There are problems of a simple kind that can be solved within the intellectual limits represented by clockworks and balances, others require the more complex framework of systems that respond to the environment. It is not possible to solve complex problems within a framework that is too restricted. International relations cannot be analysed sensibly by reference to 'balances'—harping back to the simple conceptual notions that relate to clocks. Indeed, the problem area of social organization requires the symbolic image of 'system'. If problems seem not to be solvable, if there are no 'conclusions' to be drawn from analysis, then the probability is that the models, conceptual notions and methodologies employed have not been appropriate to the level of complexity of the problems.

A REFERENCE POINT: GOALS

Why solve problems? One value judgment must be made: that human civilizations are worth preserving. Having made that one judgment the question is, how? This is not a question that can be answered scientifically on the basis of value judgments. If the objective is the preservation of social organization, then it is a false start to restate it by reference to the preservation or promotion of some particular form of social organization. There is a general problem: how to preserve harmonious social relationships. How to preserve capitalism, socialism, democracy, parliamentary institutions, rights of opposition, human rights and freedoms. These are subsequent questions that are relevant only when it has been discovered what is required to preserve societies, all types of societies. There is a probability that when that discovery is made these other questions will be answered more readily.

For this reason there is a need for a reference point that has nothing whatsoever to do with ideologies, belief systems or social goals other than the goal of persistent harmonious social organization. What are the conditions required to ensure a social organization that does not have built-in self-destructive elements? Societies require resources of many kinds and a reasonably conducive physical environment. These exist. The problem area is in relation to the social and human requirements of societies.

This area falls within the wide field of knowledge and investigation designated as sociobiology. Sociobiologists and anthropologists can trace, as one would expect, the origins of societies back to most primitive organisms. There must, obviously, be organizational reasons why, in changing circumstances, some species have survived while others have become extinct. Human societies are different from others to a significant degree in that they have the intellectual ability to discern elements in the normal social and evolutionary process that could be destructive or self-defeating and take steps to offset them. However, they can do this only if there is an awareness and a valid analysis of likely problems. Ideologies do not necessarily provide this awareness or analysis. The question, how to detect self-destructive elements, is a scientific one and has a scientific answer. Sociobiology and associated studies seem to be pointing strongly to certain universal human needs that must be satisfied if social organizations are to survive without high levels of violence which, in conditions of advanced technology, could lead to their destruction.

As has been argued on p. 75 there is little precise knowledge and less general agreement on what these needs are. This is not as important as critics of such an approach would suggest. The deduced hypothesis that there are needs provides a reference point, even though their precise nature may not yet be known. That they relate to stimulus, recognition, security, identity is not in doubt: the disagreements occur when these broad terms are operationally defined for purposes of policy-making. This is not a reason for not using needs as a reference point: there will not be agreed operational definitions until there is a wide experience in their use. Some of the ordinary processes of trial and error, recorded falsifications, are part of the discovery and learning process. The important scientific requirement is that the policies so tested are based on interpretations of needs and not on ideologies and belief systems that have no foundation other than prejudice, personal interests and value systems.

The needs to which reference has been made are social and non-material: they relate to being, not having: the satisfaction of material wants, even to a high level, does not necessarily promote human needs. The traditional emphasis has been on having a more even distribution of resources and the good life. The attraction among intellectuals to socialism in the post-war period reflected a belief that a better distribution of resources, implying control of resources by 'the state', would solve social problems. The possibility that control by 'the state' would destroy a sense of participation, control and stimulus was not adequately considered because the needs of being were subordinate to the basic requirements of having. In industrial disputes and generally in a society which is plagued by theft and personal violence, the assumption traditionally made is that the motivation of behaviour is a material goal, because this is the observed and articulated goal. The unobserved and unarticulated motivations, to which needs and expectations draw attention, are likely to be those non-material needs that must be satisfied if protest behaviour and social unrest are to be avoided.

The needs factor creates a major dilemma in contemporary times in relation to political and economic structures. Socialism can create distributive justice, but is likely to deny identity, control and stimulus. Capitalism provides opportunities for some for recognition, control and stimulus and in doing so creates distributive injustices that the state has to modify. Both sides of the political divide recognize this dilemma and both sides find it difficult to discover the changes that would retain the advantages of present structures and eliminate the disadvantages. The historical process is a search, not for a structural 'ism', but for one that concentrates on processes by which structures can change and evolve in the quest for the fulfilment of needs: process and needs are the ingredients of the ideal 'ism'.

THE PROBLEM OF CHANGE

While sociobiologists and other behavioural scientists have pointed in the direction of human societal needs as a reference, they have not, as yet, been greatly helpful in regard to processes of change. The current sociological literature is predominantly concerned with power as the organizing force in society, with problems of socialization, coercion and compliance, reflecting a law and order or institutional approach to social problems rather than a problem-solving one. There is, thus, a logical inconsistency: needs are more and more widely perceived as the navigation point of policy, but the defence of social institutions and authority still takes priority. Ways are explored of inducing the individual to conform and explanations are found that explain why he does not, such as those appearing in the studies of one-parent families, family break-ups, low intelligence, only children and drug addiction. There is a meagre literature on processes of structural and institutional change by which social and political environments can be made more conducive to harmonious behaviour. There seems to be a widespread acceptance that: 'The transfer of authority may be viewed as a process moving through a series of changes in the balance of power between insurgents and incumbents' (Janos, 1964, p. 137). Bennis complains, justifiably:

> Unfortunately, no viable theory of social change has been established. Indeed, it is a curious fact about present theories that they are strangely silent on matters of *directing* and *implementing* change. What I particularly object to ... is that they tend to explain the dynamic interactions of a system without providing one clue to the identification of strategic leverages for alteration. They are suitable for observers of social change, not for practitioners. They are theories of *change*, and not theories of *changing*. (Bennis, 1970, p. 64)

Once there is any question of power as the organizing force in society and attention is drawn to problems of coercion and compliance, some important re-thinking of many traditional notions is required. The relationship of compliance to law is clear and unavoidable. If problems of compliance reveal the need for changes in thinking about responses to authority, then they no less reveal the need for changes in thinking about the processes of law. The traditional argument is that the function of law in any society is to enable its members to calculate the consequences of their conduct. Thus, it has been argued, law controls behaviour. However this is true only to the extent that there is compliance. Experience shows that this is not necessarily the case.

One reason why there is resistance to authorities is that legal norms tend to reflect the interest and cultures of elites, values of elites, and related cultural norms and is administered accordingly. White-collar crime carries lighter penalties and crime by white-collar workers is, according to statistical surveys, less frequently punished. (Merton (1957, p. 144) has a discussion of 'White-collar crime' and reference material relevant to this phenomenon.) However, another reason, to which not sufficient attention has been given, is that there is a gap between law and compliance that is inexorable. A trivial crime, inviting even severe penalties, will not necessarily be prevented by legal processes. Sites comments:

> If an act is labelled deviant, it merely means that the person or group that does the labelling has more control over the situation than does the individual or group committing the act so labelled. It does not mean that those who are labelled deviant have no control in the situation. The very fact of the labelling response and the necessity of carrying out whatever action is deemed necessary ... forces the 'non-deviant' individual or group to behave in certain ways.

He instanced activities of the police during a riot by young people in Chicago in 1968 when the police, having labelled the young people as deviant (which others did not), were thus 'forced' to take certain action. 'Some observers made the case at the time that the young people were in complete control, for the police did just what they wanted them to do in order to expose them as "brutal pigs"' (Sites, 1973, p. 112).

Failure to appreciate the limitations of control leads to more law and more penalties as law fails, without necessarily reducing crime. Just administration becomes more difficult because of the increased complexities. The tendency persists to perceive some behaviour by members of minority ethnic groups as punishable and the same behaviour by respected citizens as a minor breach. The local administrator, be he the policeman or the judge, is given more and not less discretion, the more detailed and specific the law is: the more particularized law is, the less relevant it is to breaches that do not fit exactly into the specifications. One lawyer has concluded, after examining the situation empirically, that: 'the more a legislator specifies the terms of law to an administrator, the less predictable the administration of the law must become' (Pepinsky, 1976, p. 13). Elsewhere he asserts: 'the pattern of popular response dictated by the form and substance of the written criminal law in the United States is a necessary and conceivably sufficient condition for the growth of crime rates in the American social system' (Pepinsky, 1976, p. 6). Less written law and more problem-solving in the total context of the criminal behaviour is his recommendation.

These observations about conditions that apply in the most mature of social and political systems draw attention to the conclusion that legitimacy by itself is not a sufficient test of leadership. Legitimized leadership that reflects the wishes of those over whom authority is exercised does not necessarily reflect their interests and the future interests of society. Adaptive leadership is more than, though not inconsistent with, legitimized leadership. Leadership is more than transforming needs into wants: it is injecting an input into social relationships of knowledge and of planning. Herein lies the political problem of decision: who is to decide what is in the interests of individuals and societies, how can it be ensured that leadership is making decisions in the interests of society rather than in the narrow interests of elites? Without some navigation point, without some objectively determined goals, without some guides of policy that transcend ideology and interest, there can be no such assurance. It is specified human needs that provide this guide and this standard against which leadership performance can be measured.

One such need is participation by parties involved in a relationship in the defining of their problems and in the application of means to attain their goals. Leadership is, therefore, required to inject, also, an input of processes of change into social relationships. Indeed, it could reasonably be argued that processes of change are more important as navigation points than needs in that it is through these processes that situations are defined and problems are solved: processes reveal needs. The Sites list of needs, unlike the lists offered by biologists, are derived from observations, from the analysis of many situations at all social levels. Processes of resolving conflicts, processes of solving problems that are successful, reveal human needs and patterns of behaviour. It is not for leadership to determine and interpret needs: it is for leadership to provide the means by which problems are solved.

THE SEARCH FOR A THEORY

In prescriptive terms the search is for a theory, a set of givens, that have a universal application, on the basis of which policies can be formulated and reliably achieve their objectives. It is a theory that is sought, not an ideology. The difference is that the former is, first, based on propositions that can be generalized across cultures and times and, second, is subject to verification and falsification; while the latter is, first, based on culture, class or value systems and certain forms of political and social structures and, second, is not subject to change.

The theory relevant to social control is one concerned with relationships with authority and, therefore, with the needs of those relating to authority and with the nature of authority. To arrive at such a theory, to understand relationships and the nature of legitimized authorities, a reference point is required and the only one that is logically relevant to a behavioural analysis of social and political problems is one that relates to persons. Reference points that relate to institutions and structures, their maintenance and organization, are relevant only to an authoritative and coercive approach to the settlement of problems.

The sources of social and political problems fall into three categories: those concerning the needs and nature of people, their environment and the nature of authority. First, there is a continuing struggle by the individual in society to have recognized and to achieve his needs and desires. Second, this struggle takes place in an increasingly complex and, in many ways, unfavourable environment: increasing numbers of interdependent societies; increasing density of populations within each; increasing interaction among them; increasing multi-ethnic societies; the strains of modernization and population movements towards crowded urban centres; technological changes that create boredom at work; growing complexities in the job of living; increasingly centralized and ever more distant authorities and institutions. There being too many roles to enact, too many and conflicting loyalties and obligations, too many incompatibilities between social expectations and actual opportunities in an achieving society, the level of strain, of tension and of frustration becomes unacceptable. Either it invites opting out, by surrender to authority in a large organization or a prison, by freedom from obligations in a hippy colony, or it gives rise to interpersonal and intergroup tension and ultimately to violence against political authorities and political and social institutions. The ordinary man's promotion from slavery, to a role under feudalism, to a citizenship in a participatory democracy, has been a treadmill experience—as opportunities for individual fulfilment have increased with improved living standards, so have social complexities and obligations. From the point of view of human needs the ordinary man may have stood still or even suffered deprivation in this struggle to achieve happiness and development in an increasingly more complex environment. Third, there is the response, constructive, defensive or repressive, of authorities and elites to demands made on them for significant political and social change, for greater progress in solving increasingly complex problems, for an accelerated rate of attainment of human needs and desires, for a sharing of authoritative roles and for a greater measure of egalitarianism within and between nations.

There are only two means by which situations that arise out of this interaction between people, environment and authorities can be handled: by the use of power to coerce behaviour or by resolving conflictual interests and attitudes. It follows that one must adopt one of two perspectives when analysing interactions between people, environment and authorities. Either:

(i) Societies have evolved and will continue to evolve from a primitive tribal condition to their present form of centralized authorities as a result of decision-making feedback processes, conducted by the relatively powerful, as individuals and groups each seek their own immediate and long-term interests. Roles of authority and power have emerged which reflect racial and class interests and elite values have been promoted and partly internalized into social, political and economic norms. Frequently, human needs and desires have been denied so as to preserve institutions from change. The essential point of this position is that even though problems were not being solved and societies were seen to be maladaptive and even self-destructive in many ways, these structures would still be preserved in the interests of elites who hold power;

or:

(ii) Societies have evolved to their present stage, in which they are experiencing self-defeating consequences of decision-making at all levels as is in evidence in law and order problems;

but they possess and are beginning to employ increased knowledge of human needs and interests. Communication and organization are more and more horizontal (i.e. among social equals and interest groups) which offsets elite power; adaptive processes are coming to be recognized even in the short-term as necessary for the survival of societies. More knowledge about the bases of social relationships and about problem-solving would hasten these developments as they would demonstrate to elites and to people generally that the pursuit of human needs and interests reflected in adaptive policies was also in their interests.

Certain propositions emerge from each perspective:

(a) Power and arbitration techniques employed in the handling of social problems are those that are most relevant to maintaining social organization. They succeed by reason of the realities of power politics and the enforcement of associated legal norms; or:

(b) Problem-solving techniques, which involve participation and seek acceptable outcomes, resolve social problems, even in cases where there are class and role interests to protect.

From each of these perspectives it is possible to arrive at some general conclusions regarding social and political problems: they will be settled by power or not at all or they will be resolved by adjustment to needs by altered conditions. In this study it has been argued, first, that the power or 'political realist' theory of behaviour is inadequate as an explanation of human affairs and that the above proposition (a) is false. This has been done by examining the assumptions that underlie the theory and by reference to events unexplained by it.

A selection of classical and traditional notions have been discussed that seem to be reflected in consensual thinking and seem to explain contemporary policy approaches to authority problems now followed in most societies and in the international system. There can be argument concerning and varying interpretations of each; but their validity as a set of assumptions is reasonably questioned merely by setting down such alternatives and modifications. There is reason to believe that some widely held notions of law and order, of authority relationships and of political and social theory, may be quite inconsistent with human behaviour and with experienced events. The policies based on them are likely, therefore, to be self-defeating. These are notions that have emerged over time as societies have developed, they are notions based on experience, on interests and values, on ideologies and belief systems. None of these bases is necessarily reliable. Experience cannot be assumed to provide a foundation for a stable and individually fulfilling society unless we are prepared to assume that whatever happens to evolve in a society is not only inevitable and 'natural', but also in the best interests of it and its members. The troubling possibility is that structures and rules that have so developed over time by power differentiation and socialization may have built-in to them self-destructive consequences, i.e. inherent elements that make societies unstable and destructive of its members. This could be a part of the 'natural' process of evolution.

The conventional assumptions taken together form a general theory of behaviour which, for convenience, we have termed 'power theory'. It is essentially a theory of natural law, relating to survival of the fittest and rights conferred by reason of power. The definition of power need not concern us: it is given a variety of meanings. For our purposes it is the ability to persuade or force behaviour or, more broadly, the ability not to have to adjust to others, the ability to force the burden of adjustment on to others. The power of authorities is their ability to ensure conforming behaviour and the ability not to have to alter the codes and processes of society. If power is available this is the most straightforward and direct means of dealing with a social problem. Experience is, however, that it may not be the most effective means in the long term: it may be self-defeating by generating resistance. Power in a closed system, such as a mechanical system, can be exercised with precision and certainty to bring about a result. In an open system, such as the human or social system, the consequences are rarely predictable. Usually when some specific behaviour is prevented or enforced, other non-conforming behaviour takes place.

This study has elaborated, second, the needs and problem-solving perspective of behaviour and some evidence that it offers an approach with greater explanatory and prescriptive potential. It points towards a different theory of behaviour, one that does not deny the realities of power, but one which encompasses elements that limit the effectiveness of power. It is a general theory that no less accepts certain 'natural' elements, in particular human needs. It hypotheses as part of the 'natural' or genetic process some deliberate inputs into social organization designed to offset those influences that are the central core of power theory. In short, the alternative appears to be the negation of power theories because of the hypothesis that power elements are constrained by greater societal influences, no less 'natural', namely, the satisfaction of human needs.

Finding the solution to a problem is a more complex process than envisaged within a power framework. It involves an accurate analysis of the total situation, knowledge of the reasons for social behaviour, probably altered attitudes and, perhaps, changed environmental conditions. The processes are not those adversary ones that characterize traditional institutions, involving debate and decisions by majorities. Problem-solving processes exclude fault, 'norms', precedents, bargaining, voting and other techniques associated with zero-sum relationships and rest on processes relevant to the search for positive sum outcomes. What has been argued is that the first perspective—while probably realistic within the framework of many political and social structures at present known to us and within the limitations of our present knowledge of control mechanisms—does not sufficiently take into account some longer-term trends that have emerged, some new thinking that is taking place and some inventive possibilities that are already being explored and applied in societies and social relationships.

What emerges is a theory of behaviour which is in sharp contradiction to beliefs on which authority has traditionally been based—in the home, in the school, in industry, in respect of public order, in national and international affairs generally—i.e. that there are certain conventional norms that must be observed by individuals and groups and enforced by the relevant authorities. By contrast, what emerges is the individual and group pursuit, at all these social levels, of needs and interests that no set of enforced rules or institutional framework can permanently frustrate save at the cost of social disintegration; consistent with this, a requirement at each of these levels of leadership of a kind that creates structures that make possible this pursuit; and the view that the only source of influence on which authorities at each of these levels can rely is the value attached to relationships with authorities that arises out of such leadership.

Protest behaviour—legal, antisocial and all forms—emerges as the symptom of a significant gap between human needs and expectations, on the one hand, and opportunities within the institutional structure for satisfying these, on the other.

It is a symptom of this gap because the deviant or antisocial act need bear little relationship to the structural situation that led to it: the actor—an individual or a group—may not know what changes are possible or required. He merely seeks fulfilment in the conditions as they are perceived. 'Deviance'—to use the traditional term—is merely a warning that a gap is being experienced between personal or group need fulfilment and that which seems possible. In some cases the lack of fulfilment may be due to lack of awareness of options open and the lack of information, requiring a minor institutional alteration; in others it will be due to circumstances outside the immediate control even of authorities, e.g. unemployment, lack of resources, inadequate educational opportunities, class and race prejudice. The protest act will not demonstrate how these structural problems can be overcome.

On one side of the gap are human needs and expectations. Human needs will be pursued. In an acquiring and achieving society, achievement will also be pursued because recognition and identity relate in part to social expectations. It is in this way that values and wants are associated with needs: the need is recognition, the values and wants are one means of achieving it in some circumstances. On the other side of the gap are opportunities that relate to the interests and capabilities of the person or group. A markedly inegalitarian system or one that lacks distributive justice, is unlikely to make possible the satisfaction of needs and expectations. Protest behaviour occurs when the gap is behaviourally significant. Significance is a function of the size of the gap and, also, of a tolerance factor in behaviour. The extent to which, in particular cases, a gap can be experienced without protest behaviour occurring, relates in part to processes of socialization and processes of law, but far more to values attached to relationships. The probability is that those who are most deprived of needs satisfaction are also those most deprived of valued relationships that would induce conforming behaviour. Indeed, any valued relationships that do exist are likely to be with others who experience the same deprivation and who are apt themselves to be alienated.

Because needs require reciprocal relationships, because values are attached to relationships and because these become controlling influences that over-ride coercive constraints, the convenient term for this general theory can be termed 'relationship theory'. The alternative thesis is that:

(i)   there are certain human needs and desires that are specific and universal;

(ii)   these *will* be satisfied, even at the cost of social disruption and personal disorientation;

(iii) some structures and institutions that have evolved over time, as a result of differentiation of power and of socialization, do not necessarily, either in the short or the long-term, reflect these needs and desires and frequently frustrate them;

(iv)   disruptive behaviour is the consequence of interaction between the pursuit of human needs and the institutional framework created by power differentiation;

(v)   in the interests of social organization and to avoid destructive behaviour there is a call for a deliberate or conscious input by authorities designed to create conditions conducive to fulfilment of human needs;

(vi)   such an input at the human level is consistent with genetic inputs at other levels that are described as adaptive behaviour;

(vii) the nature of this input is determined not by ideology or belief systems, but by reference to such adaptive processes as empirically appear to be required of social organizations that survive;

(viii) the changes required in societies as a result of such an input involve adaptations by power elites and, therefore, call for problem-solving processes that ensure behaviour at the individual and group levels that accords with the adaptive needs of society;

(ix)   the application of problem-solving processes assumes rational behaviour; but problem-solving processes themselves avoid bargaining and power confrontations and contribute to rational behaviour; and

(x)   values attached to relationships provide the control mechanisms that lead to an acceptance of these processes.

'Relationship theory', however, is not adequate as a causal description: relationship is a control mechanism. The ultimate reason for social and political problems is change and adjustment to change: it relates to the dynamics of social organization. In so far as a general theory is useful, unsolved social and political problems could reasonably be regarded as a function of altering relationships. Gurr, in bringing together the findings of his colleagues who examined the history of crime in several cities, observes: 'A recurrent issue of conflict has been the demands of rising classes for a greater share of goods and power; but open combat over these and other issues has erupted at different times, displaying different forms and intensities, and bringing varied consequences' (Gurr *et al.*, 1977, p. 619).

This observation can apply to all system levels and, therefore, to all crime, from civil disorder, to terrorism, to communal, to interstate conflict. It is far from certain that East–West tension and conflict is, as popularly thought, a function of ideological differences. It could be that the significant source of tension among great powers may be their greatness and, in particular, their relative stages of growth to greatness. All great powers are or have been expansionist—expansion is a necessary prerequisite to greatness. Industrial, trade, communications, and diplomatic expansion are inevitable features of growth. Rome, the United Kingdom, Japan, the United States and the Soviet Union have gone through stages of growth that alter the relative pecking order in international relations. Probably China will also. It is not difficult to hypothesize a systemic process. Changes in technologies, environmental conditions and political and economic structures, lead to uneven rates of development giving opportunities to lesser powers to catch up to greater powers in industrial output and political influences. They lead to increased capabilities to shape the world system. To begin with there is a struggle for parity so that there can be equal participation and an absence of domination. This struggle for many reasons that are both psychological and systemic, becomes a struggle for superiority. There seems to be no decision-making process by which a halt can be called. In growth in industry and in social and political organizations, there is ample evidence that capabilities are exploited to the full despite possible reactions and consequences. At the international level a sphere of influence acquired by a developing state needs to be protected by extensions beyond the sphere. If there is the capability it will be so protected. Then these extensions require protection, until there are 'foreign bases' scattered far from the national boundaries. This expansion process, like all expansion processes, has inbuilt limits. Each extension is more costly than the last. There is the factor of distance; but more important in the modern world, there is the factor of political resistance in the intervened regions. Once a state goes beyond what are regarded by world opinion as 'legitimate' security needs, political resistances are generated. In due course, it seems, competition for resources needed for expansion—armed forces, subsidies and foreign expenditures—and for resources needed for the satisfaction of consumer expectations, gives rise to domestic resistances that can be suppressed only in the short term. Finally contractions take place in the foreign field under such foreign and domestic pressures. The United Kingdom seems to have gone through such a process. This seems to have been the experience of the United States: post-war expansionism, Vietnam, domestic unrest and foreign pressures, contraction. Are there some systemic pressures which relate to growth at work in international relations which have very little to do with types of political systems and policies?

Great powers have a special domestic problem. There is a fundamental conflict between the needs of greatness and the needs of social stability. Great powers, to be great in the traditional sense, are centralized and have within them seeds of their own destruction. After their phase of greatness has passed the demands for identity not only cannot be resisted, but do not have to be resisted for there is no longer a power requirement. Regionalism takes place, as it is taking place in the United Kingdom. Secession movements are irresistible over the longer term. When they occur in the developing world it would be expedient for great powers not to resist them. An efficient state is one that rests heavily on local identity and the promotion of a sense of participation. This may not be the recipe for international greatness in the traditional sense, i.e. greatness built on military power and threat. It may be, however, a recipe for another type of greatness, a greatness that springs from cohesion, legitimacy, stability and security based, in turn, on a sense throughout the society of indentity, participation and shared values.

Whether such a hypothesis is valid or not, it is clear that states advancing in greatness will use their influence to alter the international system and to adapt it to their interests, while relatively declining powers will seek to retain existing structures, spheres of interest and linkages. As a consequence, there are and always must be at any one time, 'revolutionary' and 'status quo' powers. Are East and West, the Soviet Union and China, accusing each other of essentially the same behaviour—the behaviour of great powers, the behaviour to be expected of states becoming powerful at relatively different rates, the behaviour associated with different stages of influence?

One reaction is to observe that no matter how the competition is generated—by ideological or systemic causes—the fact is that it is present and it is a source of conflict, especially at the stage at which a status quo power believes that it is being threatened in a zero-sum (winner-takes-all) struggle. However, there are some important political differences between a relationship defined, on the one hand, as an ideological struggle, involving cultures, values, institutions and 'ways of life', and, on the other, a systemic process leading to different pecking orders and, therefore, different competitive advantages, without necessarily threatening these non-material values. In the latter case the conflict is not defined as a winner-takes-all struggle. Such a conflict would more readily be perceived as presenting a universal and continuing problem in world society, not unlike the internal regional and class problems that all states face. In the interests of all, these problems require a solution that does not inhibit uneven rates of development but mediates their consequences.

Thus, the phenomenon that Gurr and his colleagues (1976) observed in relation to crime in cities may not be different from the same phenomena at the other system levels. Unsolved problems would seem to be systemic, not behavioural, in origin, calling for no-fault processes of solution.

It needs to be emphasized that the development of an alternative paradigm and theory is not an exercise designed to alter reality—either behavioural responses to the environment or the environment—but to alter the base from which reality is perceived and from which decisions are taken about deliberate changes in it. This study has been concerned with an altered system of thought about problems, not an alteration to the problems which is the reality that is to be discovered and understood. Whether this alternative way of viewing reality is more realistic is finally determined by the relative quality of prediction and the effectiveness of problem solving that emerges from the two approaches.

A qualification to the second perspective is, however, necessary. Societies have evolved as a result of a mix both of power influences, in which human needs are subordinated to the requirements of social stability and to the promotion of elite interests; and of social goals, in which attempts are made to resolve conflicts of interest. Because there is this mix, role defence frequently tilts the balance in favour of power solutions to problems, at least in the short-term, despite increased experience of the self-defeating consequences of role defence and of increased knowledge of problem-solving means of achieving change.

Such a theory draws attention to a problem inherent in civilizations: how to institutionalize or structure leadership roles and to build in role and leadership change, such that leadership will be adaptive and not merely or primarily protective of its own role interests. Such a theory has the familiar ring of idealism: if only there were wise and altruistic leadership! However, there is a difference: the policies and qualities of leadership can now be defined more precisely. We have the outlines of an alternative set of hypotheses which give some different insights into the nature of social and political problems and into the nature of processes by which change can be effected. Political scientists from Machiavelli and before to the present day have given most attention to ways and means of preserving authorities and existing institutional structures, if necessary against the demands of human needs. The persistence of serious social and political problems is evidence that they have failed. An alternative set of assumptions is thus relevant, even in the interests of elites and authorities. It also draws attention to means of promoting harmonious behaviour within a legitimized authority structure that avoids the self-defeating and self-fulfilling features of control policies that have been so frustrating to those concerned with policy and administration.

The combination of conceptualizing an acceptable alternative analysis and approach and a felt need for it, together create a condition in which conscious adaptation is likely, subject only to the discovery of acceptable processes of change and control.

APPLIED THEORY

Prescription or policy flows from analysis and diagnosis. Analysis and diagnosis flow from theory. However, theory is 'pure': it is directed towards problem-solving on the assumption that there exists a desire to solve that particular problem in the particular way prescribed by that theory. It takes no account of political value judgments. Hence, theory is an insufficient basis for prescription. Pure theory may point the way to a solution of a problem; but political judgments may counsel against solving it once theory has indicated costs and consequences. The remedy for homelessness is, obviously, more homes; for inadequate education, more educational resources. These remedies would create other problems as resources are limited. The remedy for violence or unemployment could be, depending on their definition, altered social or economic structures; but such a remedy would involve altering social institutions, wealth distribution and other changes that might not be acceptable to authorities. The policy decision would then be to accept the social costs and inconveniences of violence or unemployment as part of the price to be paid to secure other economic and social goals. Hence, pure theory is different in character from applied theory and policy.

Authorities usually endeavour to solve problems on the basis of some theory, but with modifications to suit political considerations. The relationship between theory and applied theory is, then, the decision-making latitude that is possible in solving a problem within the limits of theory: a too great diversion from the 'pure' destroys the application of the theory to the point at which policies fail, become self-defeating, accentuating the problem.

Political decision-making thus involves value judgments, a balancing such that policies do not stray too far from theoretical solutions. It is important to decision-makers—and to the society—that the balancing is informed. When the level of unemployment, of crime, of dissidence becomes unacceptable because of mistaken balancing, there are serious consequences for authorities and societies. Legitimized value balancing gives place to non-legitimized decision-making and possibly to role and structure defense against change.

One of the tasks of political scientists is, therefore, to determine decision-making latitude in respect of theoretical solutions to problems—how much, in what circumstances and in what areas of decision-making can authorities deviate from theoretical solutions, without the problems to be solved becoming so accentuated that they threaten the values and social structures the departure from theoretical remedies was designed to preserve.

Traditional legal theory gave no such guidance: 'The law is what the state, through its appropriate organs, i.e. the legislative and judicial, says it is' (Scarman, 1977). A less traditional legal view gives some guidance: 'There is a natural law springing from man's own humanity which must be incorporated into the positive law of the state' (Scarman, 1977). It is for the political scientist, the behaviouralist and not the lawyer, to give content to this general statement: what are the demands of 'man's own humanity', to what extent do they limit decision-making latitude and in what particular circumstances? If decision-makers had precise and certain knowledge in respect of these questions, the value judgments they make would not have self-defeating consequences.

Consequently, there are two academic goals: first, to find the thought system from which it is possible reliably to define situations; and, second, to determine what decision-making latitude is possible for decision-makers in deviating from remedies and in what circumstances. The two are clearly related. An accurate definition of a situation will rest very much on those elements in it which are fundamental in human terms and it is those same fundamental elements that determine the boundaries within which policies need to be framed, if not to be self-defeating.

What is required of pure theory is a definitive statement of necessary requirements in any application. Policy-makers require navigation points and boundaries. In the famous film *Roots* the initiation ceremony includes a dialogue between tutor and novice: 'What do you do when you have surrounded your enemy on three sides? Novice: Close the gap. Tutor: No! leave an escape route so the enemy can retreat. Novice: But will he not return if he is not killed? Tutor: You can never kill an enemy; on the contrary, you merely provoke further conflict'. No theoretical reasoning was offered; but the reasoning was sensible in terms of experience, though perhaps quite incompatible with applied political policies. The policy-maker needs the theoretical reasoning, the navigation points that were in the mind of, but not articulated by, the tutor.

Social theories, such as coercion and value theories, do not offer any such navigation points. They are *social* theories. Public policy affects persons; industrial policy, constitutional issues, development, economic policy, foreign policy, communal policy, all have a behavioural aspect. The level of policy, whether it be handling the individual, the minority national group or a health service, makes no difference in this respect. Consequently, the search is for a system of thought, which includes the set of human constraints that is common to all behaviour relationships, within which decision-making can reliably take place.

It follows that whatever the system of thought, the individual must be the unit of analysis, because it is individual human needs that ultimately have to be catered for in the interests of public policy at all levels. If the argument is valid that certain human needs *will* be pursued, by one means or another, then public policy decision-making is severely constrained, except in the short term and decision-making latitude in some cases is non-existent. Decision-making latitude will exist only where human needs are marginally affected, where definition is not precise and where knowledge and experience give no clear pointer to means.

If it can be demonstrated that there are certain human needs to be pursued, that they *will* be pursued and that structures must accommodate to them if there is to be harmonious social organization, then authorities are faced with a clear option: either alter structures in an orderly fashion or witness their disorderly disintegration. If tools are fashioned for the use of authorities such that they are able to enact an adaptive role, avoiding self-defeating policies, they will at the same time be making possible the pursuit of human needs. It is authorities, not the mass of people, who need tools such that they can construct policies which achieve social goals. There is no need to fashion tools of revolution: either there is opposition to unacceptable structures and policies or there will be protest behaviour as a means of achieving needs satisfaction. Either way, authorities are confronted with the necessity and inevitability of change. The task of the scientist is to demonstrate convincingly decision-making options and latitudes, the consequences of infringing the constraints imposed by human needs and the means by which goals can be achieved. When the white minority took matters into their own hands in Southern Rhodesia, there was a school of thought that favoured intervention. There was an opposing school that believed the problem had to be solved by Africans, giving the white minority a clear option, either to alter policies in an orderly way or face, in due course, disorderly alteration by violent means. The various attempts to coerce by sanctions and political means evoked defensive responses. There was little or no attempt to help analyse the consequences of policies and to spell out alternatives. The attempts at mediation followed by Britain and others were bargaining processes, not problem-solving. So, also, in the case of mugging, theft, dissidence and other forms of deviant behaviour: authorities require clear predictions, clearly defined options and processes before they can be expected to adopt policies that accord with appropriate remedies.

The problem of crime is now conspicuous in most politically developed states. The tensions caused by pursuing policies on one base (a power and material base) in an environment that is another (a transactions and need base) are in evidence in increasing delinquency, communal conflict, industrial disputes and violence generally. The transactional links within a society have now led to expectations that cannot be fulfilled in a legal and social structure calculated to inhibit social transaction and mobility. It has become increasingly necessary to punish minor crimes against property while sanctioning major manipulations in property, finance, commerce, industry, education and living generally. However, coercion does not promote conformity. The initial punishment of first offenders is perceived by the subject as an attempt to enforce on him a code of behaviour that society does not itself observe: he perceives that a minor infringement of social norms is punishable, while a major one is legal. Stealing is forbidden by law and socially; tax evasion only by law and financial manipulation by neither. His response is to commit another crime, this time against property or person, sometimes for no personal gain other than the release of frustration. Policies that deviate from needs are demonstrably self-defeating.

PROCESS

What, then, is the connecting link between applied theory and policy: how are needs to be defined operationally in relation to particular situations and how is decision-making latitude to be determined in particular situations?

The tendency has been for scholars and practitioners to endeavour to apply theory and principles by exercising their judgments, first, as to what is the logical application of a theory and, second, as to what are the practical possibilities and the modifications that must be made in the particular· circumstances. In the physical sciences this is the only possible procedure. It is the skill of the designer and engineer to apply principles in new situations and to discover the degree to which pure theory can be modified, the degree of deviance that is possible without threatening the desired outcome. However, in the behavioural sciences—dealing with open systems in which actors and environments are changing even while they are being examined and treated—such judgments introduce subjective influences associated with political and personal prejudice, interests and values. Not only are there few generally accepted and valid principles, as has been shown by questioning some traditional assumptions, but these subjective influences are frequently the dominating ones. The traditional arbitrator or mediator makes orders or proposals and believes he is applying principles of justice and reasonableness. Whenever important interests are at stake he fails to bring agreement between parties concerned. Courts make judgments which purport to apply principles; but only after argument and disagreement as to what the principles are and how they should be applied. There is no certainty and in any event the decisions may be legal ones that do not reflect the motivations and interests of the persons concerned, resulting in outcomes that are not regarded by them as just or appropriate. Policy-makers endeavour to decide what is just and politically feasible. This subjective approach does not provide a link between pure and applied theory: the deviance from pure theory is sometimes total and decision-making latitude exercised frequently has more to do with the interests of the decision-makers than of the parties affected by the decisions. In an open system the link must be one that relates to the behaviour and the changing environment of the actors concerned: it is only they that can make the judgments necessary as to how to interpret principles and what deviance from them will not be self-defeating.

This is not to suggest that the mediator has no role or that the decision-maker is not required to make decisions. On the contrary, the mediator and the decision-maker have two particular, professional, exacting leadership roles to perform—far more exacting and responsible than those traditionally associated with mediation and decision-making. These are, first, to articulate and to translate into terms that are relevant to a particular situation the pure theory—the principles on which decision-making in behavioural relationships must take place (argued here as need and relationship theory); and second they have the role of ensuring that the actors concerned are involved and that their involvement is a problem-solving one and not one of confrontation, competition, bargaining or power.

This third party or leadership behaviour in relation to needs and their application is 'process': it is the instruction on the label on the bottle; it is the facilitating of decision-making by injecting knowledge into the communication between actors; it is the application of problem-solving techniques to decisions made by actors; it is the invention of means by which is made possible the total involvement in the making of decisions of all those subject to decisions. It was for this reason that it was stated earlier that the aim of this study was to provide a framework in which practitioners in various areas of human behaviour could apply their special knowledge and skills: 'process' provides this framework.

Process—the linkage between applied behavioural science and policy—overcomes the problem of violence. Process, being the means of change in the specific direction of human needs, is the link between evolution and revolution, it is the means by which change takes place continuously in directions controlled by a combination of needs theory and participatory discussion in respect of particular issues. As such it is the means by which violence can be avoided.

The significance of the notion of process may not at first be appreciated fully because of the influence on thought of traditional approaches. The classical and conventional focus has been on institutions, structures, society, the values of society and the rights of its members. This is essentially a static approach leading to the uncomfortable conclusion that change is possible only by revolution. Johnson has been quoted on p. 49; 'True revolution is neither lunacy nor crime.' Within an institutional approach it is necessary to accept revolution as a legitimized means of change, as war is legally accepted in the international arena. The analysis or understanding of social problems is not improved by the more sophisticated terminology that Johnson employs. 'The key to both the study and the conceptualization of revolutionary violence lies in social system analysis. Utilizing the concept of the social system, we can distinguish between those instances of violence within the system that are revolutionary and those that constitute criminal or other forms of violent behaviour' (Johnson, 1966, p. 13). Johnson here prejudges one of the main issues in the analysis of social and political problems: he assumes there is a difference between revolution and crime and uses the notion of a value-coordinated social system to differentiate the two. The tool is used to explain something that is assumed. If the assumption is false the tool is of little relevance. Gurr believes this assumption is false (see p. 210). Crime and civil protest behaviour are closely related. The activities of the IRA are defined as crime; but they would deny this. Palestinian activities are likewise defined as criminal; but in Johnson's definition their behaviour is revolutionary. Mugging and many activities that appear on the surface to be ordinary crime probably have many motivations, some of which are identical with those of the protester and revolutionary. These difficulties occur because of the institutional or system approach to social problems. A focus on process leads to quite different definitions and conclusions. Crime and revolution are in this framework perceived evidence of protest, symptoms of institutional and structural deviance, means of change. Revolution, in this perspective, is not the relevant means of change; change takes place constantly and does not await upon a situation which invites discontinuous and largely randomly directed change. Process, problem-solving with the objective of preserving and promoting human societal needs, is the means by which what is valued in institutions is preserved, what is objectionable is removed and what in addition is required is included without the 'cleansing by violence' that system theories promote.

Within a human needs paradigm, the problem of change is not the one-sided issue of resistance against authorities and the rights and constraints that should operate on authorities. It is how to control role defence, whether it be undertaken by authorities at the expense of subjects or by subjects at the expense of each other and of authorities. The concern is with the general pattern of behaviour that is followed by individuals and groups, public and private, that prevents such change and adaptation to change as appears to be required in the interests of human needs and of social harmny.

The approach adopted in a needs paradigm is a 'no fault' one. It is no fault of the individual that he pursues his interests and needs, despite frustrations and constraints imposed by his social and political environment. Nor is it the fault of anyone who has attained some satisfaction of his needs to defend this acquisition. Everyone in a society endeavours to maximize his satisfactions, especially those that relate to needs. Those enacting authoritative roles will defend them and the structures of which they are part by all the means at their disposal, including the resources they can command by reason of their role. Elites are no more responsible for the conditions of role differentiation that lead to their roles than is the rebel responsible for the conditions that lead him to seek his: to the extent that the latter cannot be regarded as at fault those defending roles are free of fault. The differentiation of power process produces certain results, favouring some in particular respects and working to the disadvantage of others. In each case the individual has behaved in the same way—maximizing his satisfactions within the limits of the constraints operating. The malign influence is the differentiation of power and the absence of off-setting processes, not the role behaviour it creates.

The structural or system approach, supported by experience

in all civilizations, has led to the assumption that those in positions of authority with means at their disposal to preserve their roles, will do so. The assumption has been that only violence can dislodge non-legitimized authorities prepared to employ violence in their defence. Yet, despite the historical experience, there is no evidence to suggest that role defence is not a behavioural pattern that prevails in the absence of recognized processes of change. Needs are universal; they are experienced by elites and authorities. Non-legitimized authorities lack recognition, security and valued relationships and it can be assumed that they would prefer to alter role behaviour to fulfil these needs. But they operate in a political environment of win–lose in which their legitimate needs are unlikely to be met if they lose. A charismatic leader, such as the many leaders of independence movements in Asia and Africa after the Second World War, is, after independence, finally forced into isolation and deposed, sometimes punished, exiled or executed. There were no processes by which the transitional problems inherent in independence, including the problem of leadership change or role enactment change, could be dealt with outside violence. Such conditions inevitably lead to escalated role defence, repression, increased opposition and open warfare. If, on the other hand, a no-fault approach were adopted, then the emerging situation would be dealt with as a problem and an endeavour made to find outcomes that satisfy the needs of all parties. A no-fault approach is likely to reduce role defence because displaced role occupants could see tolerable options.

TRENDS IN POLICY AND PRACTICE

This has not been an exercise to suggest what should be in terms either of social and political goals or processes by which they may be attained. It has been concerned with what is, what is developing, trying to establish the 'historical process' in order to find what longer-term trends can, with advantage, be promoted and which shorter-term trends can, with advantage, be discouraged in the interests of the longer-term process. The basis has been set down as needs and the methods as problem-solving.

It would be logical to expect, therefore, considerable evidence that needs and problem-solving—'process'—are entering into policy and practice and, step-by-step, altering structures and procedures. If this is not the case, then either there is no continuing trend that can be described as a historical one or there has been a failure to analyse and discern its fundamental elements.

The behavioural literature is pointing in the direction of process, as references have shown. However, the literature on a subject tends to drag behind practice, being in fact stimulated by observation of practice. The evidence sought is far more likely to be found in the day-to-day reports of events, opinions and practices. There is no difficulty in finding this evidence while acknowledging that it is selected from many other events, opinions and practices that conform more with the power paradigm. The striking feature is the emergence in recent times of an awareness of needs and of problem-solving as the appropriate technique in dealing with social and political problems at all social levels. Sometimes this awareness occurs because of failures of past policies and increased costs of pursuing abortive policies. For example, the costs of jailing deviants has grown so greatly that in the United Kingdom ways have been explored of sentencing offenders to work outside prisons and, where prison still seems necessary, greatly to reduce sentences. In this climate it has been possible for many who have thought about these problems to advocate quite different approaches to crime, giving theoretical grounds for not sending criminals to prison, quite apart from the problem of costs. The Government of the United Kingdom published a document on *prisons and the prisoner* (HMSO, 1977) hoping to promote public debate. It rejected demands for longer sentences and emphasized the need to preserve and develop the prisoner's personality, questioning whether in practice this was possible in such conditions of isolation from society. At the same time the Anglican Church (Church Information Office, 1977) suggested that Courts should be required to give their reasons for prison sentences in preference to other punishments.

Courts, particularly in the United States of America, are acting on the 'no-fault' basis. This started with insurance claims and was an extension of the 'knock-for-knock' agreements on which insurance companies operated. It has now been extended to many juvenile crimes and to the settlement of matrimonial disputes. Logically it could be extended to many crimes in which there are clear circumstances inviting the crime—poverty leading to stealing, murder of a spouse under provocation. Once extensions of this kind take place it is a small step to adopt a no-fault approach to most behaviour that causes social problems. An accompanying trend is towards sentencing after consultation with social and probation workers and the logical extension of this is to place sentencing within the responsibilities of those who are responsible for the welfare and development of the individual—teachers, social workers and others. One New York lawyer, greatly concerned with crime rates in New York, is attracted by the Chinese processes whereby crime is dealt with at a local level by meetings among all those concerned. This is a problem-solving approach in the sense that not merely the crime and punishment are taken into account if this is considered desirable, but also the circumstances that led to the behaviour and how it may be avoided in the future. Many of these developments take place without any theoretical background. They are pragmatic developments required by the perceived circumstances, by the failure of other methods, by pressure on jails and many other conditions. What is important is to find the theoretical explanations of these developments so that those that are achieving their objectives can be explained and further developed. For example, the movement towards work of a social nature as a sentence was originally stimulated by pressure on prisons and a hunch that prison sentences for juveniles and first offenders was self-defeating. There were many social and probation workers who feared there would be a great deal of trouble if crime led only to such work. The reason for its success is probably in part due to the fact that it helps to overcome one of the important causes of crime, namely boredom. If this is established then other forms of 'punishment' can be encouraged.

In industrial relations Japanese firms operating in Britain have set out to eliminate as much as possible the we–they relations that characterize British industrial relations. Breaking down barriers in refreshment rooms, keeping the same times, dressing in the same style, use of the same pub, negotiating on a problem-solving basis, have apparently avoided many problems experienced by British firms. Again, this is a pragmatic approach, the theoretical explanation points to means of overcoming problems other than industrial.

The United States Congress (1978) has authorized the creation of the Commission on proposals for a United States Academy for Peace & Conflict Resolution, including a training institution for mediators, that is persons who do not necessarily have a legal training and who adopt problem-solving techniques in industry, race and other problem areas. The American Arbitration Association has moved steadily towards problem-solving—in spite of its name—in handling industrial and community conflict (Rio and Lincoln, 1975). An association of interested people, under the direction of a psychiatrist interested in applying problem-solving techniques to conflict problems, has endeavoured to sponsor a non-governmental organization for the handling of conflict situations at all social levels (see Wedge, 1971). These are but straws in the wind; their significance is not their scale or their practical importance, but the evidence of a trend in thought and practice.

PRESCRIPTION

Discovering trends and the reasons for them is the means by which the 'historical process' can be pushed ahead. This is the source of prescription. Prescription is the end-product of 'process': the theorist can observe decision-making deviance—as when financial policies cause unemployment which more than any other condition denies to the individual his human societal needs; as when planners build new towns to which people are moved who cannot cope with the break in kinship relationships and the functional ties associated with them; as when conservation of fishing is taken away from those most concerned with conservation in the interests of 'internationalism'; as when pay differentials are eroded to a point where distributive justice seems threatened; as when streaming of children in schools destroys self-image and peer relationships; as when economies of scale that are made at the expense of stimulus and identity are thought to increase productivity; as when isolation in prison is thought to be a remedy for crime that was originally induced by an absence of relationships. The theorist can also observe and suggest alterations—in parliamentary procedures to eliminate the adversary nature of debates, changes in court and sentencing procedures, alterations in management–worker relationships. However, the problem and the remedy is not for the theorist to define or to solve: he should avoid such prescription. The theorist can indicate only the procedures that can effectively be followed in defining and solving problems and the considerations that are to be taken into account in the process. The definition and resolution of a problem must remain within the jurisdiction of those concerned with the problem: it is their's, their perceptions, their interests. In this sense the theorist can act as a third party in a dispute or when parties meet to solve problems. There are no situations that would not be assisted by such a third party, SALT talks and industrial disputes of all kinds. This is an unfamiliar role for a third party; but one necessary until problem-solving as an approach becomes part of conventional wisdom and as much part of culture as is bargaining at present. It is a highly professional role for it assumes a wide knowledge of behavioural theory and an ability to communicate theory to those concerned. The main prescription that emerges from this study, therefore, is the promotion of an awareness, by educational means, by practice within existing institutions, of problem-solving in the behavioural context of human societal needs.

It is in this respect that socio-biological interpretations of human behaviour are inadequate. Genetic selection explains and is the source of needs—as Wilson (1973) persuadingly demonstrates. Evolution, left to itself, can be self-defeating in respect of these: there is nothing natural and inevitable about the fulfilment of human needs. Some species have become extinct presumably because of self-defeating tendencies. The differentiation of power in human societies is an example of a self-destructive trend: it creates conditions which, if not controlled, destroys social harmony. However, unlike earlier primates, the human species is capable of offsetting such trends, of indulging in 'process'—problem-solving to ensure the pursuit of needs. No doubt the human species is also capable of altering and suppressing needs by genetic processes, of creating a race of automats. 'Process' is also the means by which this capability can be controlled. Man's future is within his own control: 'process' is the means of control.

The conventional and almost near consensual view of behaviour is that it is governed by power, bargaining, competition and finally violence. Changes in this mental set are taking place with experience. If this change is part of a historic process it can be assisted by finding its explanation, theoretical and behavioural, by imaginative ideas as to how to introduce problem-solving as the norm of control, by altering institutional procedures and by educational means generally. The race against time is virtually won in many fields of endeavour, especially those in which trained people are in direct communication with others who have problems to solve: social workers, industrial mediators, psychiatrists, community workers, school counsellors, etc. There are, however, few signs of change at higher levels of conflictual interaction, in communal disputes, race relations, interstate conflicts. The theorist always takes his clue from his observations of practice; but having noticed events and trends he does not need to drag behind and can assist in their acceleration.

THE PREJUDICE IN FAVOUR OF COERCION AND PUNISHMENT

It is relevant to conclude with an observation on consensual thinking. There is currently in most countries a political reaction against the type of analysis contained in this book and the prescriptive deductions that flow. There is a strong feeling in many societies that terrorism, violence, brutality of all kinds, theft and even political deviance must be punished. Punishment is felt necessary for the correction or just deserts of the individual and also as an example to others. In support of this view it is pointed out that many who commit crimes are from privileged sections of societies: there are persons, groups and nations whose behaviour is antisocial and 'evil' despite opportunities and the satisfaction of most material needs. It is observed, also, that not all underprivileged persons and groups commit crimes. However, from the stand-point of this analysis, this argument is misled. It is based on the traditional and elitist view that if material needs are satisfied there are no reasons for antisocial behaviour, that conflicts of interests are primarily conflicts over resources and material possessions. This analysis has drawn attention to the controlling importance of non-material needs: security, recognition, identity, stimulation and others. The materially privileged can experience a lack of these at least as much as anyone else. Material benefits given to the unemployed do not offset a sense of alienation, nor do they remove boredom, both of which are an incentive for crime (Northumberland Police, 1977). These human needs *will* be pursued: the individual is so programmed that he has no option. Punishment is not a replacement for human needs. It may be that social workers and others who have advocated supportive approaches to the handling of non-conforming behaviour have not expressed themselves in terms that explain the nature of deviant behaviour; they may have come to their conclusions pragmatically as a result of their own personal experiences and their own assessments of the failure of punishment. Experience cannot be transferred and argument from experience is not convincing. Only a sound theoretical argument will still the disquiet that prevails about leniency and supportive approaches to deviants—be they non-conforming individuals or deviant authorities.

Behind these prejudices lies a reluctance to acknowledge social and political realities. There is no social or political system that does not require great changes. Minorities cannot be expected to live for ever as second class citizens, excluded from decision-making processes by 'democratic' or majority rule structures. Either means are found that make possible their separate identity along with their full participation in society or the need for separate nations is accepted. 'Terrorists', 'gunmen', 'dissidents' cannot be defeated; they can be made irrelevant only by processes that involve them in the solutions of social and political problems.

Sites (1973) has argued that social norms are used as tools as and when they are found to be adequate. Otherwise other tools are invented—tools that are unacceptable to society, unacceptable also to those employing them. The terrorists that declare war on their own society by kidnapping, blackmail, damage to property and violence against persons, are employing tools that appear to be the only ones available to combat injustice, defects in the economic or social system and other unacceptable conditions as perceived and experienced by them. What, then, can supplement social norms, what tools can be provided in all societies that would prove adequate for those who, rightly or wrongly, perceive injustice and the need for change? If certain needs *will* be satisfied and if social norms are not adequate tools, it is expedient for societies to provide some that are adequate in the eyes of those seeking them and acceptable to the rest of society. For society to employ the tool of punishment against the offender does not solve his problem. When an individual, a group, a minority a nation finds that within the social norms he cannot achieve his needs, then there is a problem: it is a problem for the person or group concerned and it is also a problem for the society in which he operates. Whatever the structure of society, however developed it is, however well planned, social norms will be inadequate unless supplemented by the general availability of problem-solving institutions that can be used effectively as tools by which to pursue needs within the limits that are perceived to be possible. Sites referred to some needs as 'desires'. They could not be secured immediately; but it is, nevertheless, a need that the possibility of achievement, that the prospect of success, that a path to a goal is at all times perceived.

The difference between a traditional law and order approach that relies on punishment in a particular set of circumstances and a wider problem-solving approach reflects the difference between puzzle-solving and problem-solving. The former is a convergent approach: there is a concentration on the particular, on known means, on a narrowly defined situation. Problem-solving reflects a divergent approach: it is less concerned with the immediate symptoms of types of behaviour, with the particular case, with immediate remedies. It is problem-solving in the sense that it seeks options not previously considered, it seeks remedies that meet the requirements both of the individual and of society, it seeks outcomes that satisfy and involve all parties. Perhaps conflicting approaches, those that favour punishment and those that are supportive, those that try to settle disputes and those that try to solve problems, reflect personality types or attitudes engendered by education: it is divergent and wide-ranging, exploratory attitudes that are likely to solve problems.

Singer encapsulates this view:

> Finally, my conviction is that we must, in one fashion or another, break away from the normative assumptions which seem to be implicit in so many of the formulations found in contemporary social science. Whether the orientation is toward national interests, social order, political stability, economic growth, or one or other of the many structural–functional paradigms, we seem to be in increasing danger of forgetting that the basic unit of any social system is the individual human being, and that any scientific formulation must take cognizance of that fact. In my judgment, no theory which ignores the single person is scientifically adequate or morally defensible. In sum, what is proposed here is that we begin some systematic research which can simultaneously 'think big' and 'think small', and which embraces in a rigorous synthesis both the lone individual and all of mankind. (Singer, 1970).

Bibliography

ARDNEY, ROBERT (1966) *The Territorial Imperative*, Dell.

BARKUN, M. (1968) *Law without Sanctions*, Yale.

BAY, CHRISTIAN (1958) *The Structure of Freedom*, Stanford.

BELL, D. (1973) *The Coming of Post-industrial Society: A Venture in Social Forecasting*, Penguin Books.

BENNIS, W. G. (1970) 'Theory and method in applying behavioural science to planned organizational change' in W. G. BENNIS, K. D. BENNE and R. CHIN (eds) *The Planning of Change*, Holt, Rinehart and Winston.

BLAKE, R. R., SHEPARD, H. A. and MOUTON, J. S. (1964) *Managing Intergroup Conflict in Industry*, Gulf Publishing Co.

BLAU, P. M. (1964) *Exchange and Power in Social Life*, Wiley.

BODENHEIMER, EDGAR (1971) 'Philosophical anthropology and the law', *California Law Review*, **59** 3, May 1971.

BOEHM, W. W. (1958) 'The Nature of Social Work' in *Social Work*, **3** 2, 1958.

BOULDING, K. E. (1956) 'General systems theory – the skeleton of science', *Management Science*, **2**, 1956.

BOULDING, K. E. (1970) *A Primer on Social Dynamics*, The Free Press.

BOX, S. (1971) *Deviance, Reality and Society*, Holt, Rinehart and Winston.

BRECHT, ARNOLD (1967) *Political Theory*, Princeton.

BURNS, JAMES MACGREGOR (1977) 'Wellsprings of Political Leadership', *The American Political Science Review*, **LXXI**, March 1977.

BURTON, J. W. (1969) *Conflict and Communication*, Macmillan.

BURTON, J. W. (1972) 'Resolution of conflict', *International Studies Quarterly*, **16** 1, 1972.

CHURCH INFORMATION OFFICE (1977) *Prisons and Prisoners in England Today*, Church Information Office, London.

COSER, L. (1956) *The Functions of Social Conflict*, Routledge and Kegan Paul.

COWAN, THOMAS (1971) 'Law without force', *California Law Review*, **59**, 1971, p. 690.

CURLE, ADAM (1971) *Making Peace*, Tavistock Publications.

DAHRENDORF, RALF (1959) *Class and Class Conflict in an Industrial Society*, Routledge and Kegan Paul.

DAVID DAVIES MEMORIAL INSTITUTE (1966) *Report of a Study Group on the Peaceful Settlement of International Disputes*, David Davies Memorial Institute, London.

231

232   *Deviance, Terrorism and War*

DAVIES, J. C. (1963) *Human Nature in Politics*, Wiley.
DAVIES, J. C. (ed.) (1971) *When Men Revolt and Why*, The Free Press.
DE BOND, EDWARD (1971) *The Use of Lateral Thinking*, Pelican Books.
DE REUCK, A. and DE REUCK, M. (1974) 'Value Systems and Value Change', *Science and Absolute Values*, 1, 1974. (Proceedings of the Third International Conference on the Unity of Sciences. The International Cultural Foundation, Inc.)
DEUTSCH, KARL W. (1963) *The Nerves of Government*, The Free Press.
DRUCKER, P. F. (1950) *The New Society: The Anatomy of the Industrial Order*, Heinemann.
DUNCKER, KARL (1943) *Psychological Monographs*, no. 58.

ECKSTEIN, H. and APTER, D. (eds) (1963) *Comparative Politics*, The Free Press.
EIBL-EIBESFELDT, IRENAEUS (1971) *Love and Hate, The Natural History of Behaviour Problems*, Holt, Rinehart and Winston.
ENLOE, CYNTHIA (1973) *Ethnic Conflict and Political Development*, Little, Brown and Company.
EPSTEIN, A. L. (1978) *Ethos & Identity*, Tavistock.

FRIEDRICH, C. J. (1963) *Man and his Government*, McGraw-Hill.
FROHOCK, F. M. (1967) *The Nature of Political Inquiry*, The Dorsey Press.
FROMM, E. (1961) *May Man Prevail?*, Doubleday.

GAGNE, ROBERT M. (1973) *The Conditions of Learning* (2nd edn), Holt, Rinehart and Winston.
GALTUNG, JOHAN (1969) 'Violence, peace and peace research', *Journal of Peace Research*, no. 3, 1969.
GOULET, DENIS (1973) *The Cruel Choice*, Atheneum.
GREEN, R. (1977) *The Urban Challenge*, Follett.
GREENSTEIN, F. (1969) *Personality and Politics*, Markham Publishing Company.
GURR, T. R. (1970) *Why Men Rebel*, Princeton.
GURR, T. R. (1976) *Rogues, Rebels and Reformers*, Sage.
GURR, T. R., GRABOSKY, PETER and HULA, RICHARD (1977) *The Politics of Crime and Conflict*, Sage.

HALSEY, A. H. (1978) *The Reith Lectures*, One.
HAWLEY, ANOS (1963) 'Community power and urban renewal success', *The American Journal of Sociology*, 68, 1963.
HEILBRONNER, R. L. (1959) *The Future as History*, Grove Press.
HIRSCH, F. (1977) *The Social Limits of Growth*, Routledge and Kegan Paul.
HMSO (1977) *Prisons and the Prisoner*, HMSO, London.

JANOS, A. C. (1964) 'Authority and violence' in H. Eckstein (ed.) *Internal War*, The Free Press.

JOHNSON, CHALMERS (1966) *Revolutionary Change*, Little, Brown and Company.

KELMAN, H. C. (1977), 'The Conditions, Criteria & Dialectics of Human Dignity' *International Studies Quarterly* Vol. 21 No. 3 1977.
KRISLOV, S. (1966) 'The perimeters of power' in S. Krislov, K. Bogam, J. Clark, R. Shaffer, S. White (eds) *Compliance and the Law*, Sage.
KUHN, THOMAS S. (1962) *The Structure of Scientific Revolutions*, Chicago Press.

LEVINE, R. A. and CAMPBELL, D. T. (1972) *Ethnocentrism, Theories of Conflict, Ethnic Attitudes and Group Behaviour*, Wiley.
LLOYD, DENNIS (1964) *The Idea of Law*, Pelican Original.

MACCOBY, E. E. (1968) 'The development of moral values and behaviour in childhood' in J. Clausen (ed.) *Socialization and Society*, Little, Brown and Company.
MARSH, P., ROSSER, E. and HARVE, R. (1978) *The Rules of Disorder*, Routledge and Kegan Paul.
MASLOW, A. H. (1954) *Motivation and Personality*, Harper Brothers.
MAYO, E. (1949) *The Social Problems of an Industrial Society*, Routledge and Kegan Paul.
MERTON, ROBERT K. (1957) *Social Theory and Social Structures*, The Free Press.
MOORE, W. E. (1970) 'A reconsideration of theories of social change' in S. N. Eisenstadt (ed.) *Readings in Social Evolution and Development*, Pergamon Press.
MORGENTHAU, HANS (1948) *Politics among Nations: The Struggle for Power and Peace*, Knopf.

NANCE, JOHN (1975) *The Gentle Tasaday*, Harcourt Brace.
NATIONAL ASSOCIATION OF AMERICAN SOCIAL WORKERS (1958) *Social Work*, 3 2, 1958.
NIEBUHR, R. (1963) *Moral Man and Immoral Society*, SCM Press.
NIEMEYER, G. (1941) *Law without Force*, Princeton.
NISBET, R. (1976) *Twilight of Authority*, Heinemann.
NORTHUMBERLAND POLICE (1978) Report of the Chief Constable.

OLSEN, M. (ed.) (1970) *Power in Society*, Macmillan.

PARSONS, TALCOTT (1956) 'The relations between the small group and the larger social systems' in R. R. Grinker (ed.) *Towards a Unified Theory of Human Behaviour*, Basic Books.
PEPINSKY, H. E. (1976) *Crime and Conflict*, Law in Society Series, Martin Robertson.
POLYA, G. (1945) *How to Solve It*, Princeton.
POPPER, KARL (1957) *The Poverty of Historicism*, Routledge and Kegan Paul.

POPPER, KARL (1974) 'Normal science and its dangers' in Imre Lakatos and Alan Musgrave (eds) *Criticism and the Growth of Knowledge*, Cambridge University Press.
PRINGLE, MIA (1974) *The Needs of Children*, Hutchinson.
PRUITT, DEAN (1965) *Problem-solving in the Department of State*, The Social Science Foundation and Graduate School of International Studies Monograph Series in World Affairs, Denver.

RASER, J. R. (1966) 'Deterrence research', *Journal of Peace Research*, no. 4, 1966.
RAWLS, JOHN (1972) *A Theory of Justice*, Clarendon Press.
RIP, P. and LINCOLN, W. F. (1975) *Impartial Intervention into Communal Conflict*, American Arbitration Association.
ROKEACH, M. (1976) *Beliefs, Attitudes and Values*, Jossey-Boss.
ROSENAU, J. (1954) *International Aspects of Civil Strife*, Princeton University Press.
ROSENAU, J. (1968) 'Private preferences and individual responsibilities' in J. D. Singer (ed.) *Quantitative International Politics*, The Free Press.

SCARMAN, L. (1977) 'Human rights', *University of London Bulletin*, no. 39, 1977.
SINGER, J. D. (1970) 'Individual values, national interests and political development in the international system', *Studies in Comparative International Development*, **VI** 9, 1977.
SITES, PAUL (1973) *Control, the Basis of Social Order*, Dunellen Publishers.
SMITH, C. G. (ed.) (1971) *Conflict Resolution: Contributions of the Behavioural Sciences*, Notre Dame.

THE TIMES (1977) 28 October 1977.
THOMAS, J. M. and BENNIS, W. G. (eds) (1972) *Management of Change and Conflict*, Penguin.
TODD, A. R. (1965) 'Working with what we know' in N. Calder (ed.) *The World in 1984*, Volume 1, Pelican.
TOWLE, CHARLOTTE (1973) *Common Human Needs*, E. Younghusband (ed.), Allen and Unwin.

UNITED NATIONS (1965) Report of the United Nations Mediator on Cyprus to Secretary General, 26 March 1965.
UNITED STATES CONGRESS (1977 & 1978) *Congressional Record*, **123** 14 and 15, 1977 and subsequent authorization on 15 October 1978.

WALTZ, K. N. (1959) *Man, the State and War*, Columbia University Press.
WEDGE, B. (1971) 'A psychiatric model for intercession in intergroup conflict', *Journal of Applied Behavioural Science*, **7** 6, 1971.

WICKELGREN, W. A. (1974) *How to Solve Problems*, Freeman and Company.
WILSON, E. O. (1973) *Sociobiology: A New Syntheses*, Harvard.

ZAWODNY, J. K. (1966) *Man and International Relations*, Chandler Publishing Company.
ZETTERBAUM, MARVIN (1977) 'Equality and human need', *American Political Science Review*, Volume LXXI, no. 3, September 1977.

Index

ability, and power, 86
adversary institutions, 96, 107
aggression, 34, 35; and deterrence, 89; as manifestation of need, 80
alienation, 81; and deviance, 111, 188
altruism, and human need, 78, 79
American Arbitration Association, 225
analysis, and problem solving, 118
Analysis of Conflict, Centre for the, 178
abitration, 98–9, 137
Ardrey, Robert, 75
area of inquiry, boundaries of, 13–17
assumptions, questioning existing, 160–61; and selection of facts, 41
authority, 85–6, 203; and adaptive change, 152; admission of error, 146; and coercion, 46; differentiation of power, 125–9, 221–2; erosion of, 42; and human need, 69, 184, 185, 191–2, 204, 207; legitimacy of, 14, 51, 130; and obedience, 6, 87; relevance of, xiv–xv; resistance to, 200; role of, 135–9; in system, 65, 66; transfer of, 200; *see also* leadership, power

bargaining power, 174
bargaining process, 104, 110, 113, 128
Barkun, M., 65
Bay, Christian, 43
behaviour, and action, 32; adaptive, 66; categorization of, 15–16, 17, 183–92; coercive, 137–8; control mechanism, 85–93; definition of, 28; interpretation, 32–3, 37; as response, 183; theory of, 207–8; *see also* random behaviour
behavioural systems, open nature of, 5
belief systems, challenging, 29, 30; and deterrence, 89; and prescription, 35, 38; questioning, 41
Bell, D., 148
Bennis, W. G., 200
Blake, R. R., 51, 69
Blau, P. M., 77, 125, 142
Bodenheimer, Edgar, 150, 155
Boehm, W. W., 71

Bono, Edward de, 19
boredom, 70, 178; and crime, 224, 228
Boulding, K. E., 100, 196
Box, S., 69, 89, 143, 180
Brecht, Arnold, 63
bureaucracy, resistance of, 147–8; *see also* authority
Burns, James, 59, 67, 70, 145
Burton, J. W., 116, 119, 178

Campbell, D. T., 195
capital punishment, as deterrent, 89; *see also* punishment
capitalism, and distributive justice, 199
categorization, problems of, 15–16, 17
change, 144; desire for, 173, 196; inevitability of, 217; nature of, 148–50; problem of, 199–202; resistance to, 109, 110, 160; as threat, 29–30
child, needs of, 70; and parent, 90, 132
Children's Bureau, National, 70
China, 210, 212
Churches, World Council of, 106
civil strife, 18, 151, 154; *see also* protest
class, and conflict of interests, 108, 109; and cultural norms, 60–61; and interpretation of law, 182
coercion, and authority, xv, 5–6, 126, 127, 132; and conformity, 217; as control mechanism, 85–9; dispute settlement, 100, 113; effectiveness of, 14, 19, 27, 51, 56; and integration, 45, 46, 47, 54; prejudice in favour of, 227–30; resistance to, 52; theory, 45, 46, 47, 54, 55, 76, 154; *see also* deterrence, power
coexistence, 117
coherence, and coercion, 45, 46; concept of, 44, 47, 50; and conflict, 48; lack of, 52
Common Market, 163
communication, structuring, 119
compliance, 134; and law, 200, 201
conflict, 194; communal, 14, 15, 25; functional, 48; interstate, 13, 15,

236